Brevity 3

Other Books by

guy & rodd

Brevity
NOT THE DOG ...
NOT THE DOG ...
A COLLECTION OF COMICS BY guy & rodd

Brevity 2
ANOTHER COLLECTION OF COMICS BY guy & rodd
WELL, THIS IS AWKWARD.
WORLD'S BEST GRANDAD

Brevity (Remix)
A TREASURY OF COMICS BY guy & rodd
NOW in glorious INKO-COLOR with UNWANTED Bonus features including NEVER before seen comics, stickers, and INANE COMMENTARY from guy AND rodd

Brevity 3

YET ANOTHER COLLECTION
OF COMICS BY

*guy &
rOdd*

**Andrews McMeel
Publishing, LLC**

Kansas City

Brevity is distributed by United Feature Syndicate, Inc.

Brevity 3 copyright © 2008 by Guy & Rodd. All rights reserved. Printed in China. No part of this book may be used or reproduced in any manner whatsoever without written permission except in the case of reprints in the context of reviews. For information, write Andrews McMeel Publishing, LLC, an Andrews McMeel Universal company, 1130 Walnut Street, Kansas City, Missouri 64106.

08 09 10 11 12 WKT 10 9 8 7 6 5 4 3 2 1

ISBN-13: 978-0-7407-7360-0
ISBN-10: 0-7407-7360-7

Library of Congress Control Number: 2008926292

www.andrewsmcmeel.com

──── **ATTENTION: SCHOOLS AND BUSINESSES** ────

Andrews McMeel books are available at quantity discounts with bulk purchase for educational, business, or sales promotional use. For information, please write to: Special Sales Department, Andrews McMeel Publishing, LLC, 1130 Walnut Street, Kansas City, Missouri 64106.

Guy dedicates this book to all the fun broads at ID-PR.

Rodd dedicates this book to Erin Friedrich, who single-handedly ended the Great Cartoonist War by bringing peace to all.

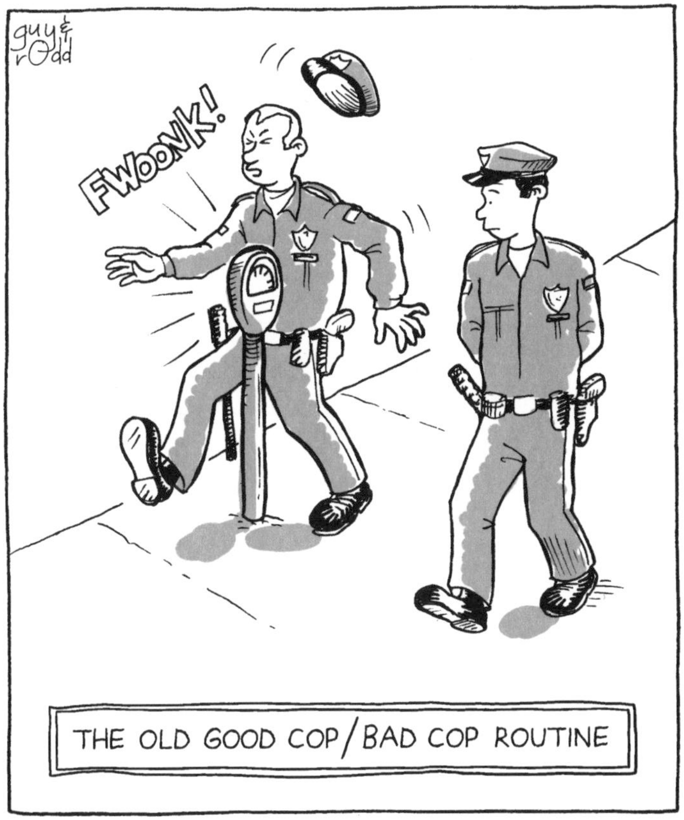
FWOONK!

THE OLD GOOD COP/BAD COP ROUTINE

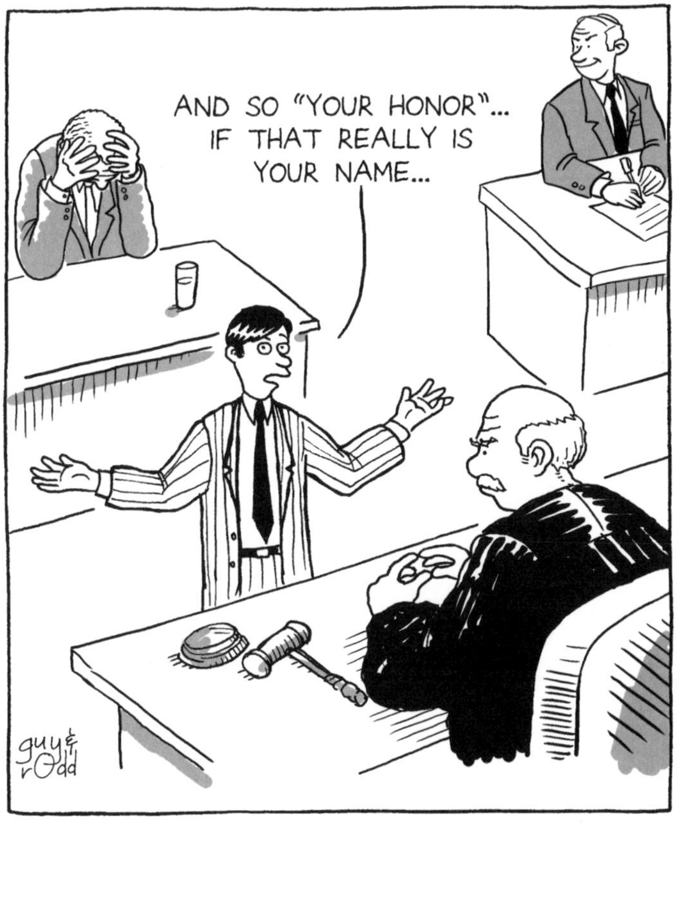
AND SO "YOUR HONOR"... IF THAT REALLY IS YOUR NAME...

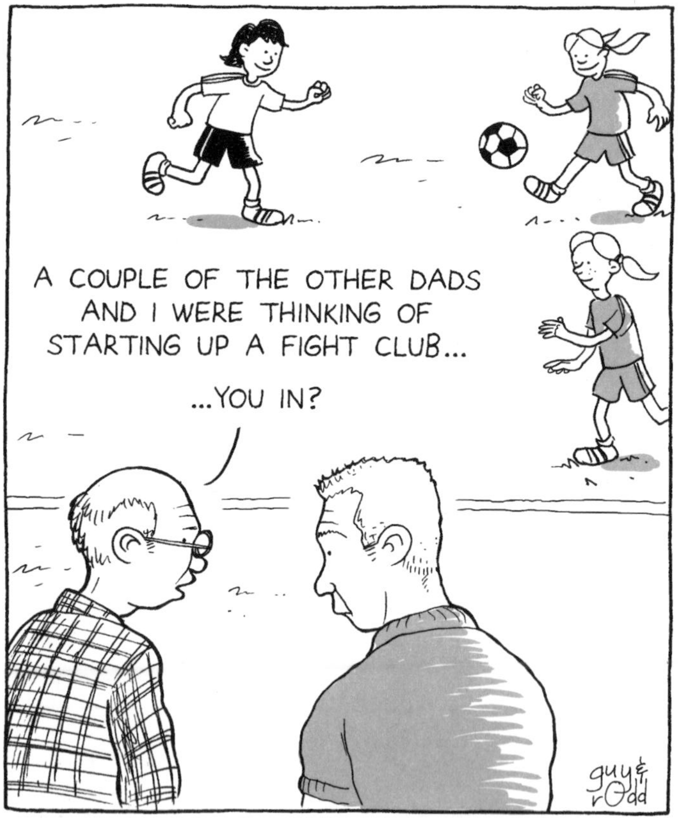
A COUPLE OF THE OTHER DADS AND I WERE THINKING OF STARTING UP A FIGHT CLUB...
...YOU IN?

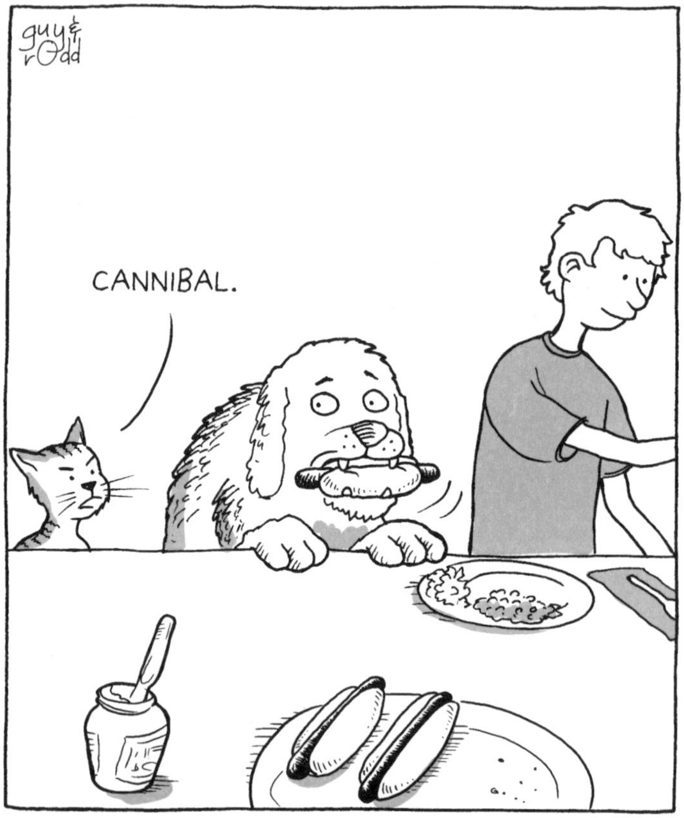
CANNIBAL.

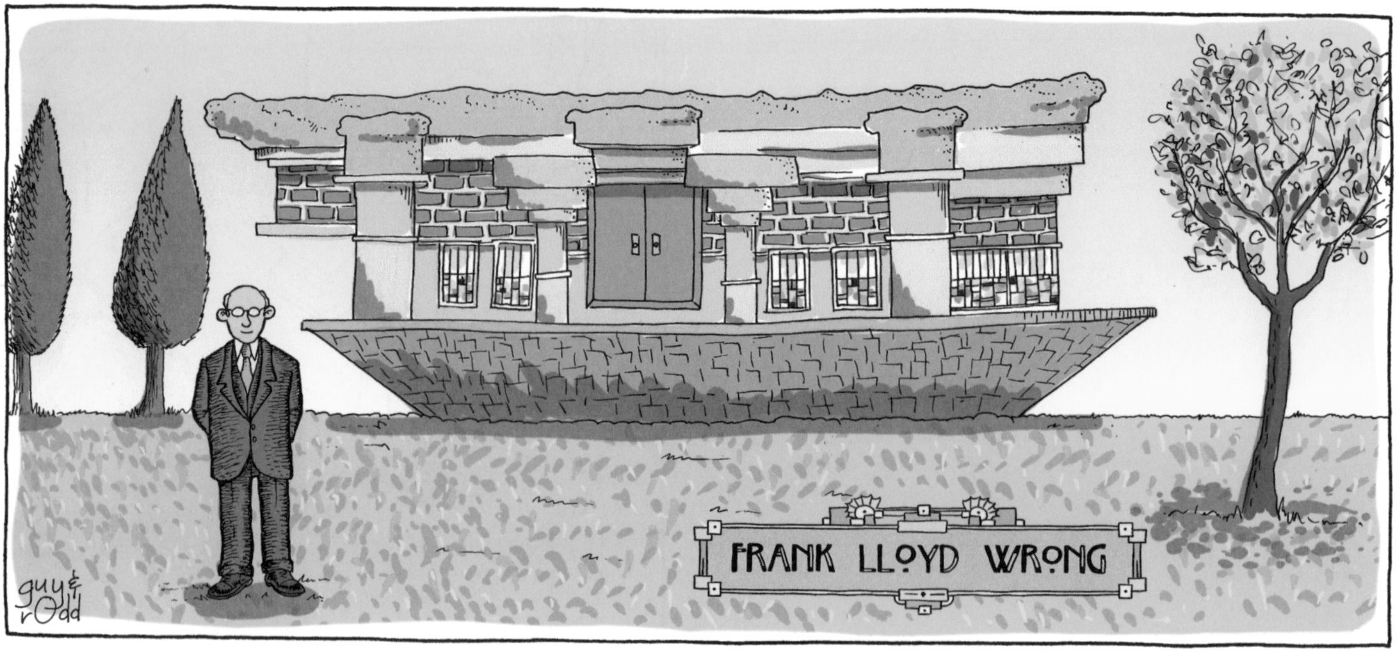
FRANK LLOYD WRONG

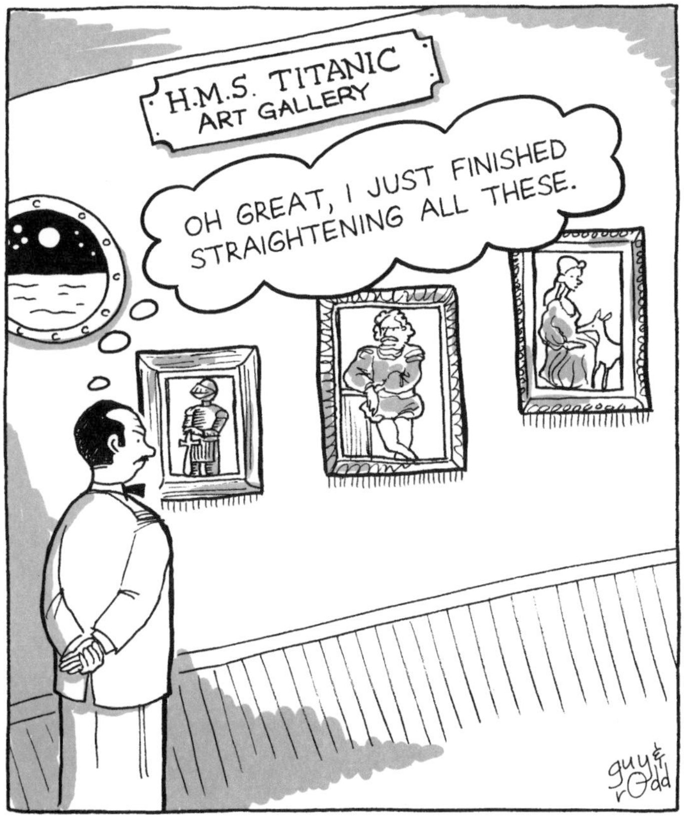
H.M.S. TITANIC
ART GALLERY
OH GREAT, I JUST FINISHED STRAIGHTENING ALL THESE.
guy & rOdd

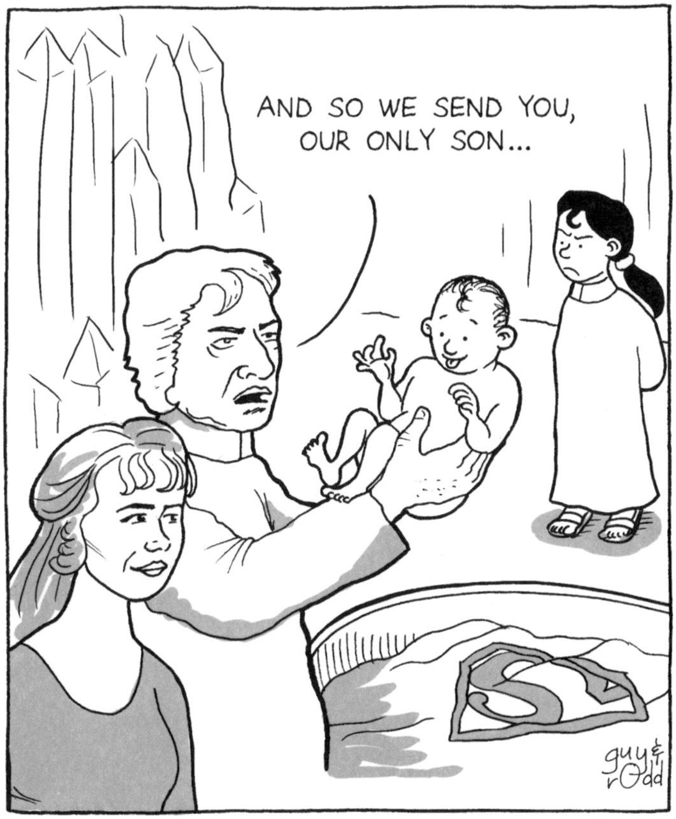
AND SO WE SEND YOU, OUR ONLY SON...
guy & rOdd

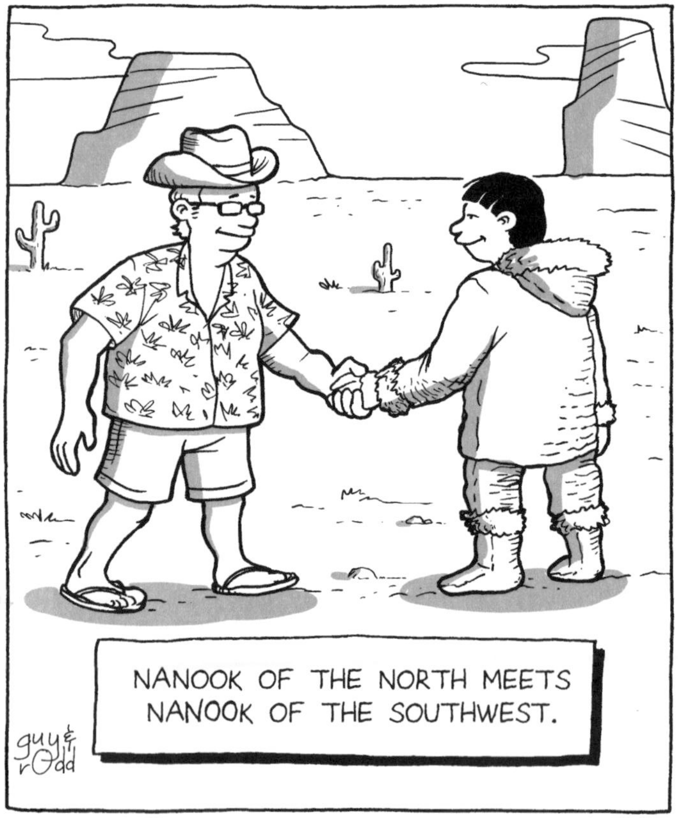
guy & rOdd
NANOOK OF THE NORTH MEETS NANOOK OF THE SOUTHWEST.

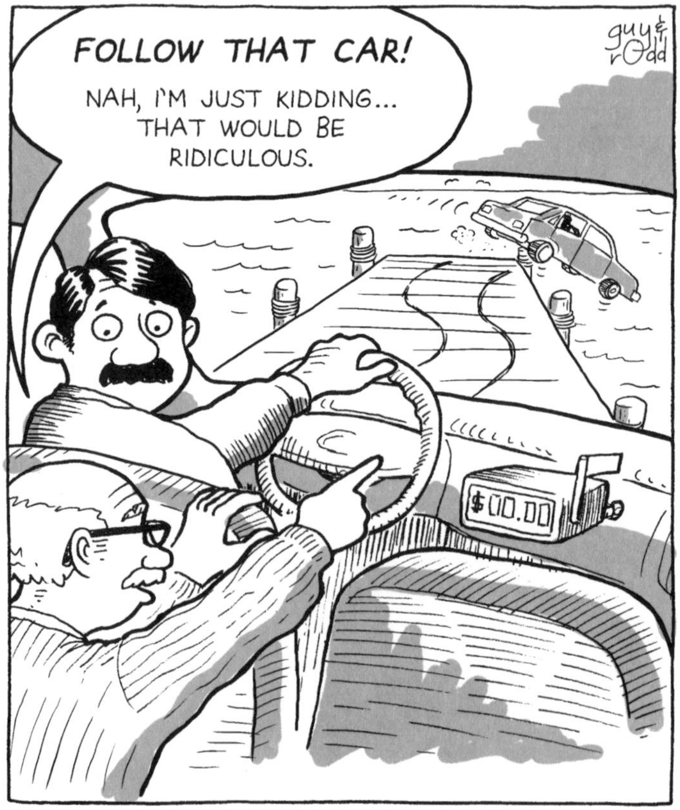
guy & rOdd
FOLLOW THAT CAR!
NAH, I'M JUST KIDDING... THAT WOULD BE RIDICULOUS.

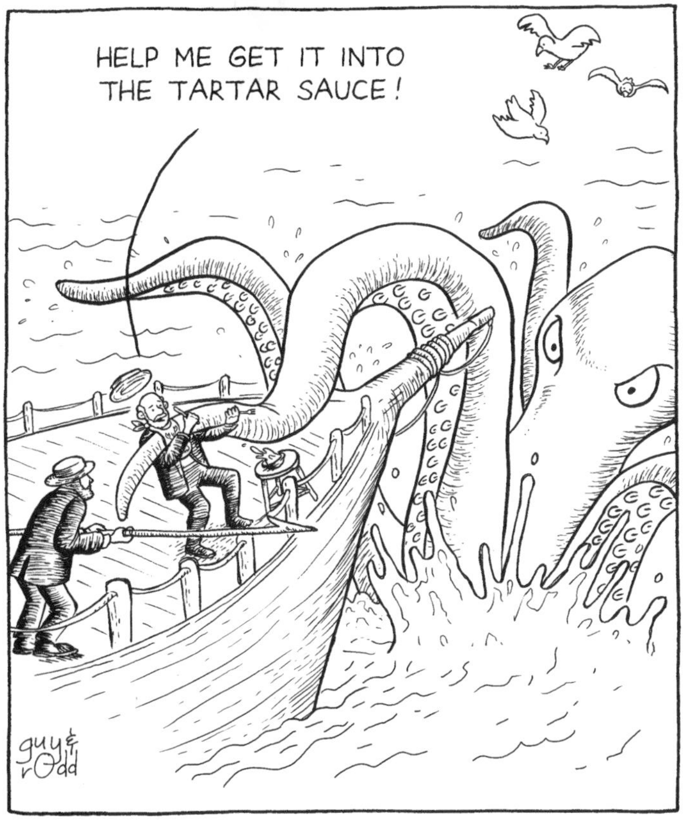
HELP ME GET IT INTO THE TARTAR SAUCE!

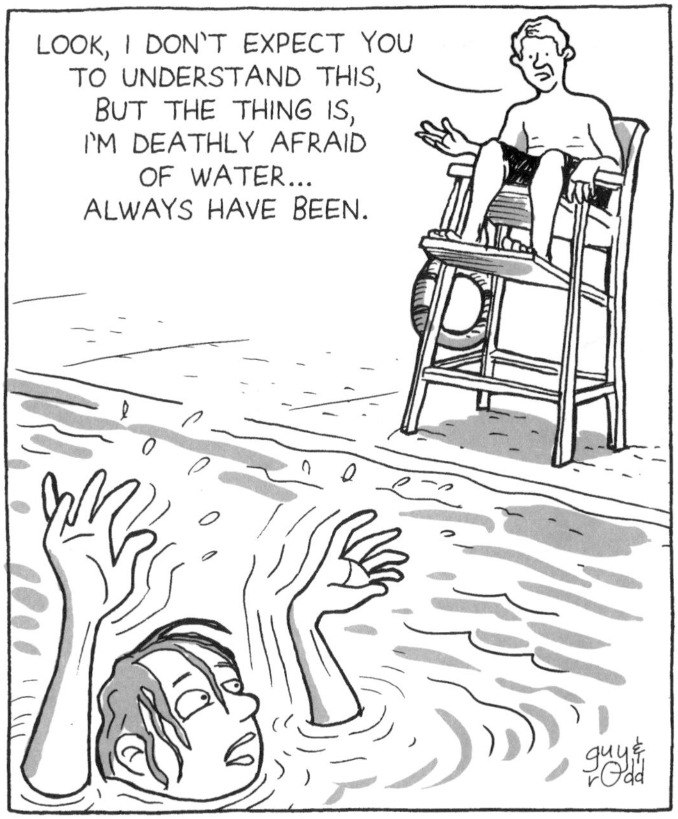
LOOK, I DON'T EXPECT YOU TO UNDERSTAND THIS, BUT THE THING IS, I'M DEATHLY AFRAID OF WATER... ALWAYS HAVE BEEN.

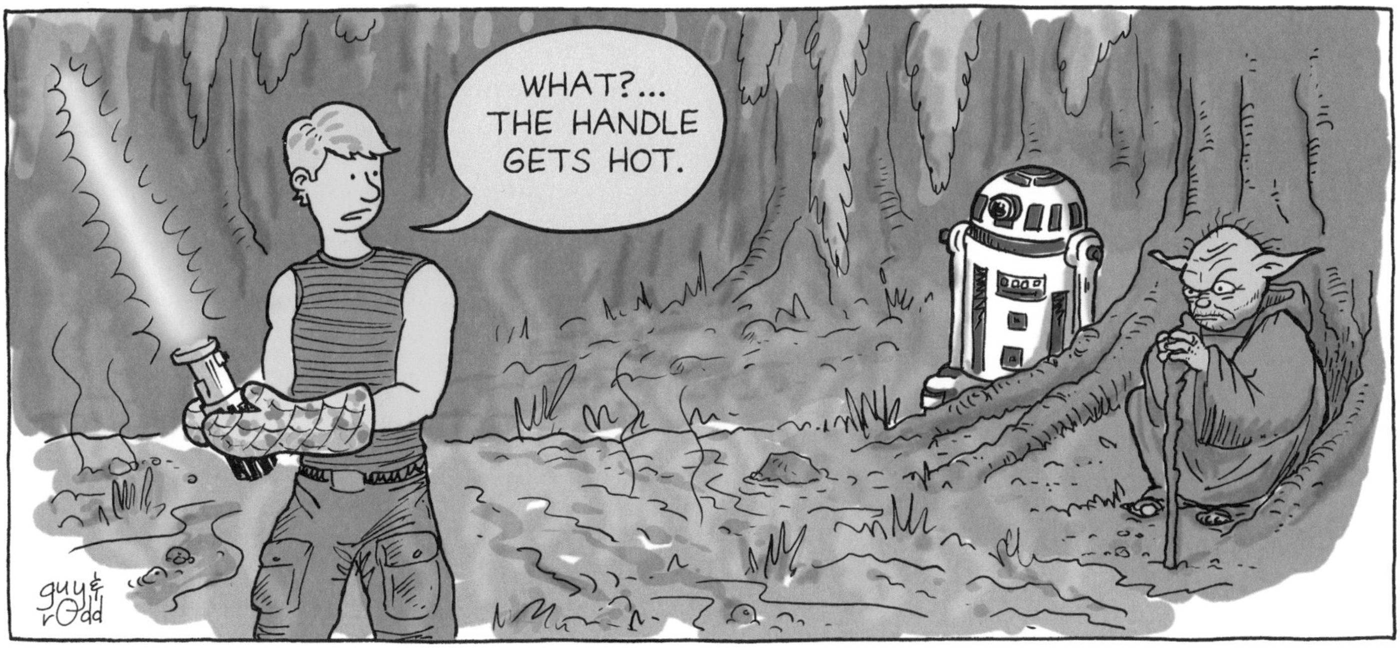
WHAT?... THE HANDLE GETS HOT.

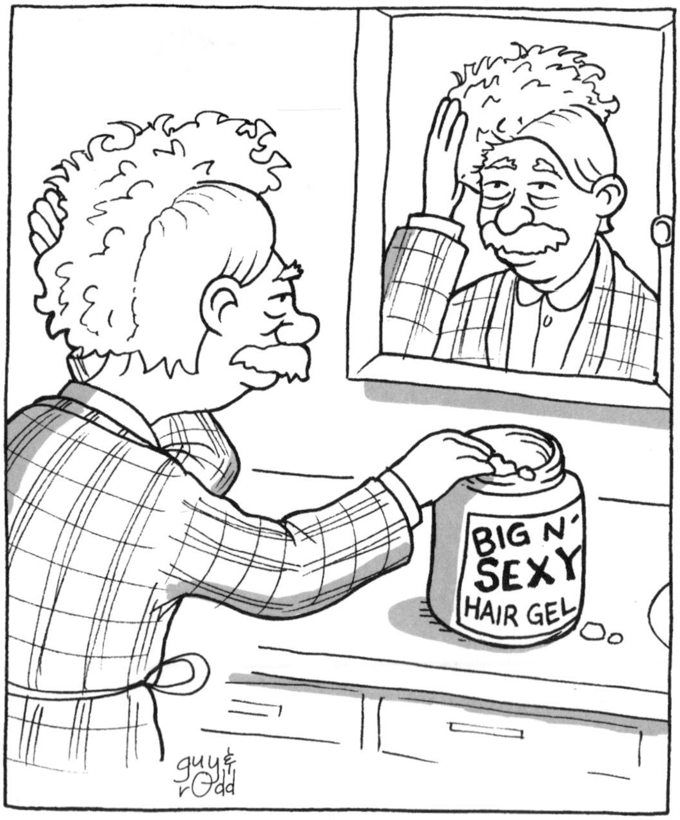
BIG N' SEXY HAIR GEL
guy & rodd

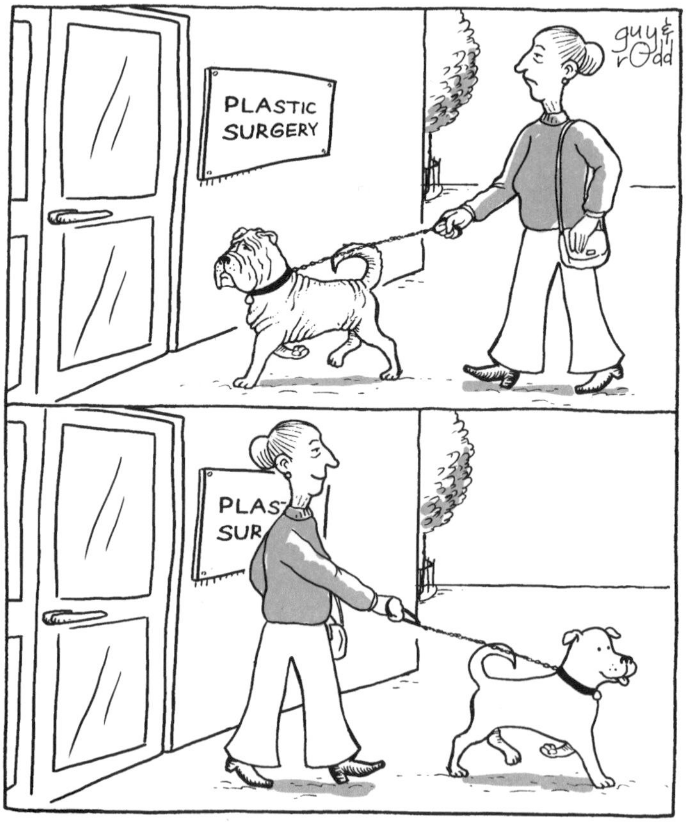
PLASTIC SURGERY
guy & rodd

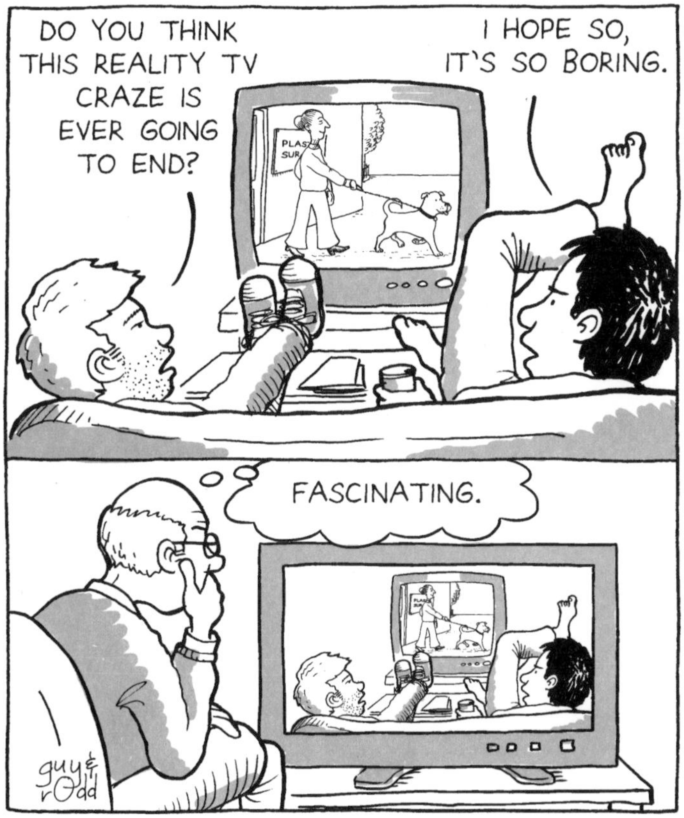
DO YOU THINK THIS REALITY TV CRAZE IS EVER GOING TO END?
I HOPE SO, IT'S SO BORING.
FASCINATING.

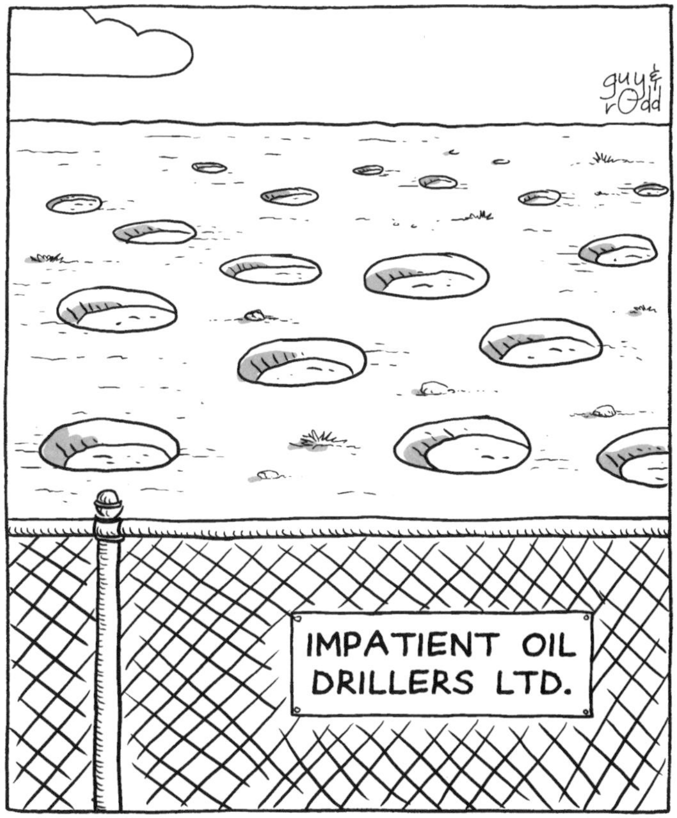
IMPATIENT OIL DRILLERS LTD.

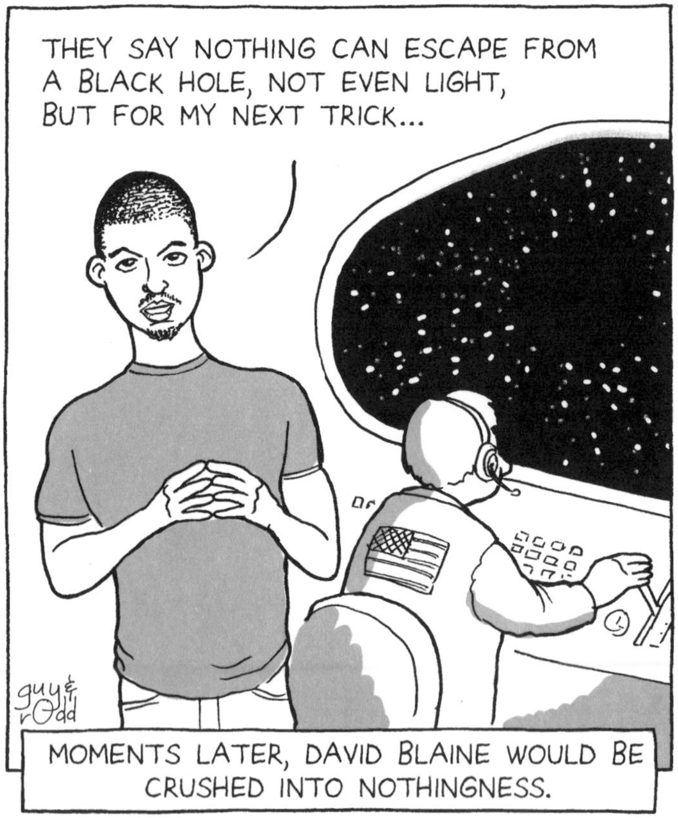
THEY SAY NOTHING CAN ESCAPE FROM A BLACK HOLE, NOT EVEN LIGHT, BUT FOR MY NEXT TRICK...
MOMENTS LATER, DAVID BLAINE WOULD BE CRUSHED INTO NOTHINGNESS.

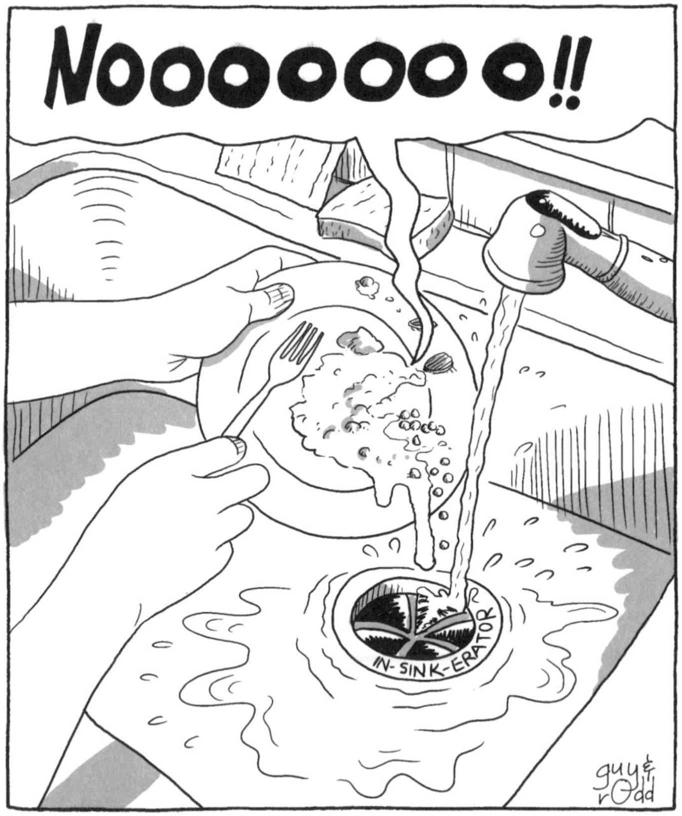
NOOOOOOOO!!
IN-SINK-ERATOR

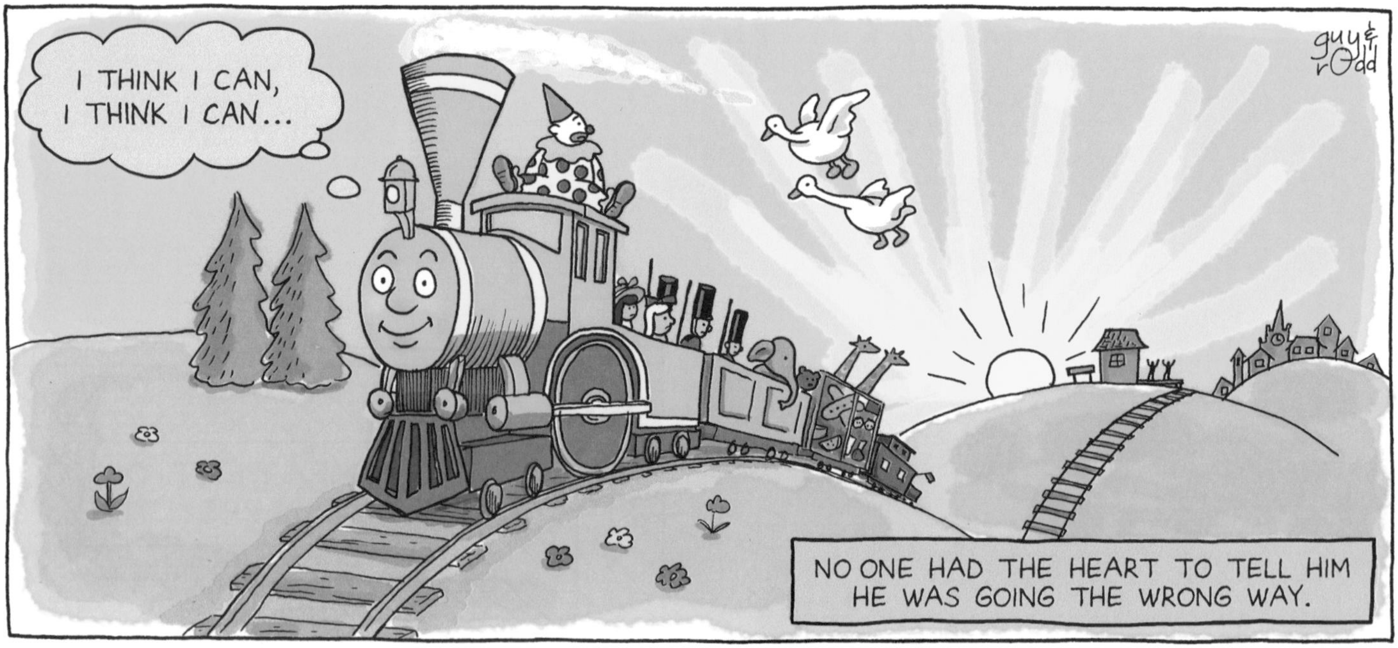
I THINK I CAN, I THINK I CAN...
NO ONE HAD THE HEART TO TELL HIM HE WAS GOING THE WRONG WAY.

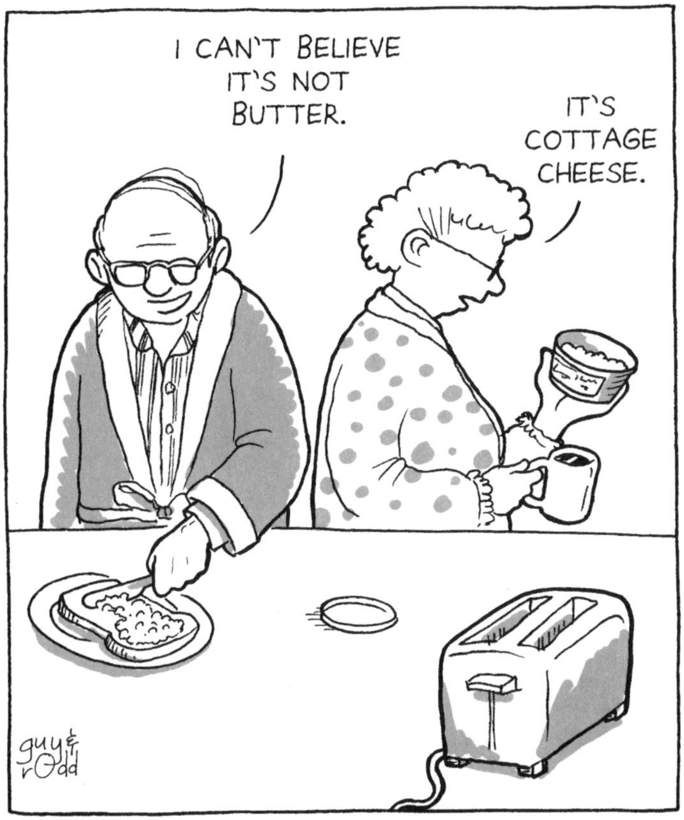
I CAN'T BELIEVE IT'S NOT BUTTER.
IT'S COTTAGE CHEESE.

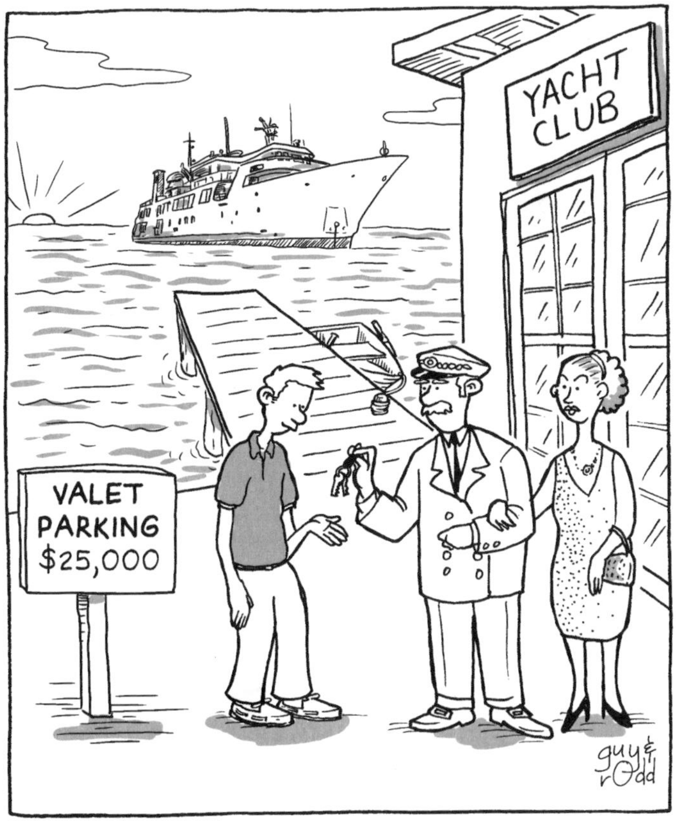
YACHT CLUB
VALET PARKING $25,000

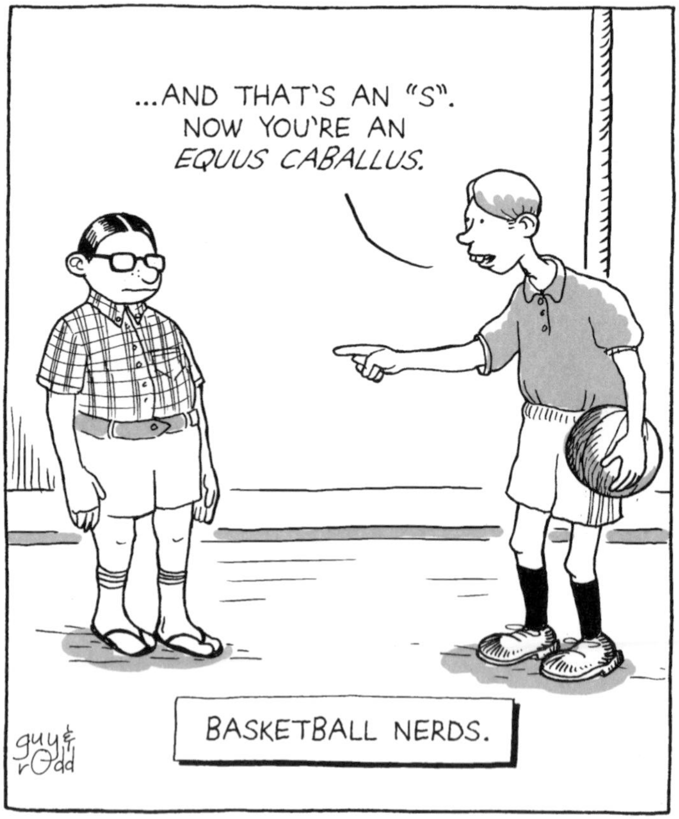
...AND THAT'S AN "S". NOW YOU'RE AN *EQUUS CABALLUS.*
BASKETBALL NERDS.
guy & rOdd

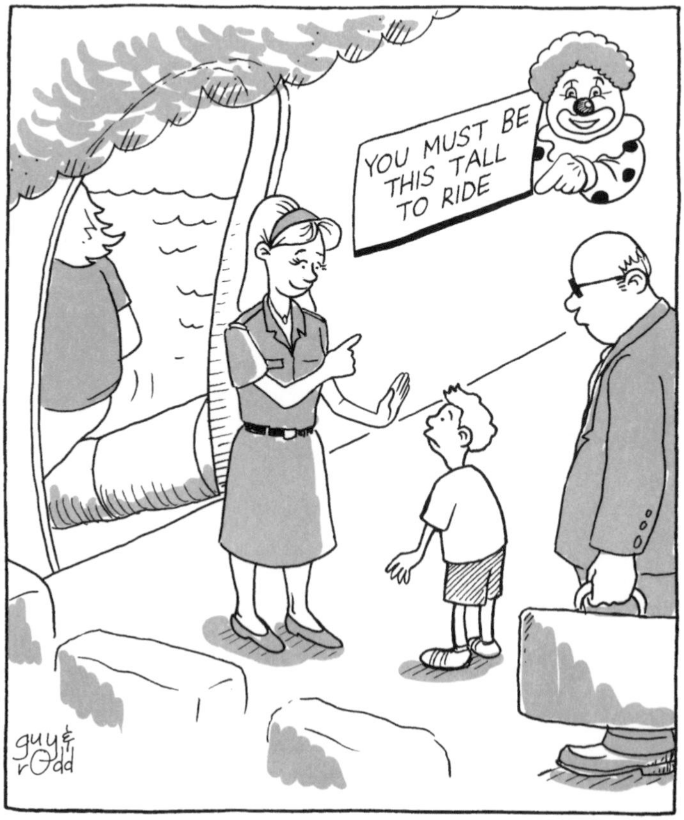
YOU MUST BE THIS TALL TO RIDE
guy & rOdd

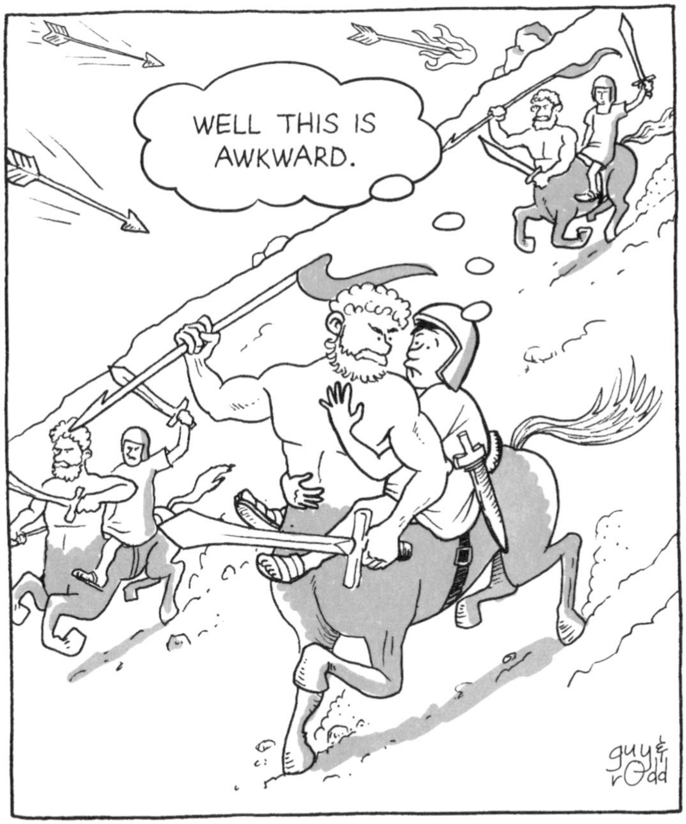
WELL THIS IS AWKWARD.

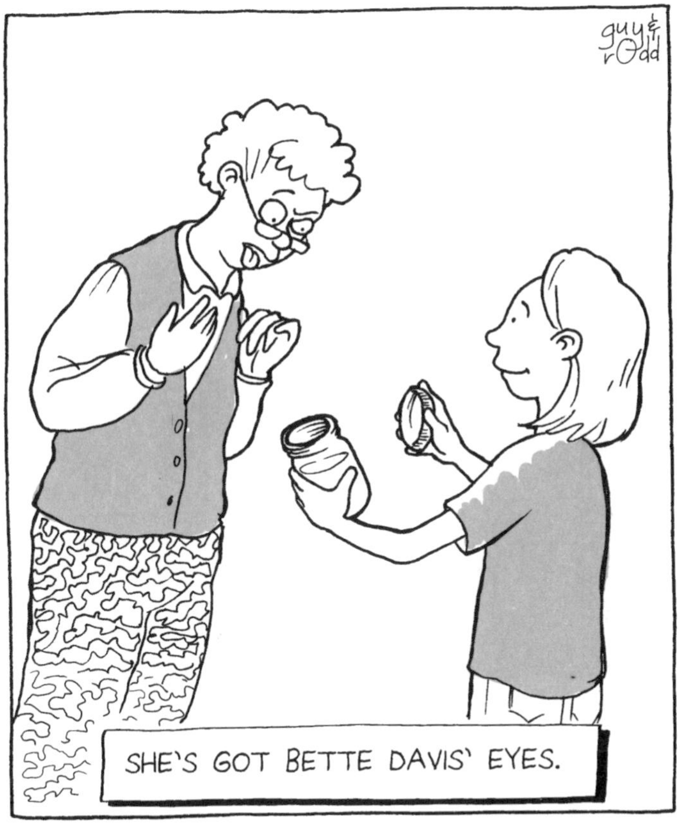
SHE'S GOT BETTE DAVIS' EYES.

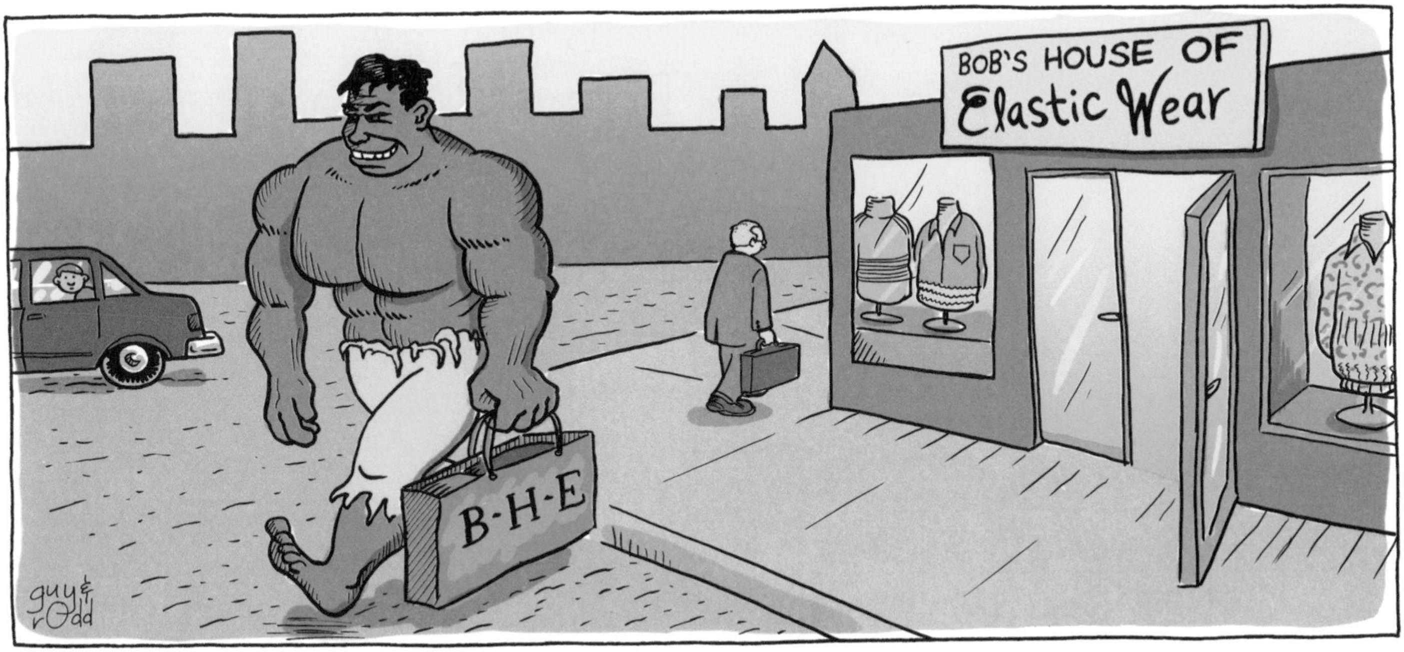
BOB'S HOUSE OF
Elastic Wear
B-H-E

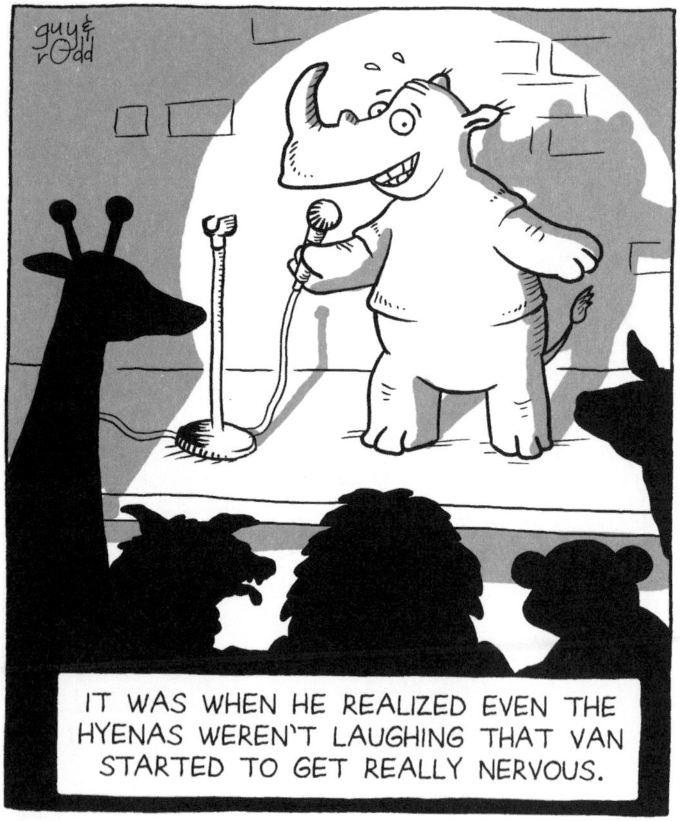
guy & rOdd

IT WAS WHEN HE REALIZED EVEN THE HYENAS WEREN'T LAUGHING THAT VAN STARTED TO GET REALLY NERVOUS.

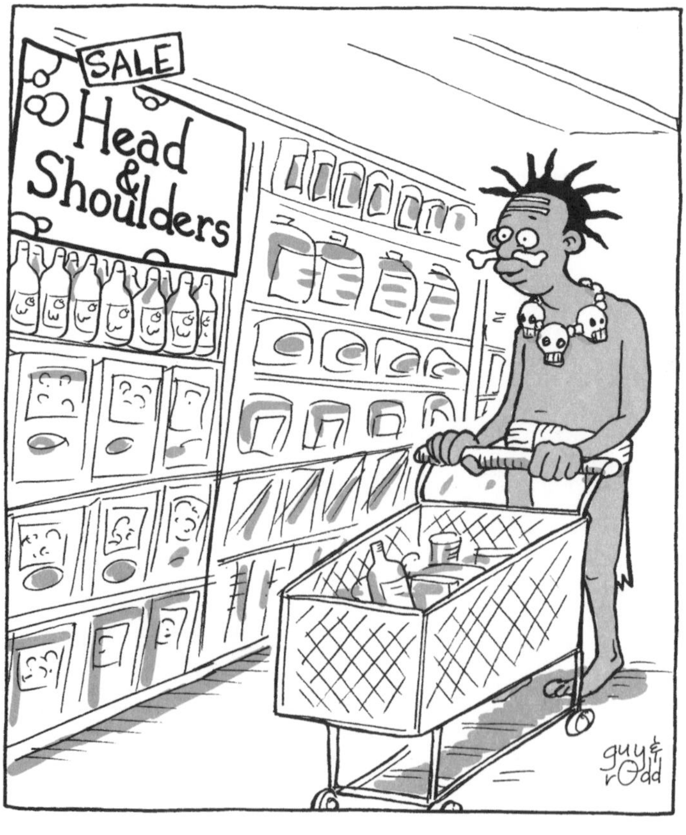
SALE
Head & Shoulders
guy & rOdd

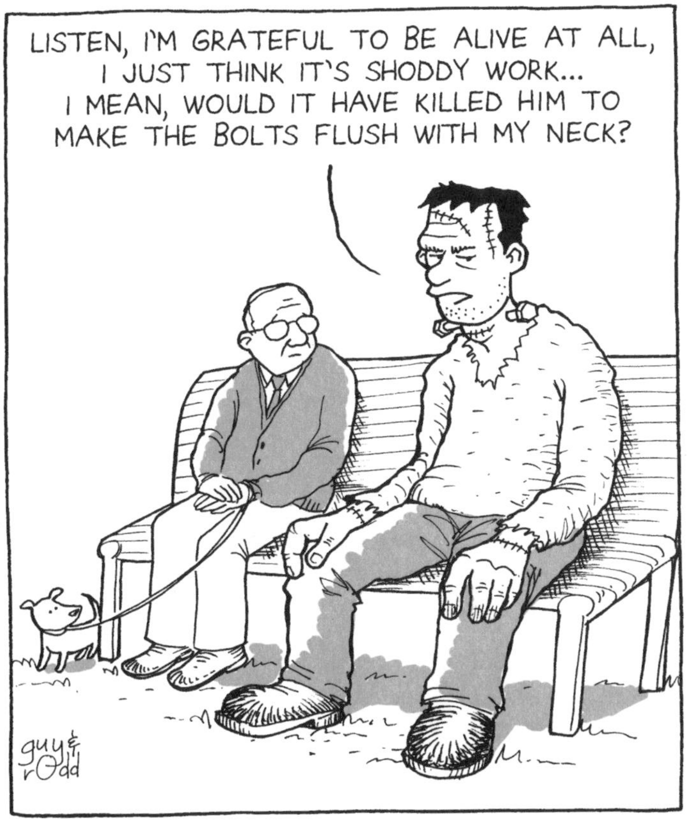
LISTEN, I'M GRATEFUL TO BE ALIVE AT ALL, I JUST THINK IT'S SHODDY WORK... I MEAN, WOULD IT HAVE KILLED HIM TO MAKE THE BOLTS FLUSH WITH MY NECK?
guy & rOdd

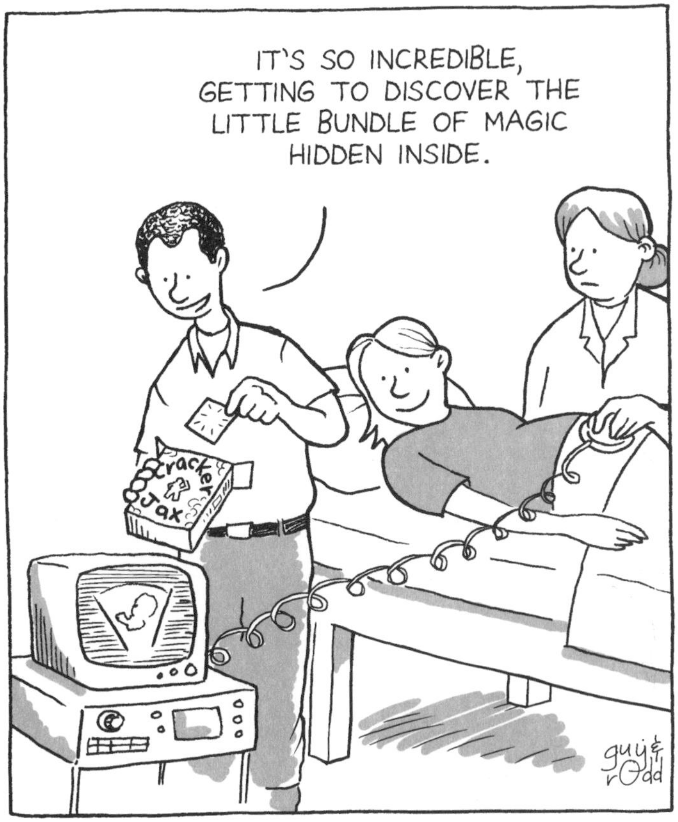
IT'S SO INCREDIBLE, GETTING TO DISCOVER THE LITTLE BUNDLE OF MAGIC HIDDEN INSIDE.
Cracker Jax
guy & rOdd

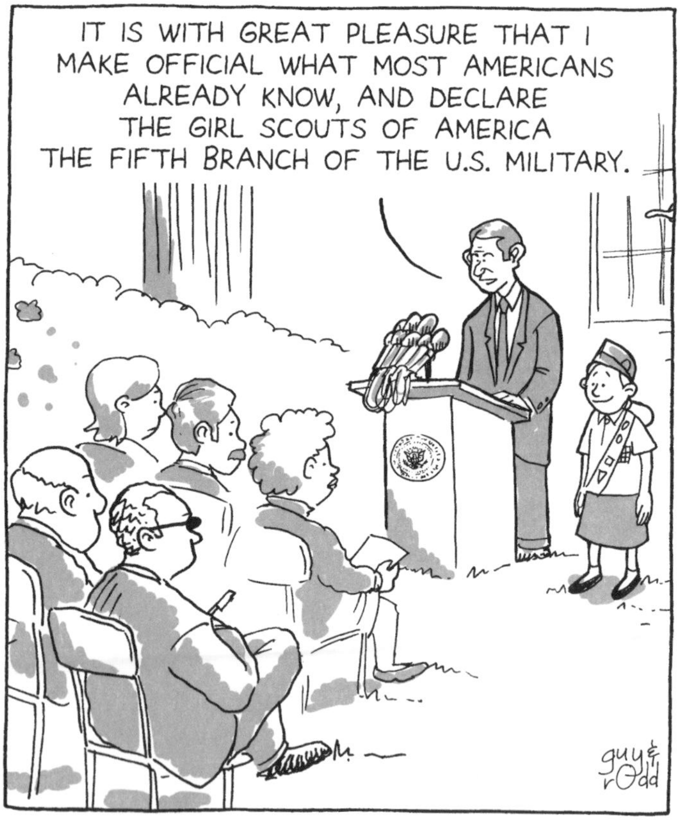
IT IS WITH GREAT PLEASURE THAT I MAKE OFFICIAL WHAT MOST AMERICANS ALREADY KNOW, AND DECLARE THE GIRL SCOUTS OF AMERICA THE FIFTH BRANCH OF THE U.S. MILITARY.

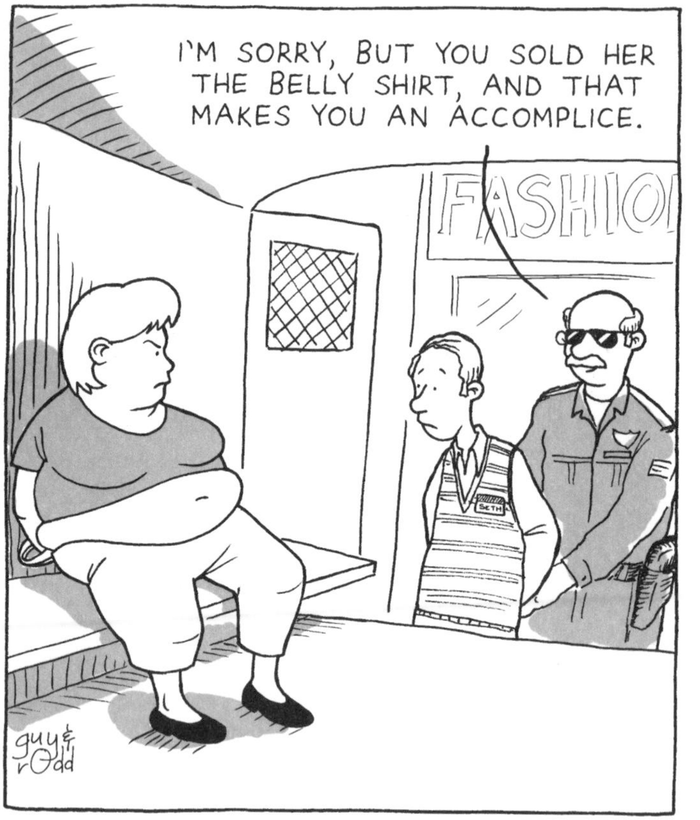
I'M SORRY, BUT YOU SOLD HER THE BELLY SHIRT, AND THAT MAKES YOU AN ACCOMPLICE.
SETH

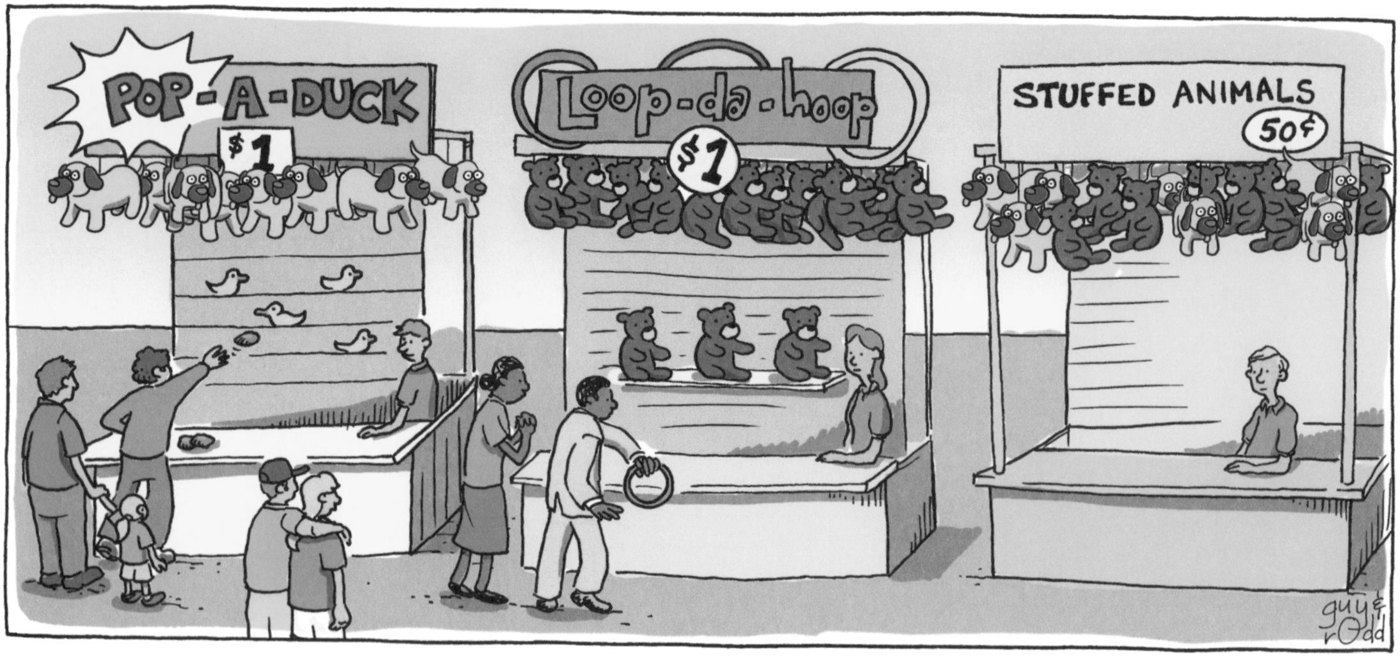
POP-A-DUCK
$1
Loop-da-hoop
$1
STUFFED ANIMALS
50¢

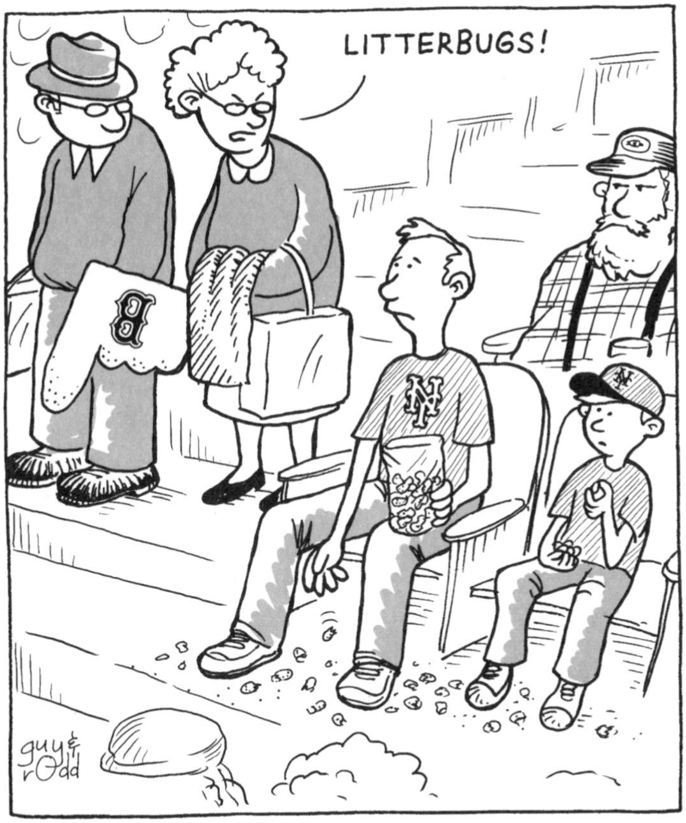
LITTERBUGS!
guy & rOdd

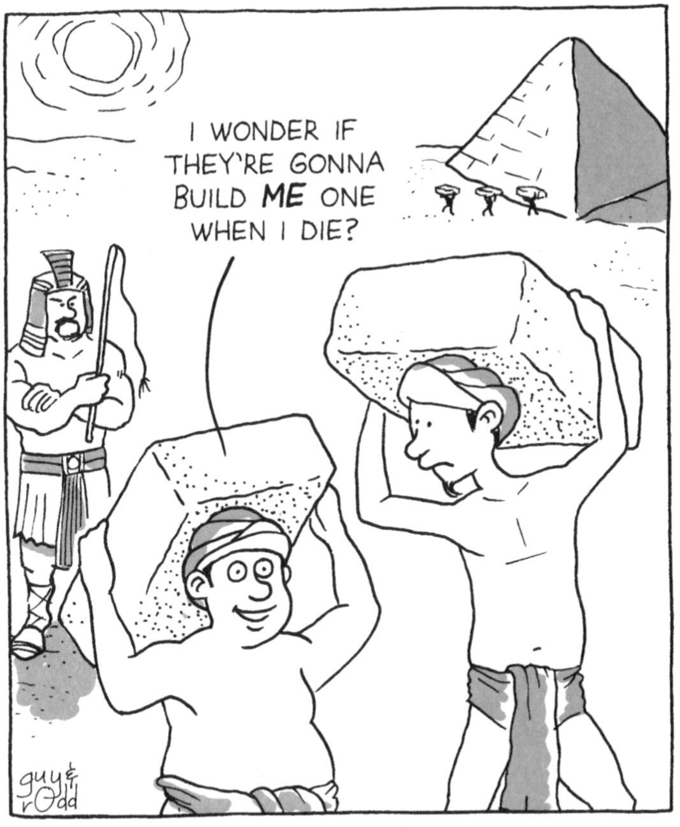
I WONDER IF THEY'RE GONNA BUILD **ME** ONE WHEN I DIE?
guy & rOdd

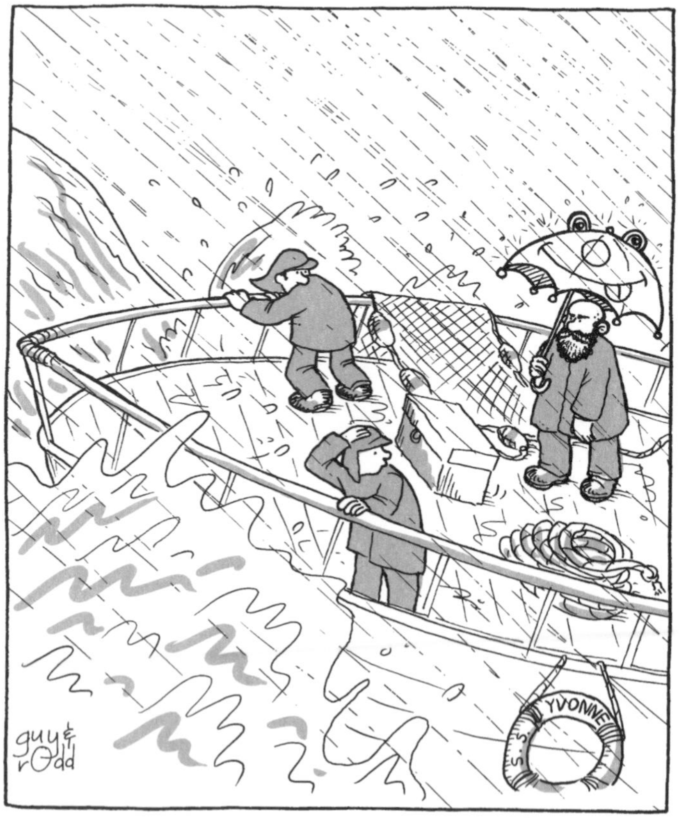
S.S.
YVONNE
guy & rOdd

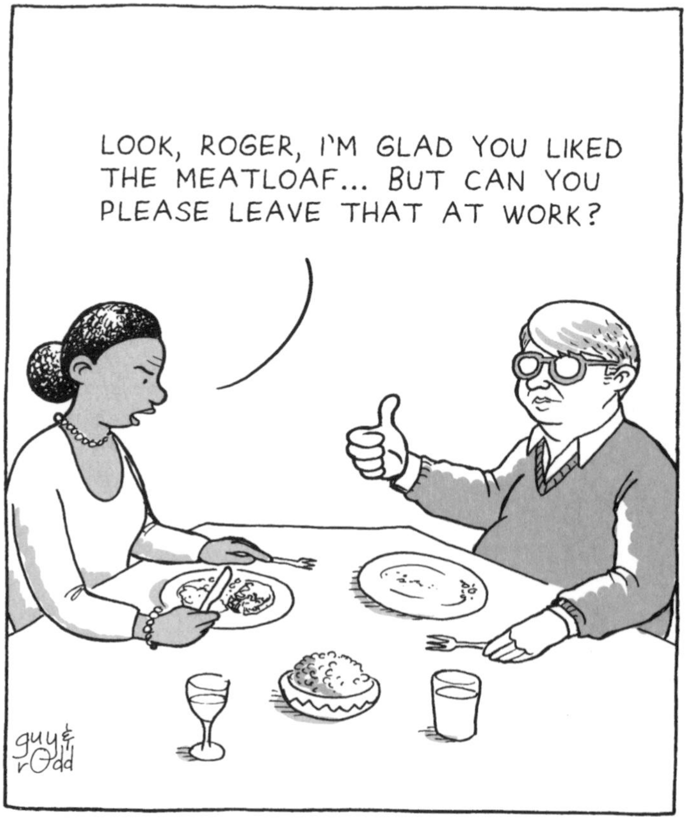
LOOK, ROGER, I'M GLAD YOU LIKED THE MEATLOAF... BUT CAN YOU PLEASE LEAVE THAT AT WORK?
guy & rOdd

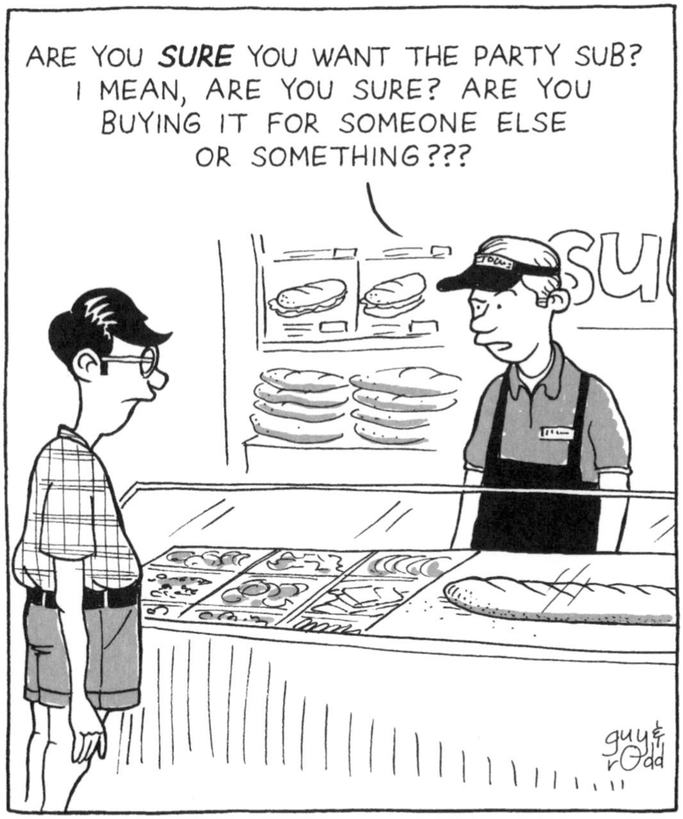
ARE YOU **SURE** YOU WANT THE PARTY SUB? I MEAN, ARE YOU SURE? ARE YOU BUYING IT FOR SOMEONE ELSE OR SOMETHING???

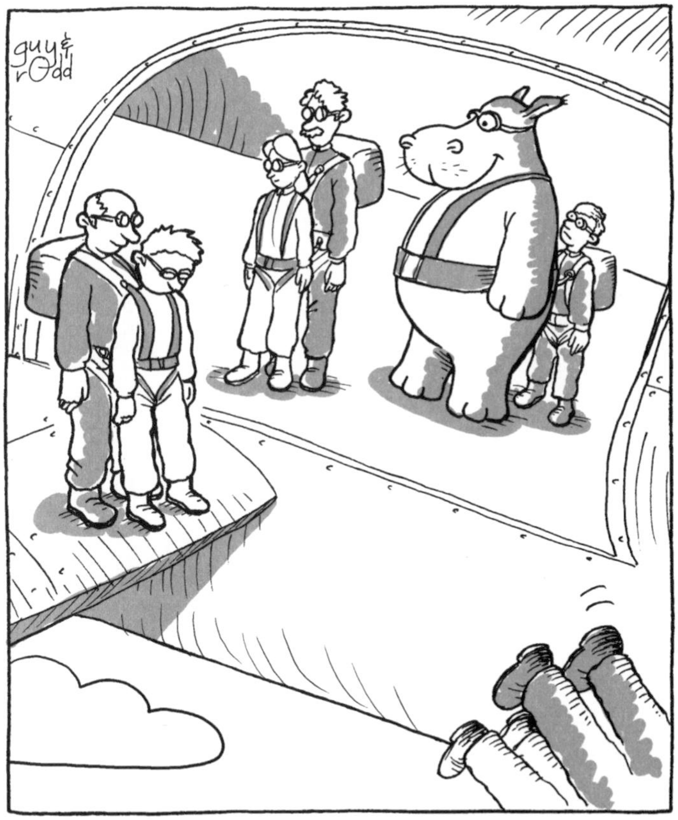

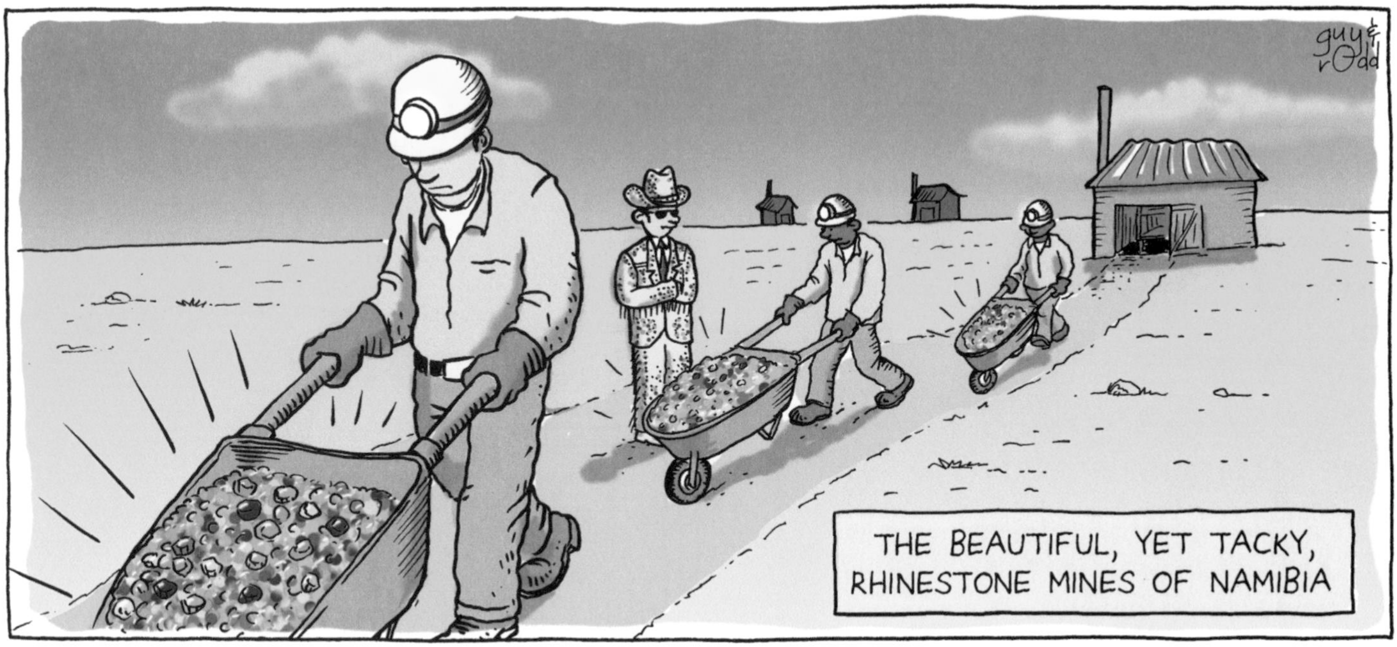
THE BEAUTIFUL, YET TACKY, RHINESTONE MINES OF NAMIBIA

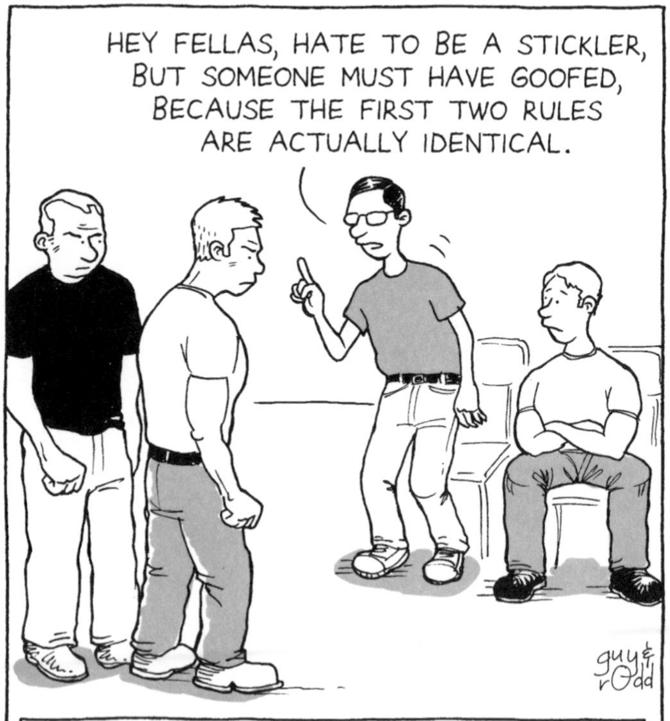
HEY FELLAS, HATE TO BE A STICKLER, BUT SOMEONE MUST HAVE GOOFED, BECAUSE THE FIRST TWO RULES ARE ACTUALLY IDENTICAL.

GENE GETS KICKED OUT OF FIGHT CLUB

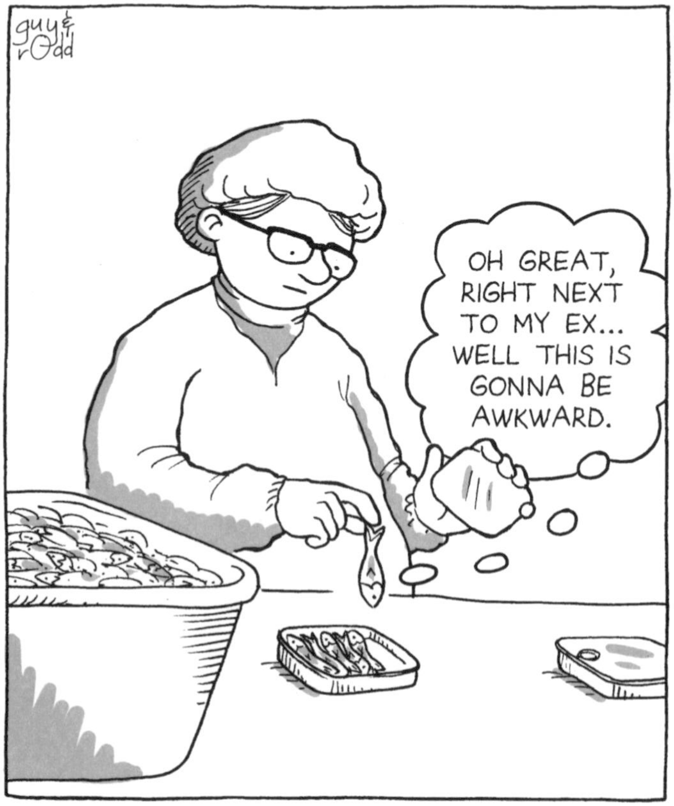
OH GREAT, RIGHT NEXT TO MY EX... WELL THIS IS GONNA BE AWKWARD.

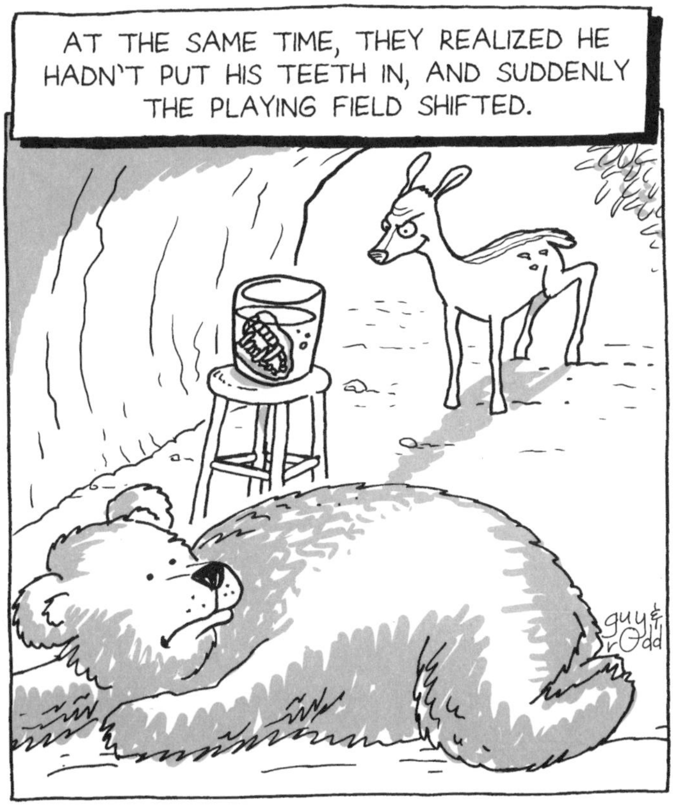
AT THE SAME TIME, THEY REALIZED HE HADN'T PUT HIS TEETH IN, AND SUDDENLY THE PLAYING FIELD SHIFTED.

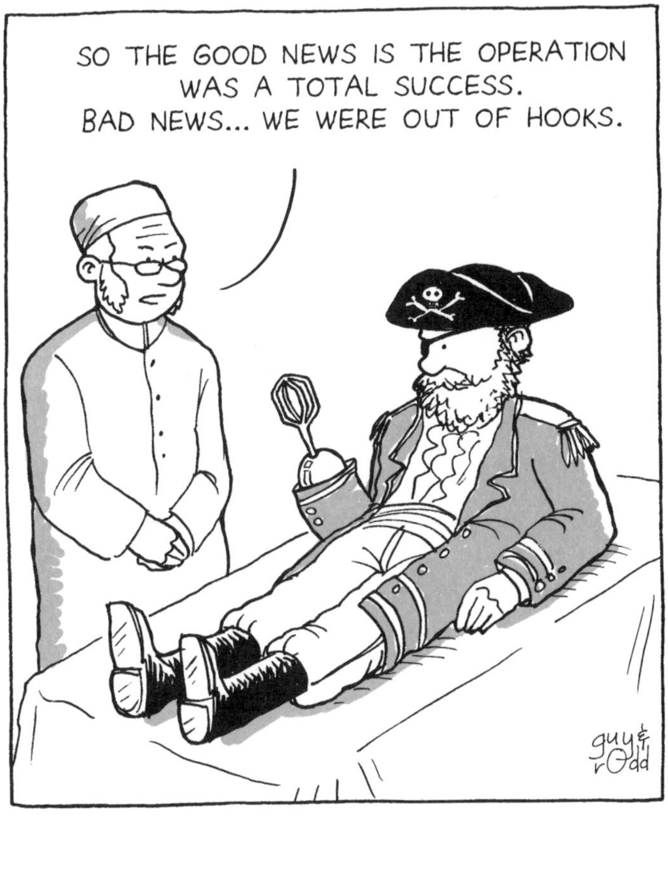
SO THE GOOD NEWS IS THE OPERATION WAS A TOTAL SUCCESS.
BAD NEWS... WE WERE OUT OF HOOKS.

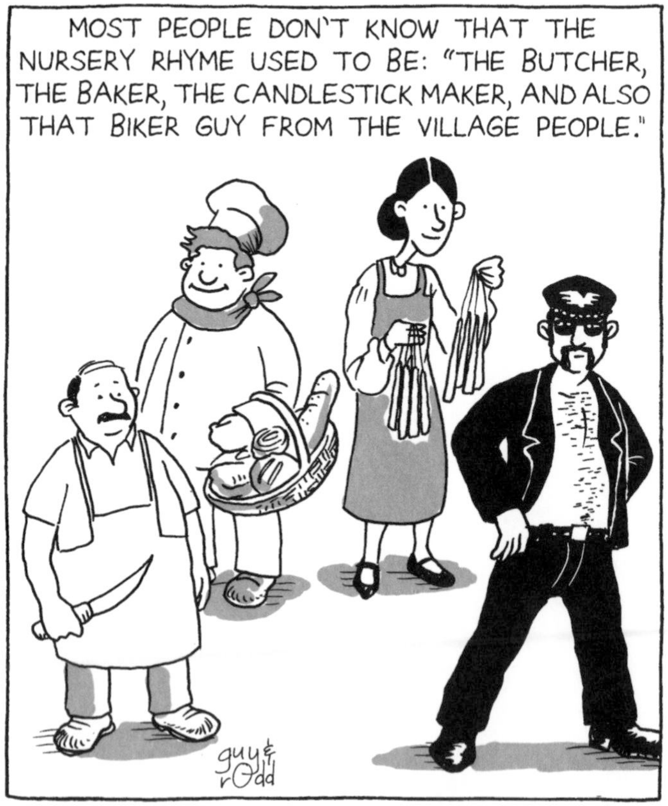
MOST PEOPLE DON'T KNOW THAT THE NURSERY RHYME USED TO BE: "THE BUTCHER, THE BAKER, THE CANDLESTICK MAKER, AND ALSO THAT BIKER GUY FROM THE VILLAGE PEOPLE."

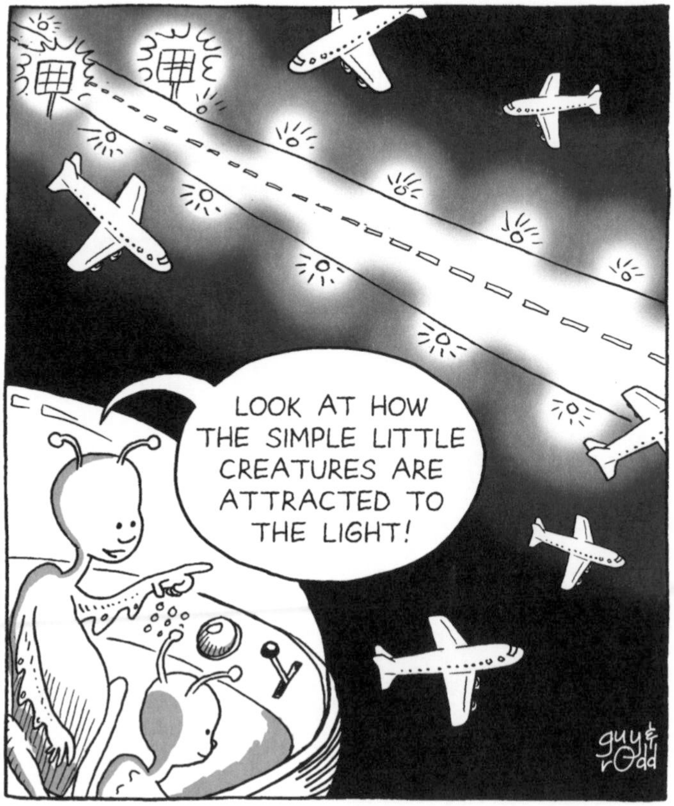
LOOK AT HOW THE SIMPLE LITTLE CREATURES ARE ATTRACTED TO THE LIGHT!

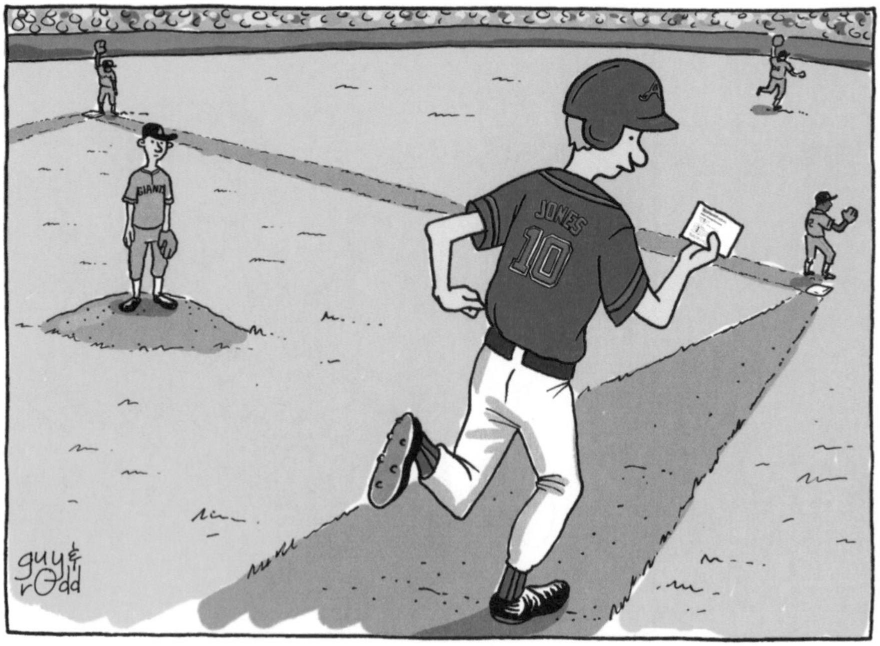
GIANTS
JONES
10

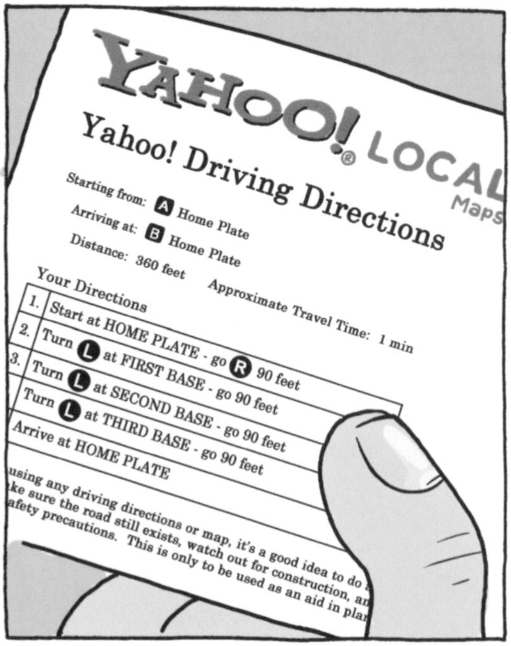
YAHOO! LOCAL
Maps
Yahoo! Driving Directions
Starting from: A Home Plate
Arriving at: B Home Plate
Distance: 360 feet
Approximate Travel Time: 1 min
Your Directions
1. Start at HOME PLATE - go R 90 feet
2. Turn L at FIRST BASE - go 90 feet
3. Turn L at SECOND BASE - go 90 feet
Turn L at THIRD BASE - go 90 feet
Arrive at HOME PLATE

BY THE YEAR 2500, 1 IN 10 ACADEMICS WILL DEVOTE THEIR ENTIRE CAREER TO DIVINING THE MEANING OF THE WORD "SUSSUDIO."

WELL, WELL, WELL, LOOKS LIKE WE'VE GOT OURSELVES A TROUBLEMAKER.

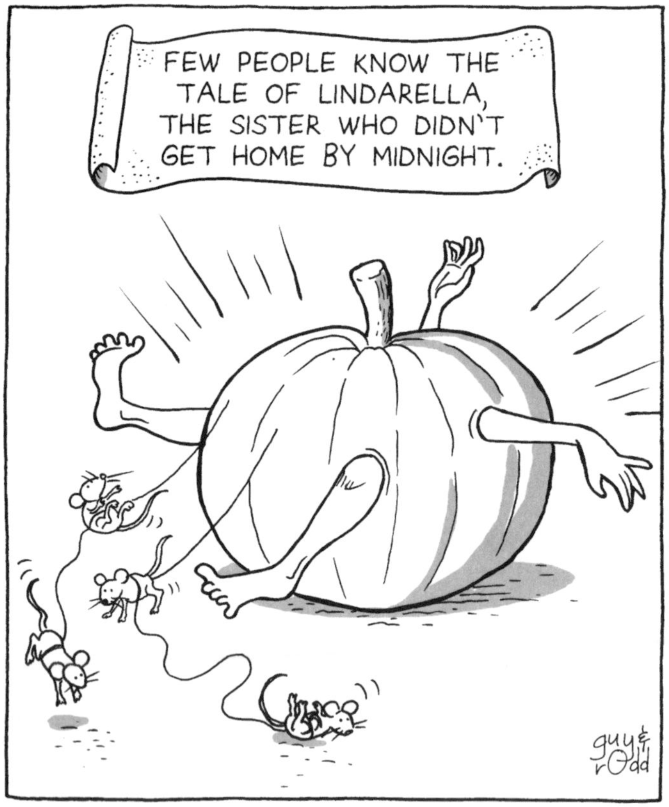
FEW PEOPLE KNOW THE TALE OF LINDARELLA, THE SISTER WHO DIDN'T GET HOME BY MIDNIGHT.
guy & rOdd

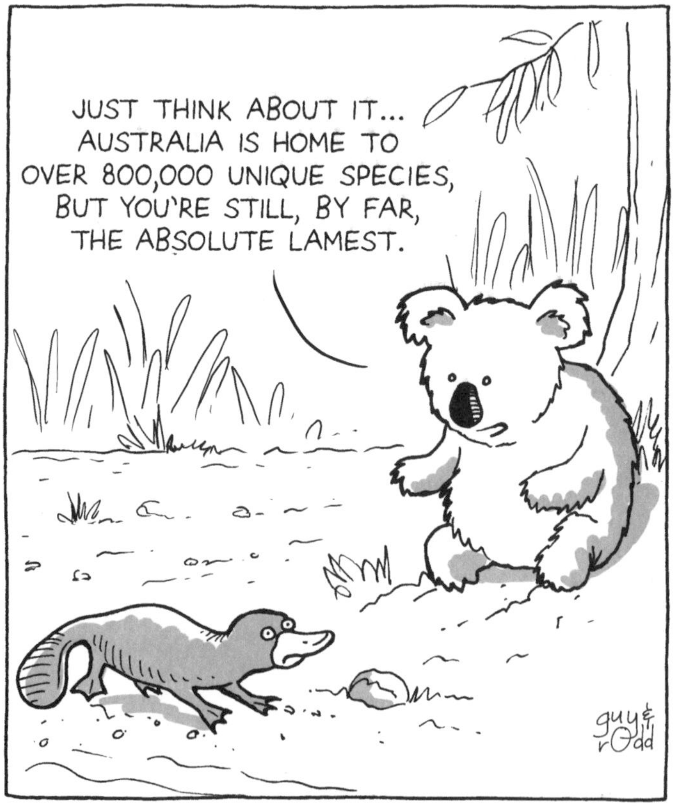
JUST THINK ABOUT IT... AUSTRALIA IS HOME TO OVER 800,000 UNIQUE SPECIES, BUT YOU'RE STILL, BY FAR, THE ABSOLUTE LAMEST.
guy & rOdd

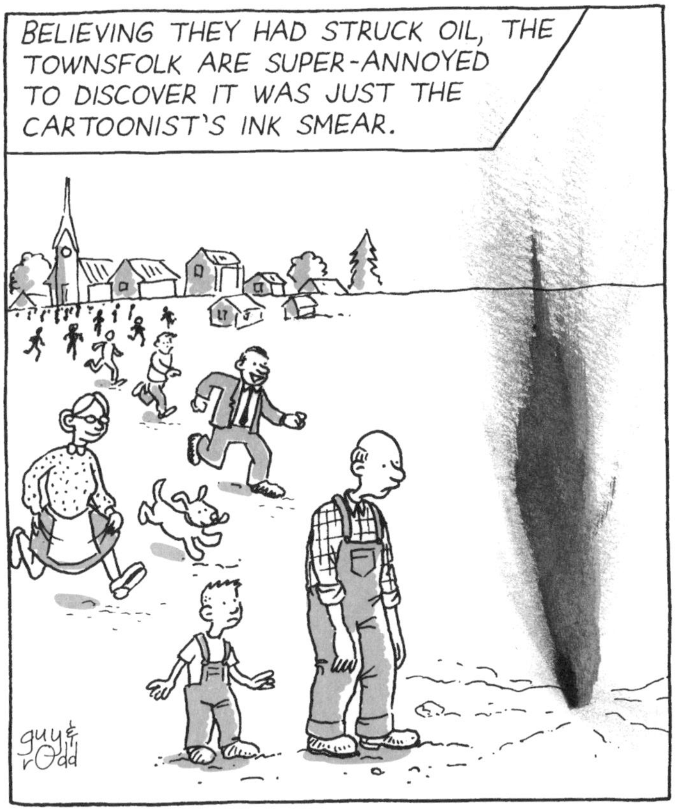
BELIEVING THEY HAD STRUCK OIL, THE TOWNSFOLK ARE SUPER-ANNOYED TO DISCOVER IT WAS JUST THE CARTOONIST'S INK SMEAR.

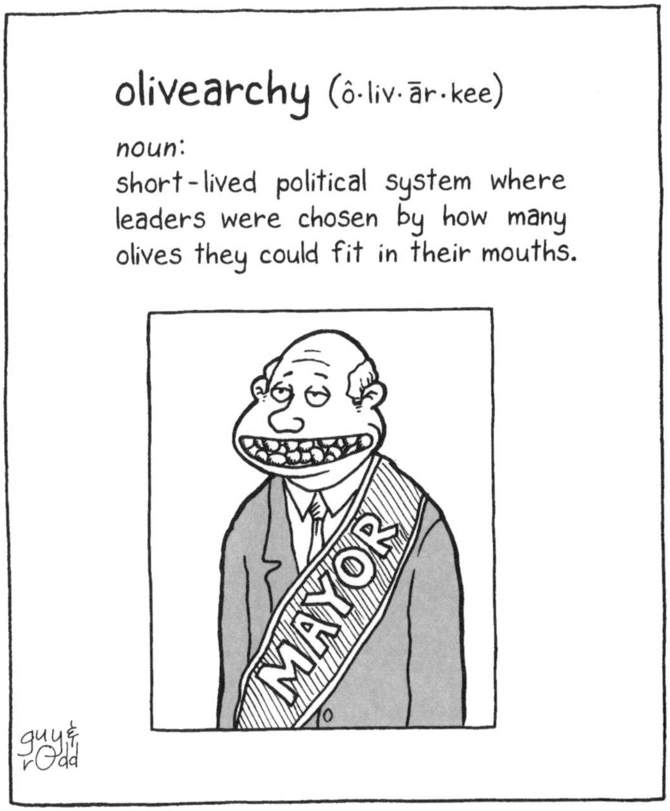
olivearchy (ô·liv·ār·kee)
noun:
short-lived political system where leaders were chosen by how many olives they could fit in their mouths.
MAYOR

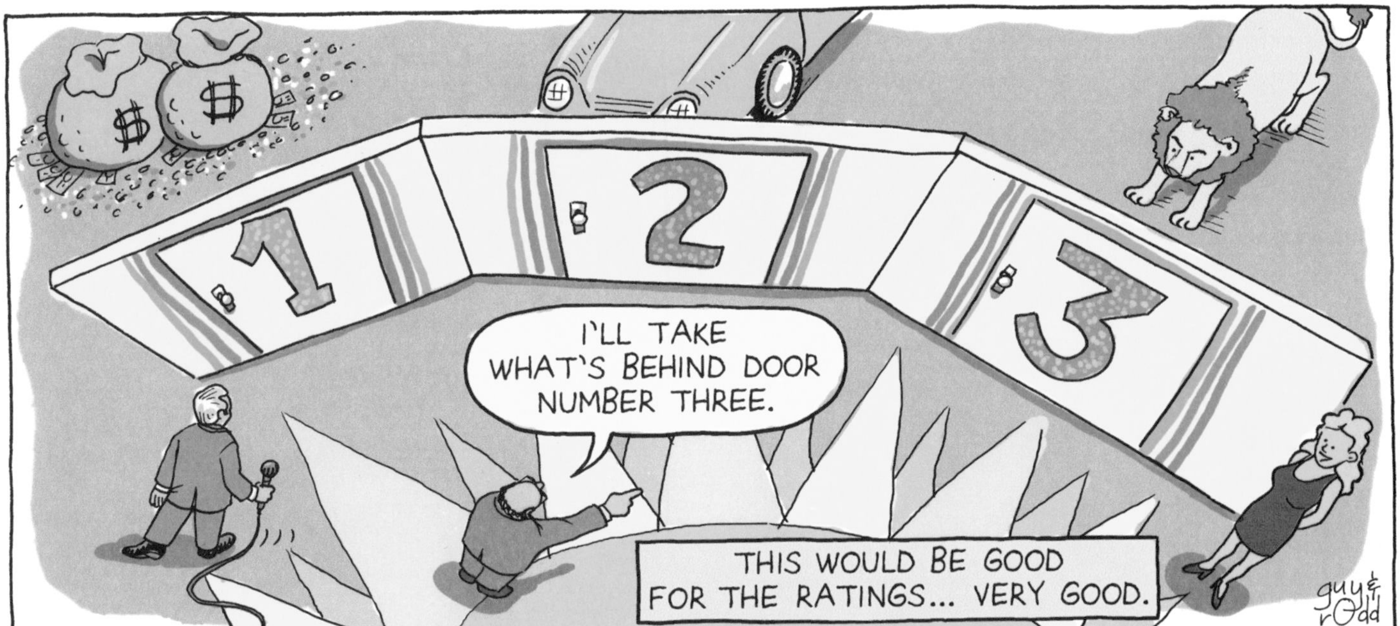
1
2
3
I'LL TAKE WHAT'S BEHIND DOOR NUMBER THREE.
THIS WOULD BE GOOD FOR THE RATINGS... VERY GOOD.

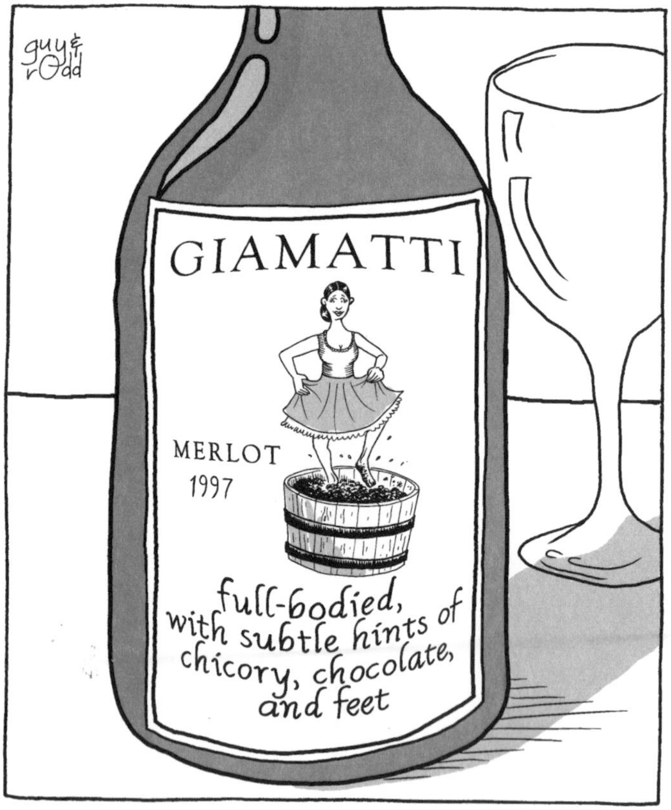
guy & rOdd
GIAMATTI
MERLOT
1997
full-bodied, with subtle hints of chicory, chocolate, and feet

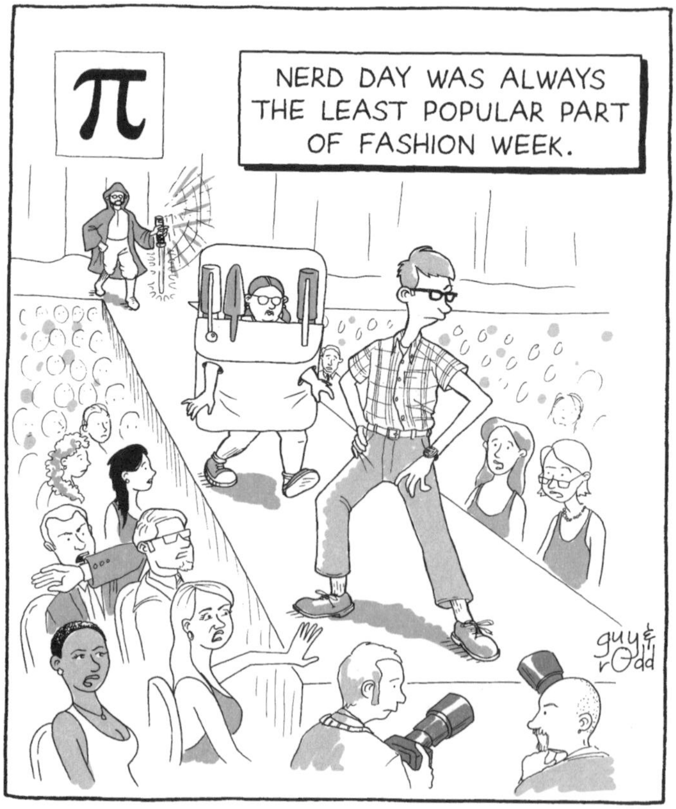
π
NERD DAY WAS ALWAYS THE LEAST POPULAR PART OF FASHION WEEK.
guy & rOdd

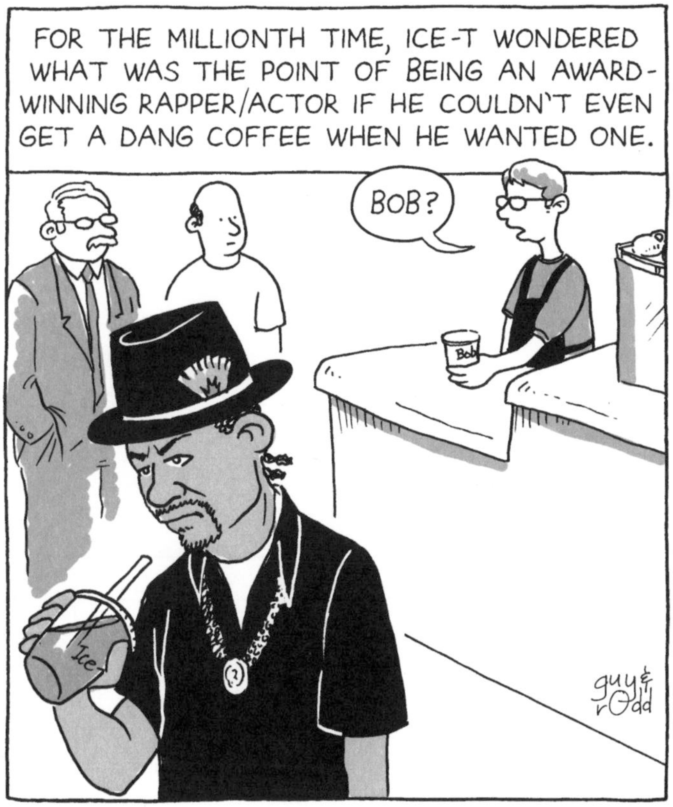
FOR THE MILLIONTH TIME, ICE-T WONDERED WHAT WAS THE POINT OF BEING AN AWARD-WINNING RAPPER/ACTOR IF HE COULDN'T EVEN GET A DANG COFFEE WHEN HE WANTED ONE.
BOB?
Bob
Ice-
guy & rOdd

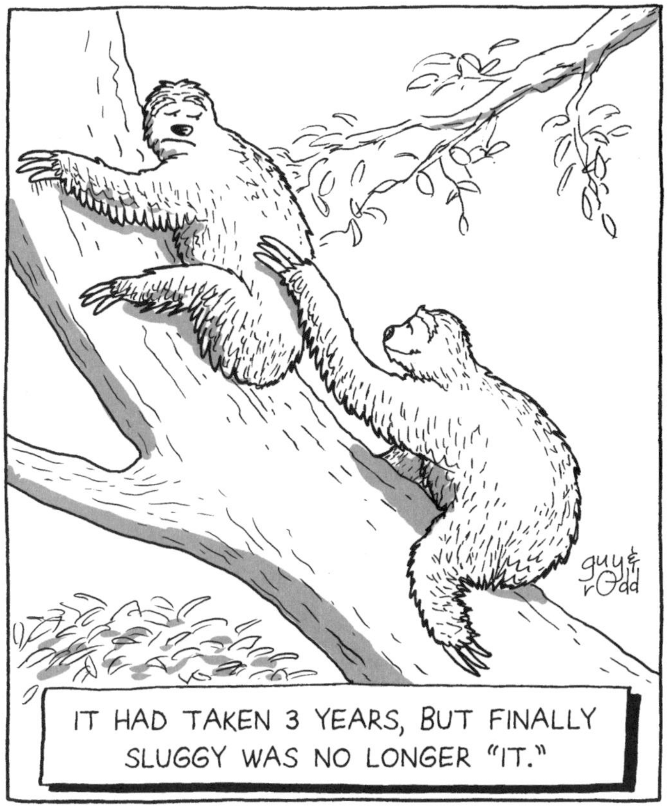
guy & rOdd
IT HAD TAKEN 3 YEARS, BUT FINALLY SLUGGY WAS NO LONGER "IT."

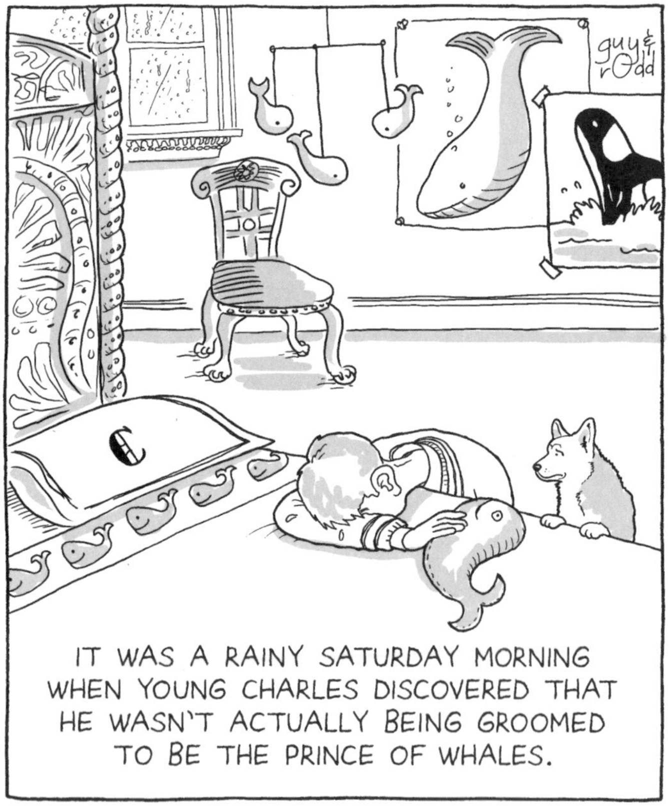
IT WAS A RAINY SATURDAY MORNING WHEN YOUNG CHARLES DISCOVERED THAT HE WASN'T ACTUALLY BEING GROOMED TO BE THE PRINCE OF WHALES.

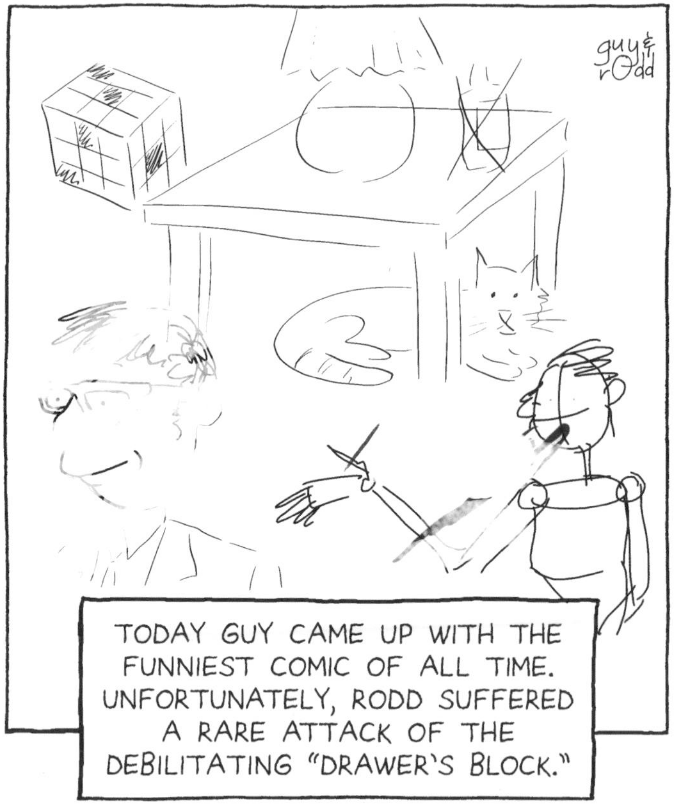
TODAY GUY CAME UP WITH THE FUNNIEST COMIC OF ALL TIME. UNFORTUNATELY, RODD SUFFERED A RARE ATTACK OF THE DEBILITATING "DRAWER'S BLOCK."

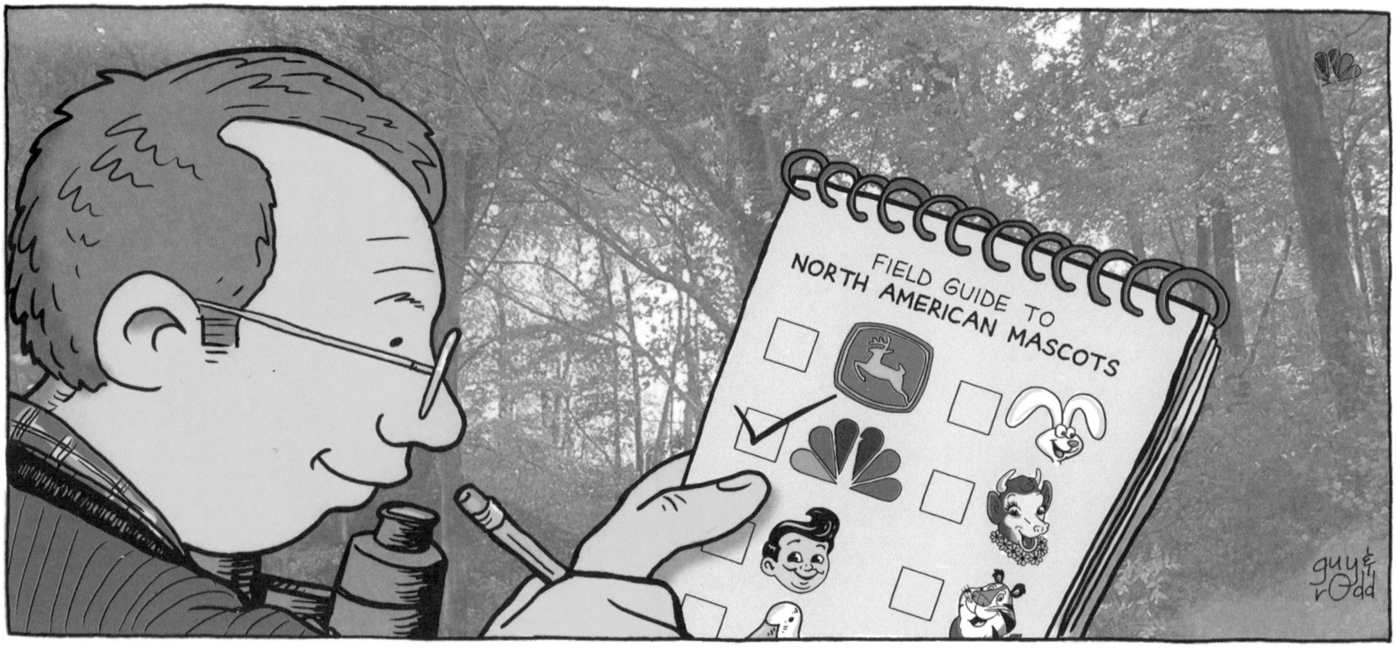
FIELD GUIDE TO
NORTH AMERICAN MASCOTS

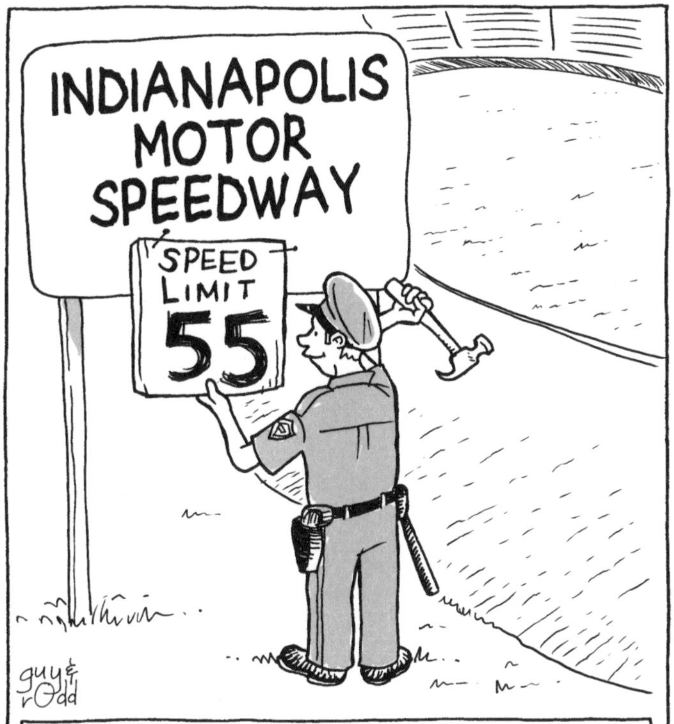
INDIANAPOLIS MOTOR SPEEDWAY
SPEED LIMIT 55

TOMORROW WOULD BE A LUCRATIVE DAY FOR THE INDIANAPOLIS POLICE DEPARTMENT.

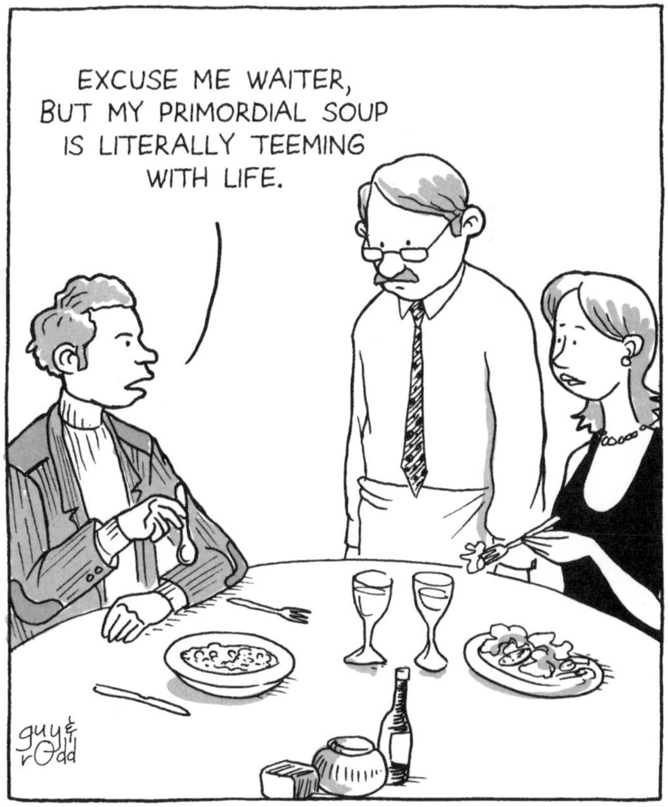
EXCUSE ME WAITER, BUT MY PRIMORDIAL SOUP IS LITERALLY TEEMING WITH LIFE.

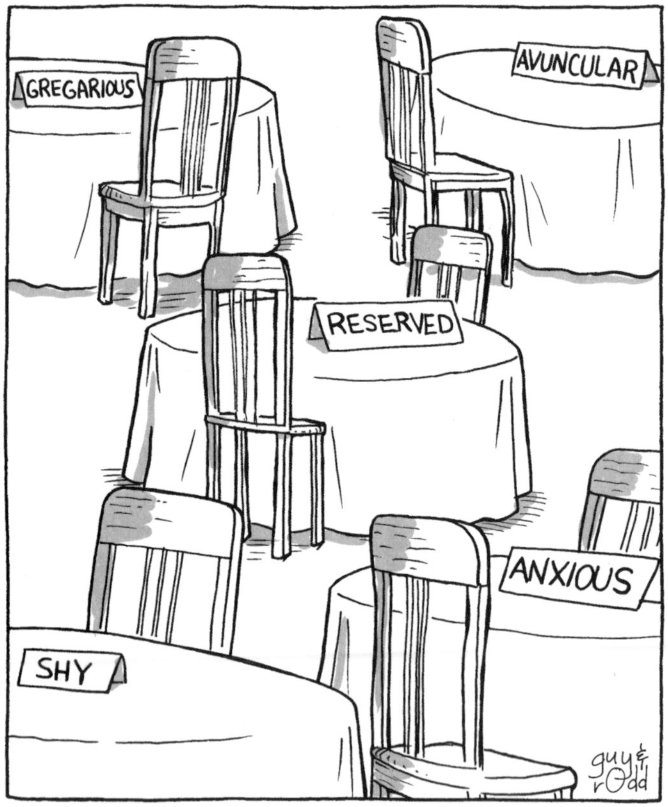
GREGARIOUS
AVUNCULAR
RESERVED
ANXIOUS
SHY
guy & rOdd

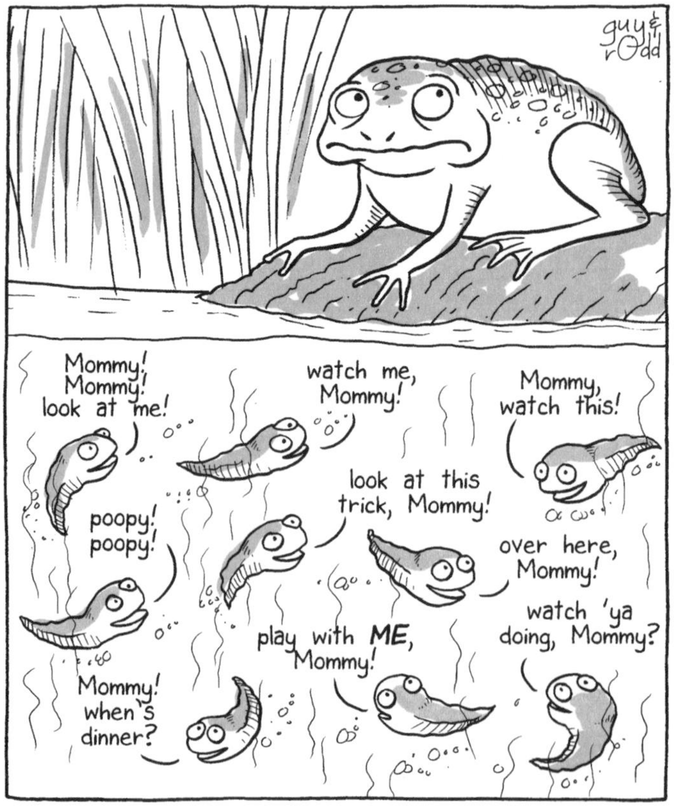
guy & rOdd
Mommy! Mommy! look at me!
watch me, Mommy!
Mommy, watch this!
look at this trick, Mommy!
poopy! poopy!
over here, Mommy!
watch 'ya doing, Mommy?
play with **ME**, Mommy!
Mommy! when's dinner?

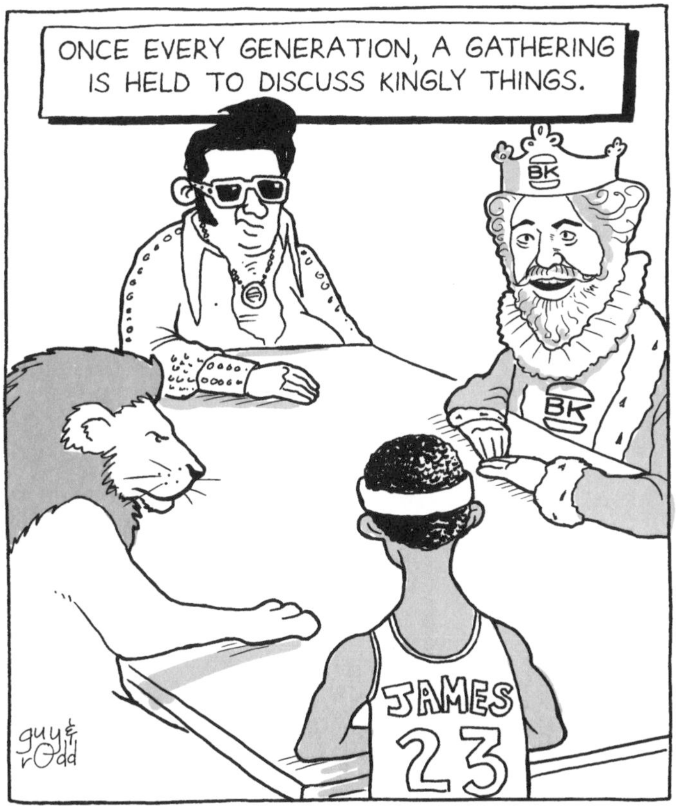
ONCE EVERY GENERATION, A GATHERING IS HELD TO DISCUSS KINGLY THINGS.
BK
BK
JAMES
23
guy & rOdd

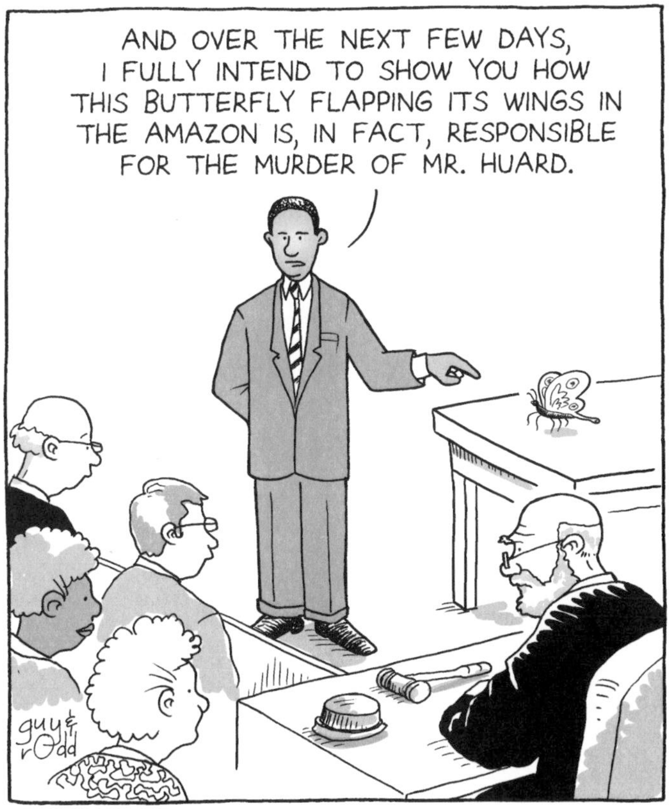
AND OVER THE NEXT FEW DAYS, I FULLY INTEND TO SHOW YOU HOW THIS BUTTERFLY FLAPPING ITS WINGS IN THE AMAZON IS, IN FACT, RESPONSIBLE FOR THE MURDER OF MR. HUARD.
guy & rOdd

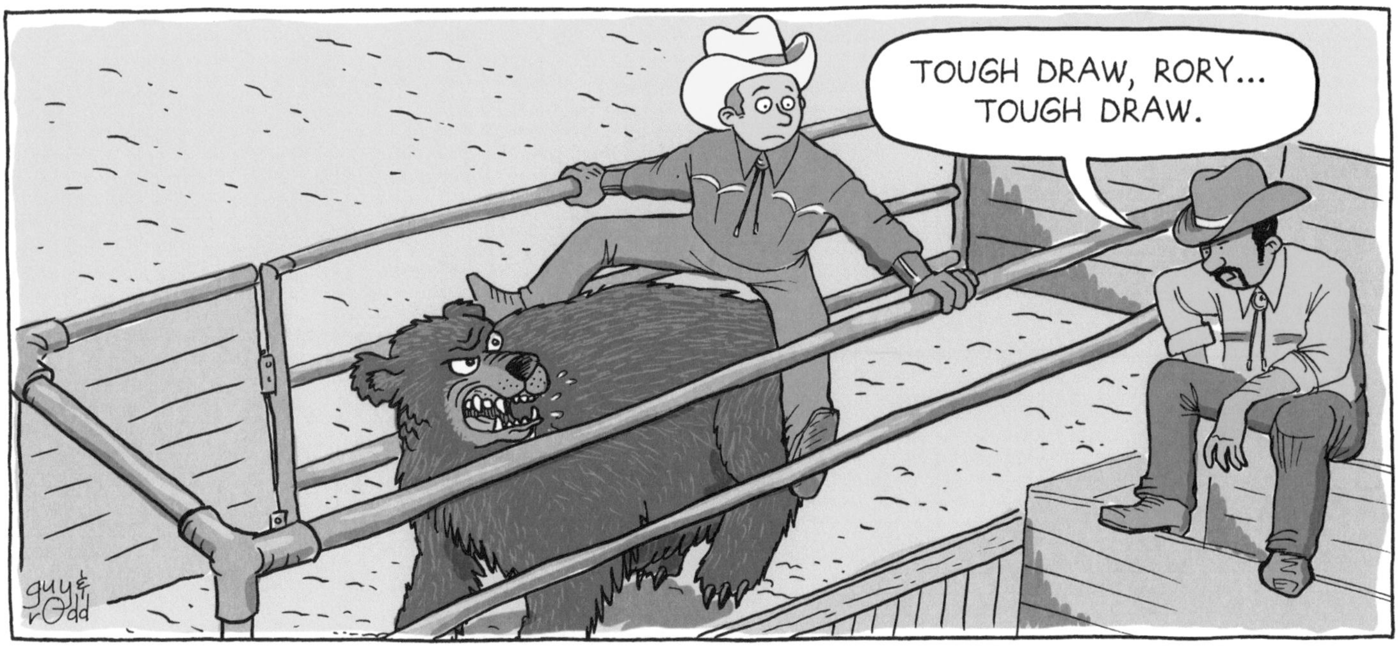
TOUGH DRAW, RORY... TOUGH DRAW.
guy & rOdd

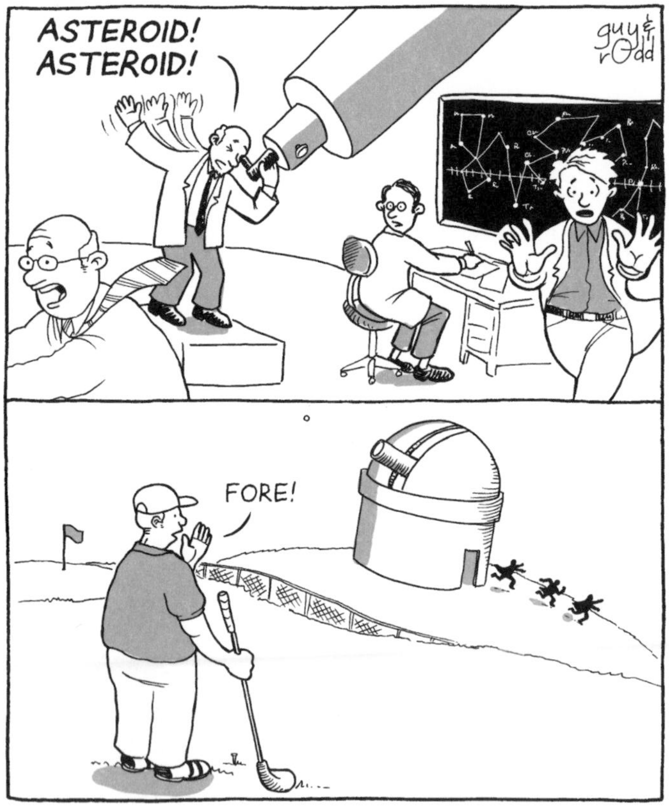
ASTEROID!
ASTEROID!
FORE!

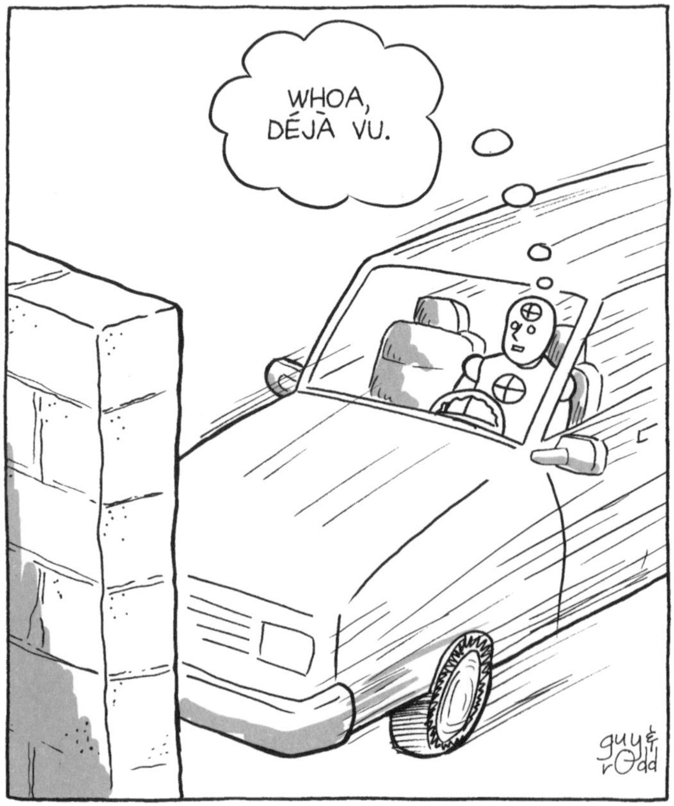
WHOA,
DÉJÀ VU.

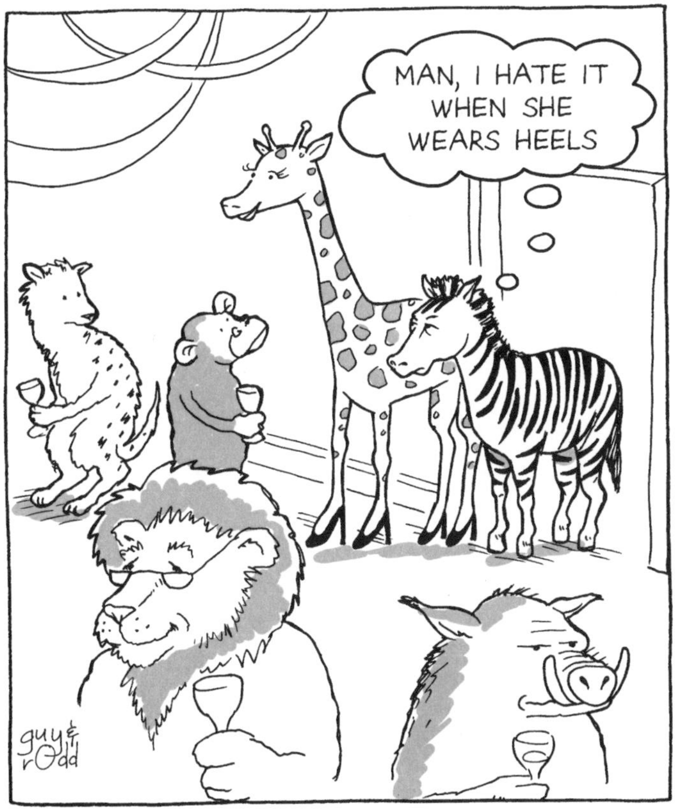
MAN, I HATE IT WHEN SHE WEARS HEELS

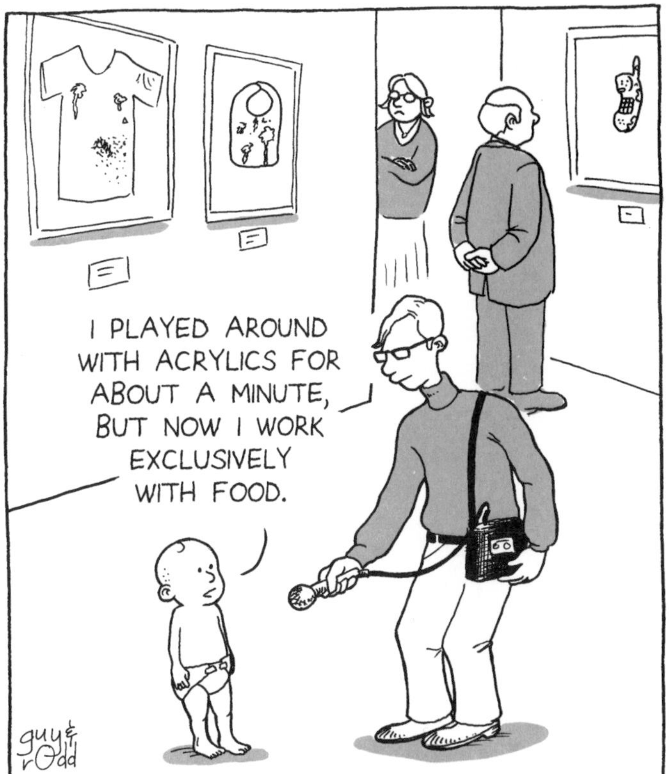
I PLAYED AROUND WITH ACRYLICS FOR ABOUT A MINUTE, BUT NOW I WORK EXCLUSIVELY WITH FOOD.

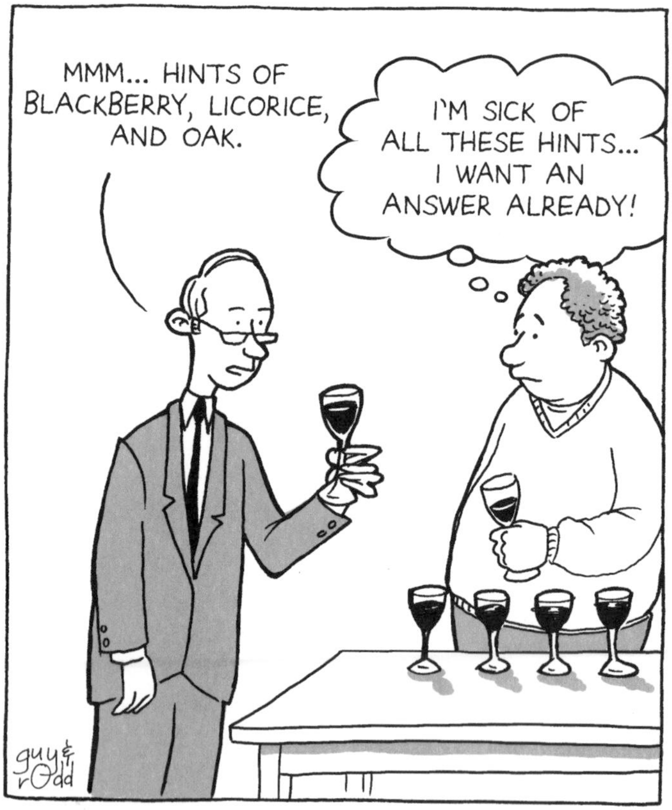
MMM... HINTS OF BLACKBERRY, LICORICE, AND OAK.
I'M SICK OF ALL THESE HINTS... I WANT AN ANSWER ALREADY!
guy & rOdd

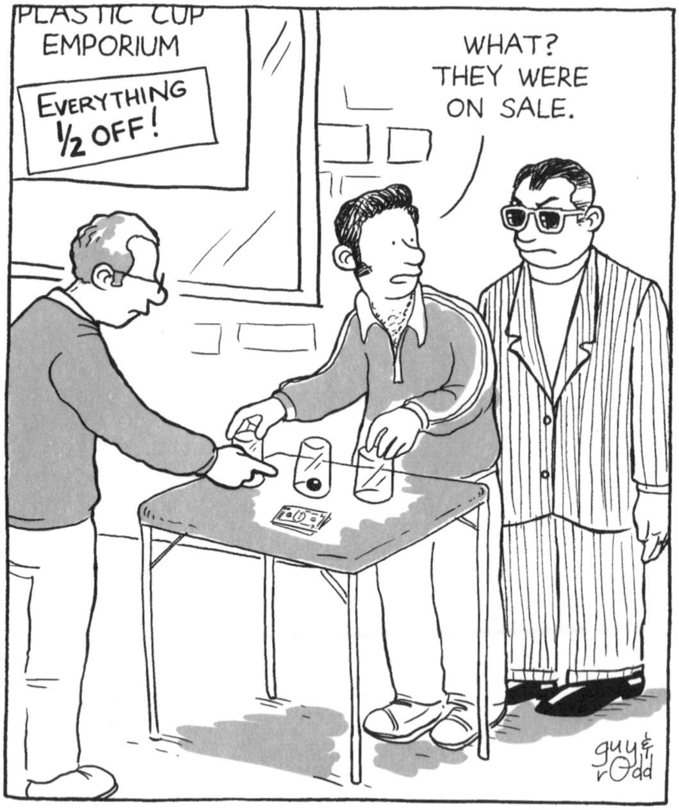
PLASTIC CUP EMPORIUM
EVERYTHING 1/2 OFF!
WHAT? THEY WERE ON SALE.
guy & rOdd

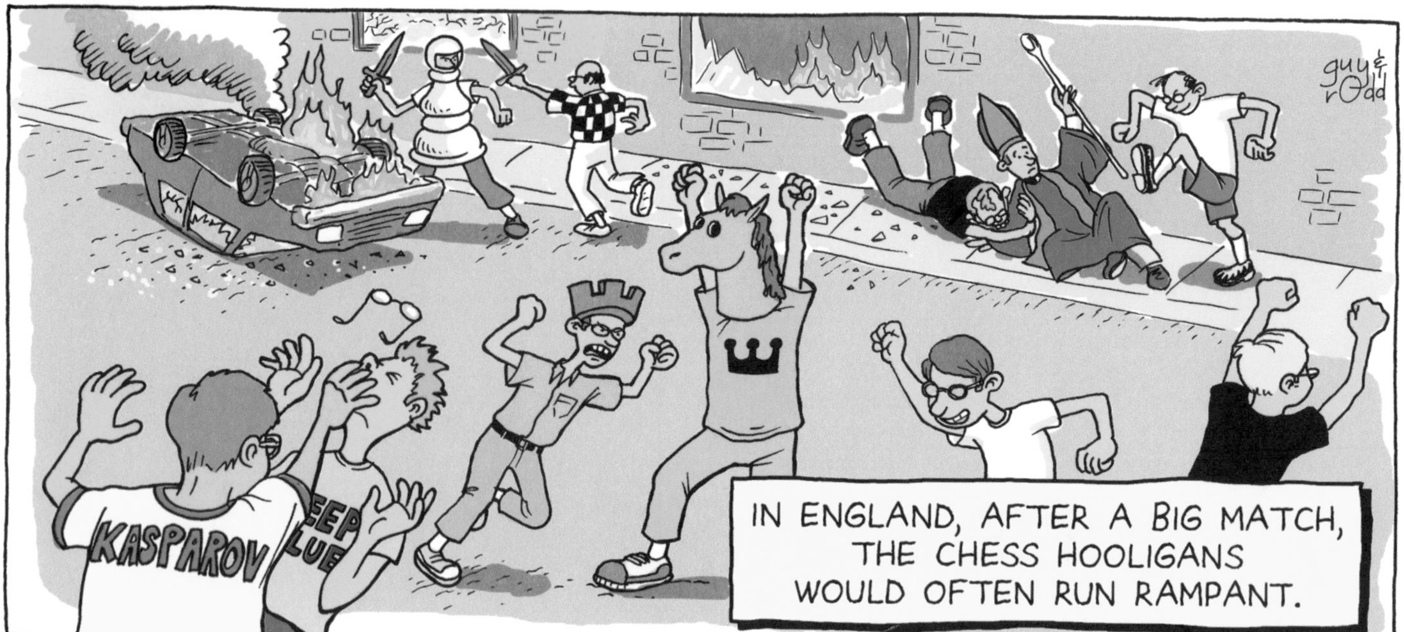
guy & rOdd
KASPAROV
EEP
LUE
IN ENGLAND, AFTER A BIG MATCH, THE CHESS HOOLIGANS WOULD OFTEN RUN RAMPANT.

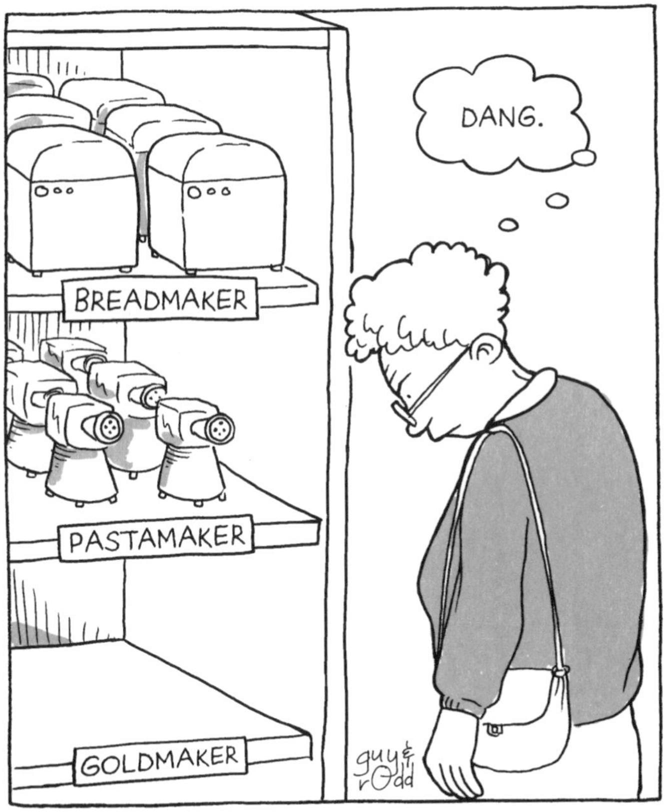
DANG.
BREADMAKER
PASTAMAKER
GOLDMAKER

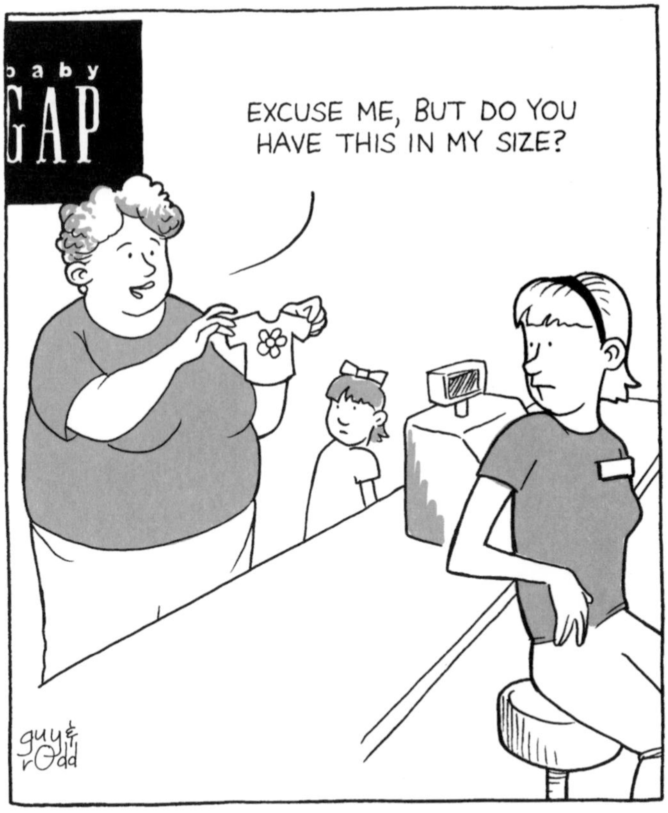
baby GAP
EXCUSE ME, BUT DO YOU HAVE THIS IN MY SIZE?

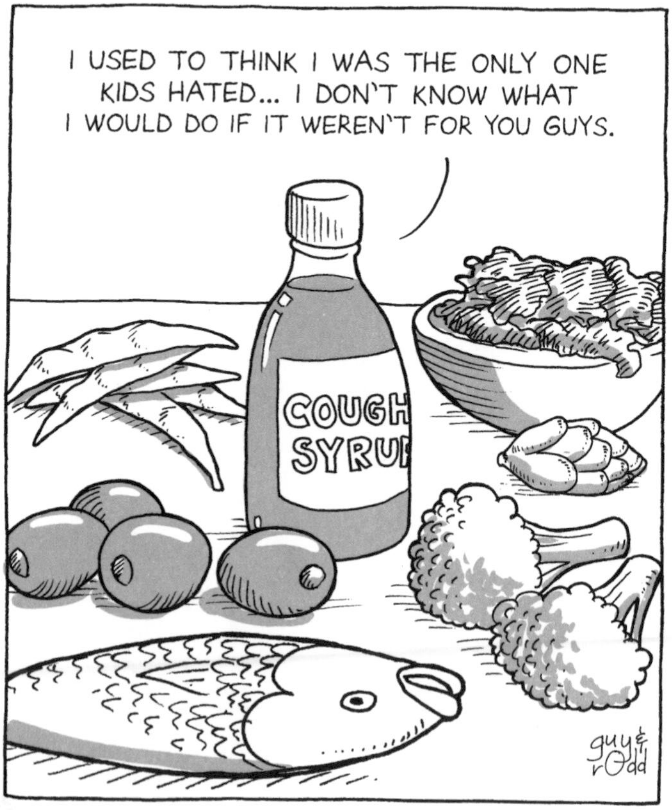
I USED TO THINK I WAS THE ONLY ONE KIDS HATED... I DON'T KNOW WHAT I WOULD DO IF IT WEREN'T FOR YOU GUYS.
COUGH SYRU
guy & rOdd

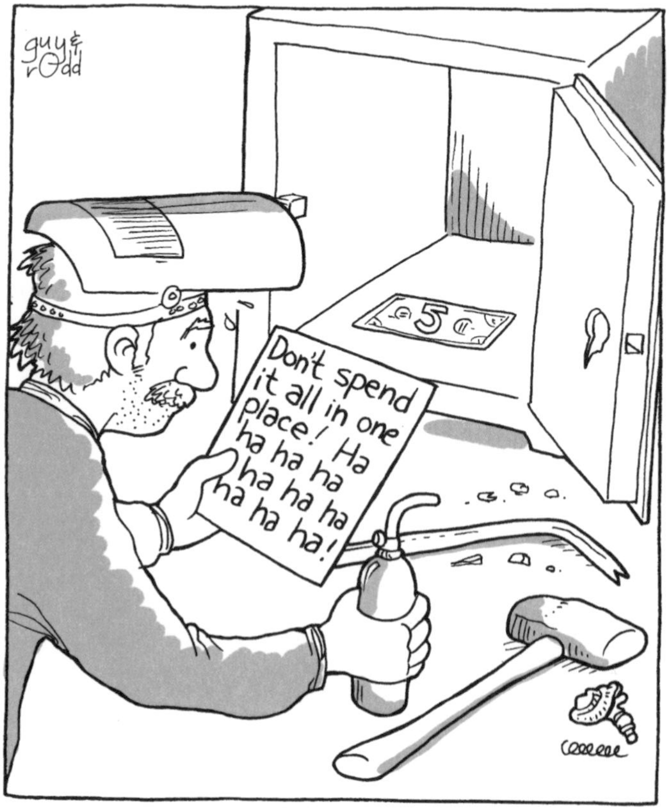
guy & rOdd
Don't spend it all in one place! Ha ha ha ha ha ha ha ha ha ha!
5

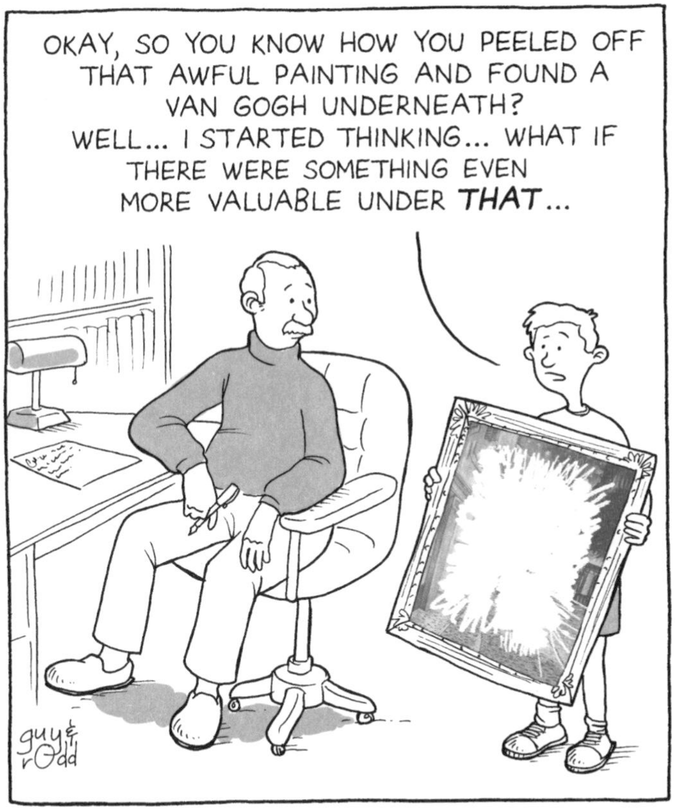
OKAY, SO YOU KNOW HOW YOU PEELED OFF THAT AWFUL PAINTING AND FOUND A VAN GOGH UNDERNEATH? WELL... I STARTED THINKING... WHAT IF THERE WERE SOMETHING EVEN MORE VALUABLE UNDER **THAT**...

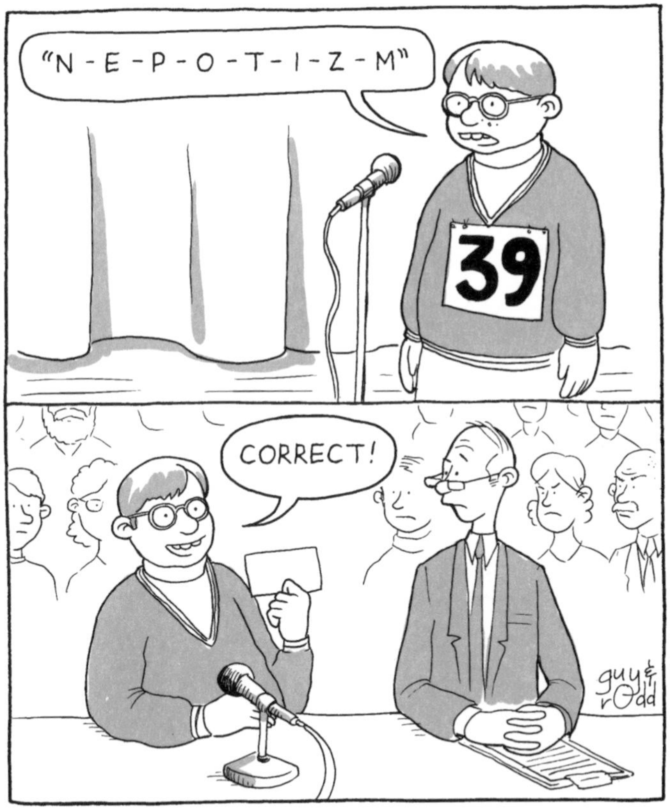
"N-E-P-O-T-I-Z-M"
39
CORRECT!

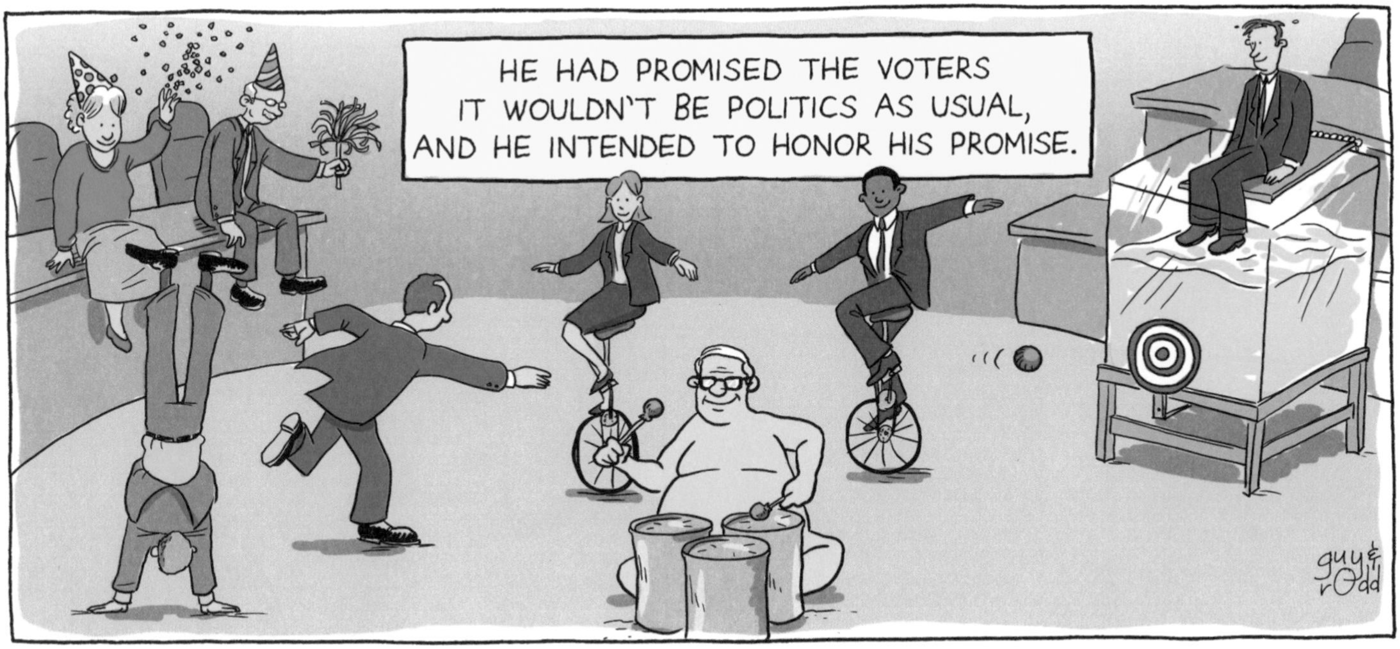
HE HAD PROMISED THE VOTERS IT WOULDN'T BE POLITICS AS USUAL, AND HE INTENDED TO HONOR HIS PROMISE.

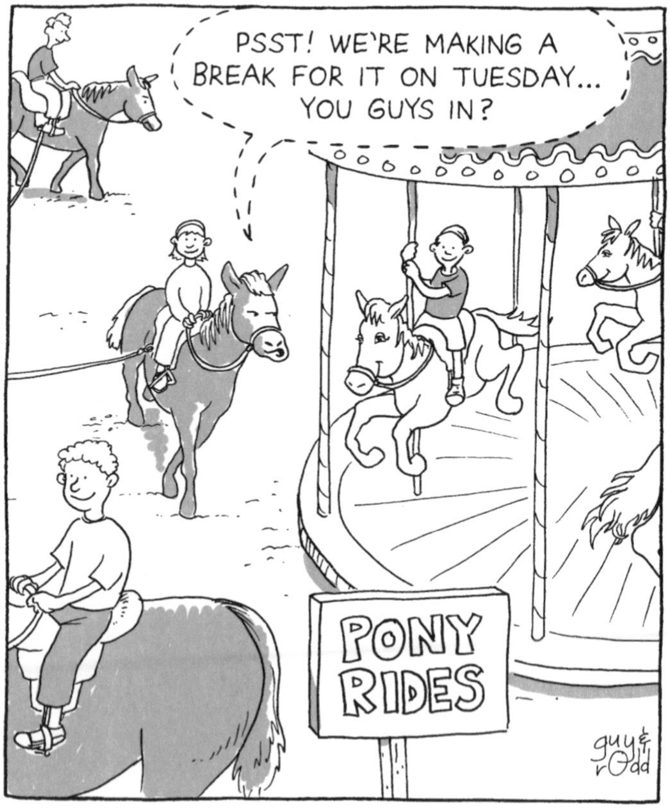
PSST! WE'RE MAKING A BREAK FOR IT ON TUESDAY... YOU GUYS IN?
PONY RIDES

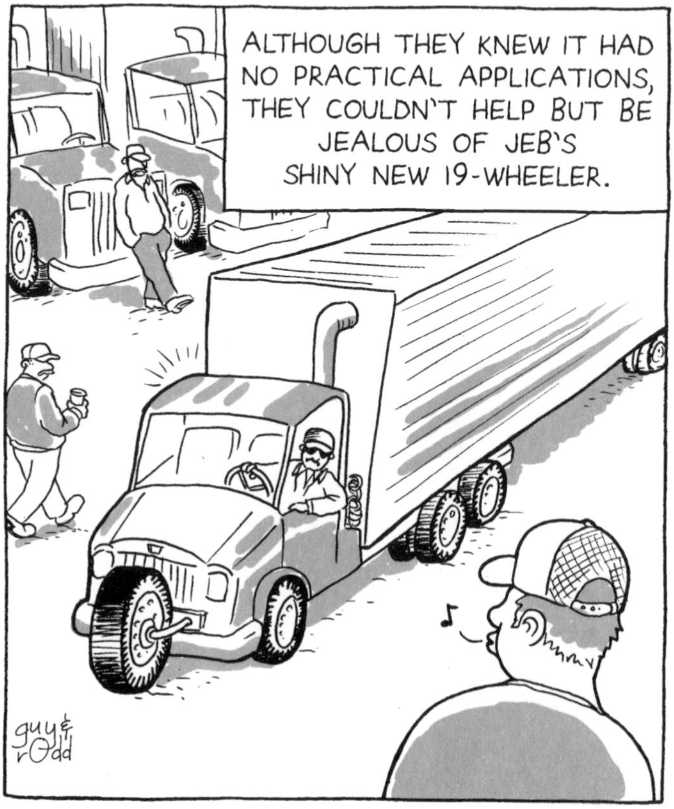
ALTHOUGH THEY KNEW IT HAD NO PRACTICAL APPLICATIONS, THEY COULDN'T HELP BUT BE JEALOUS OF JEB'S SHINY NEW 19-WHEELER.

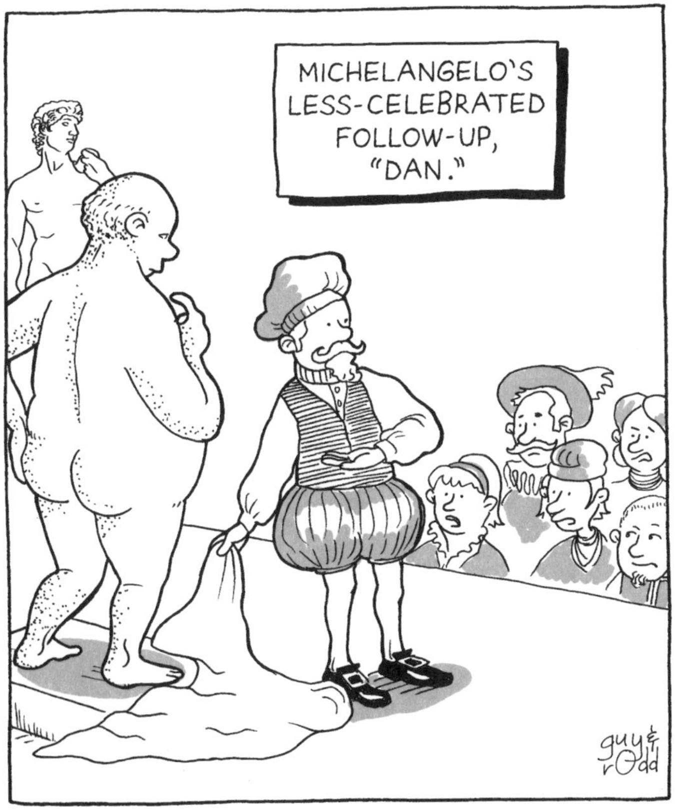
MICHELANGELO'S LESS-CELEBRATED FOLLOW-UP, "DAN."

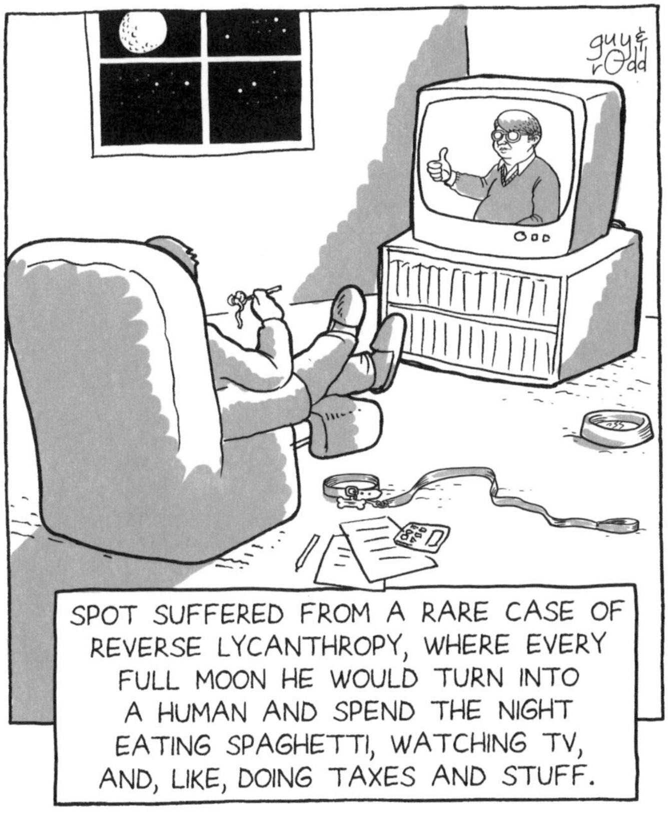
SPOT SUFFERED FROM A RARE CASE OF REVERSE LYCANTHROPY, WHERE EVERY FULL MOON HE WOULD TURN INTO A HUMAN AND SPEND THE NIGHT EATING SPAGHETTI, WATCHING TV, AND, LIKE, DOING TAXES AND STUFF.

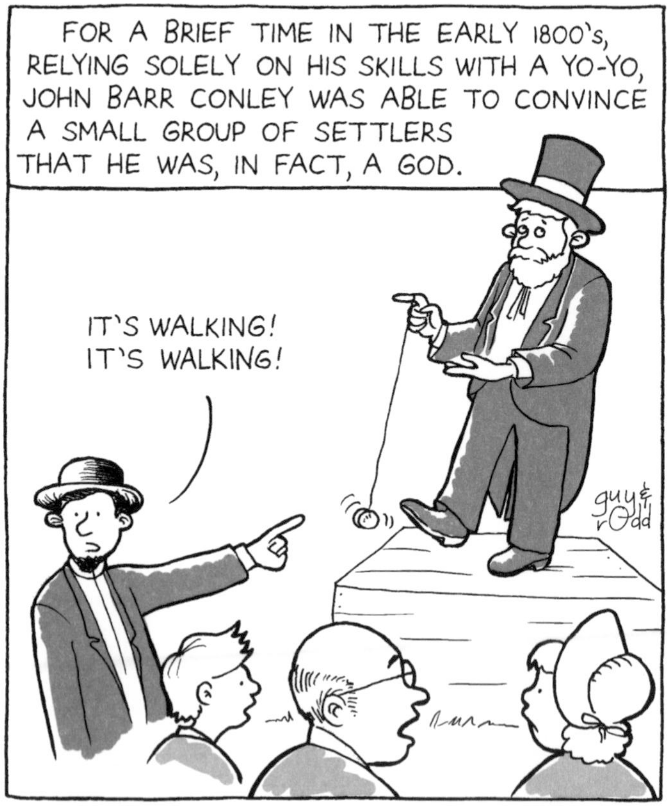
FOR A BRIEF TIME IN THE EARLY 1800'S, RELYING SOLELY ON HIS SKILLS WITH A YO-YO, JOHN BARR CONLEY WAS ABLE TO CONVINCE A SMALL GROUP OF SETTLERS THAT HE WAS, IN FACT, A GOD.
IT'S WALKING! IT'S WALKING!

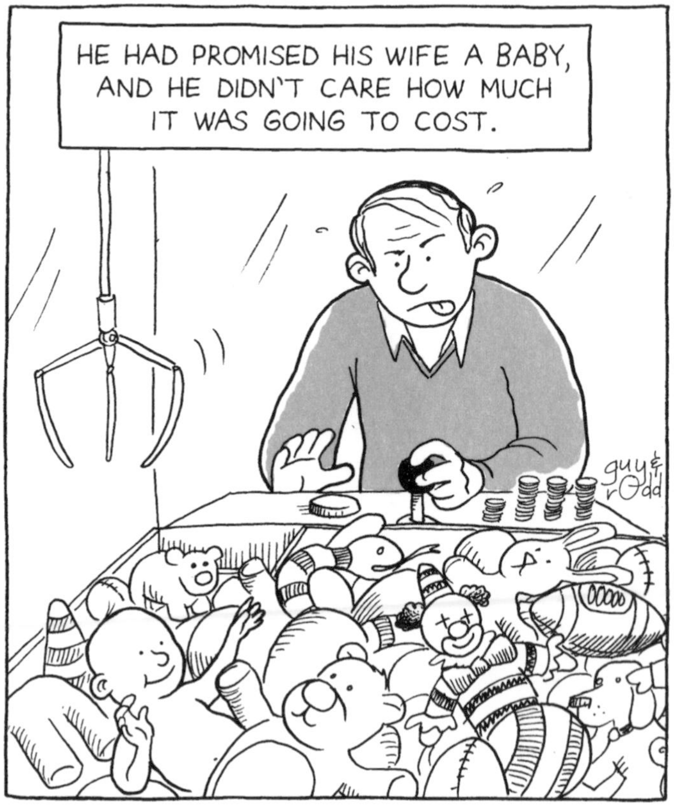
HE HAD PROMISED HIS WIFE A BABY, AND HE DIDN'T CARE HOW MUCH IT WAS GOING TO COST.

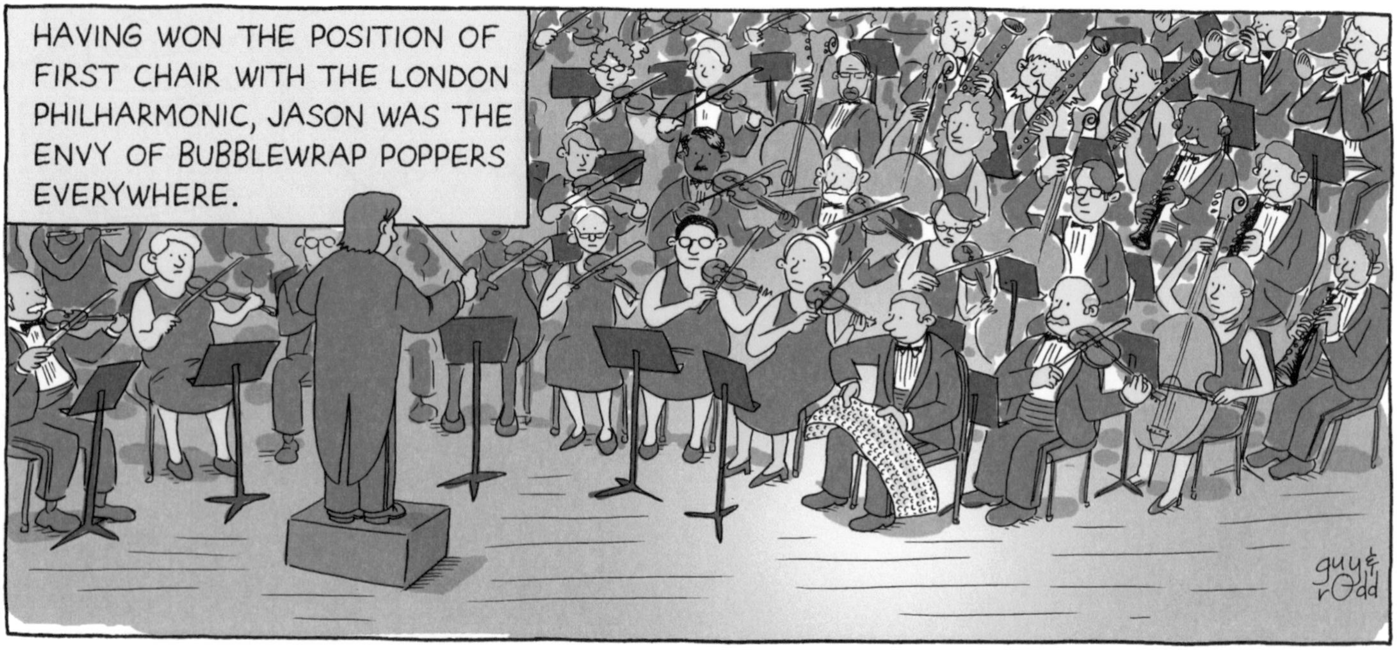
HAVING WON THE POSITION OF FIRST CHAIR WITH THE LONDON PHILHARMONIC, JASON WAS THE ENVY OF BUBBLEWRAP POPPERS EVERYWHERE.

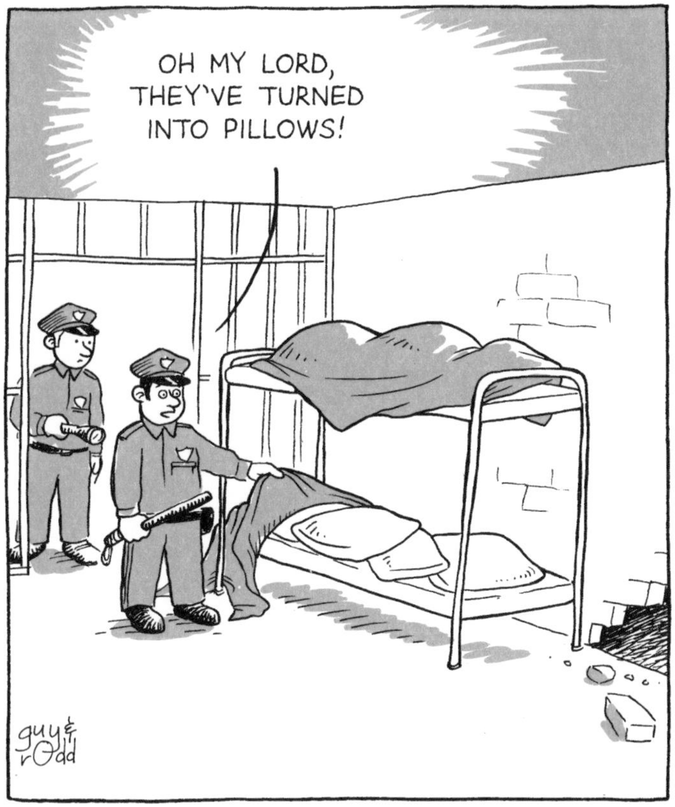
OH MY LORD, THEY'VE TURNED INTO PILLOWS!

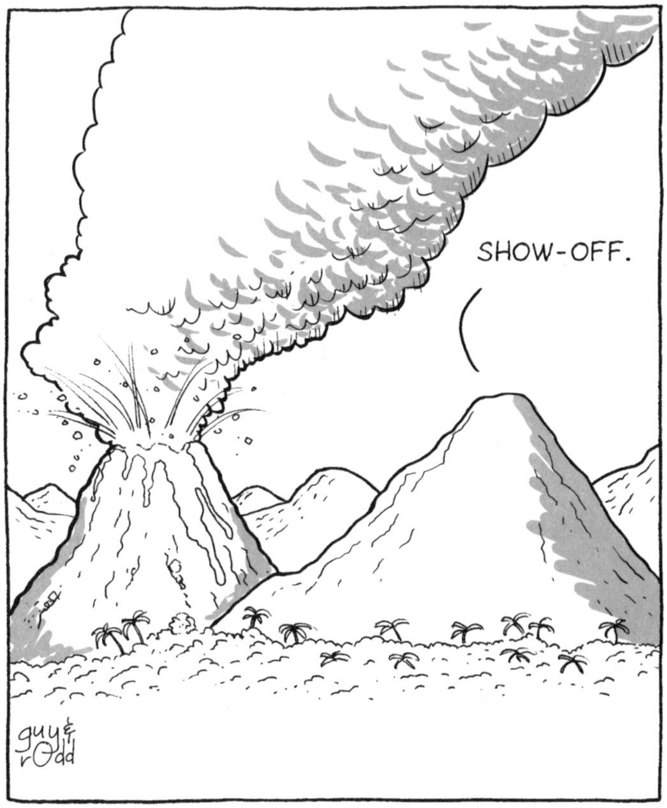
SHOW-OFF.

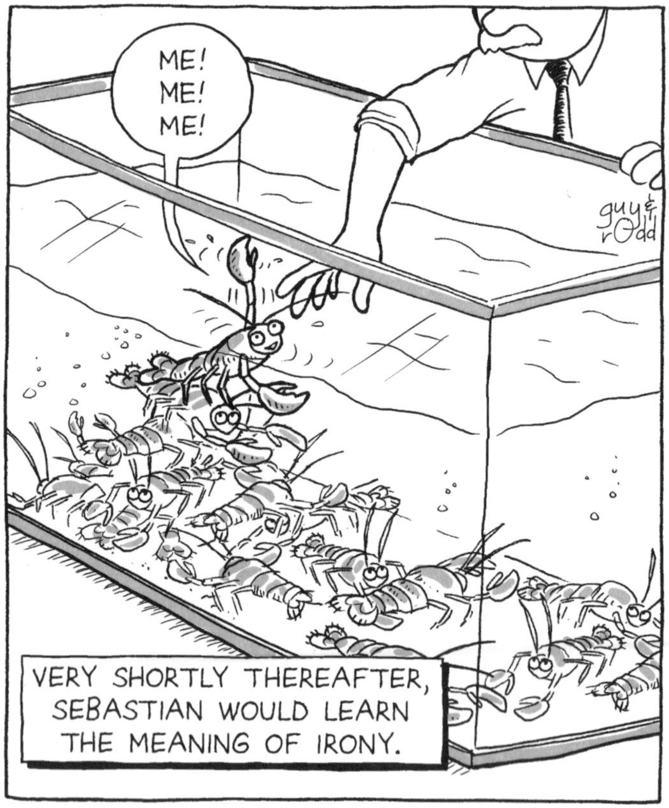
ME!
ME!
ME!
VERY SHORTLY THEREAFTER, SEBASTIAN WOULD LEARN THE MEANING OF IRONY.

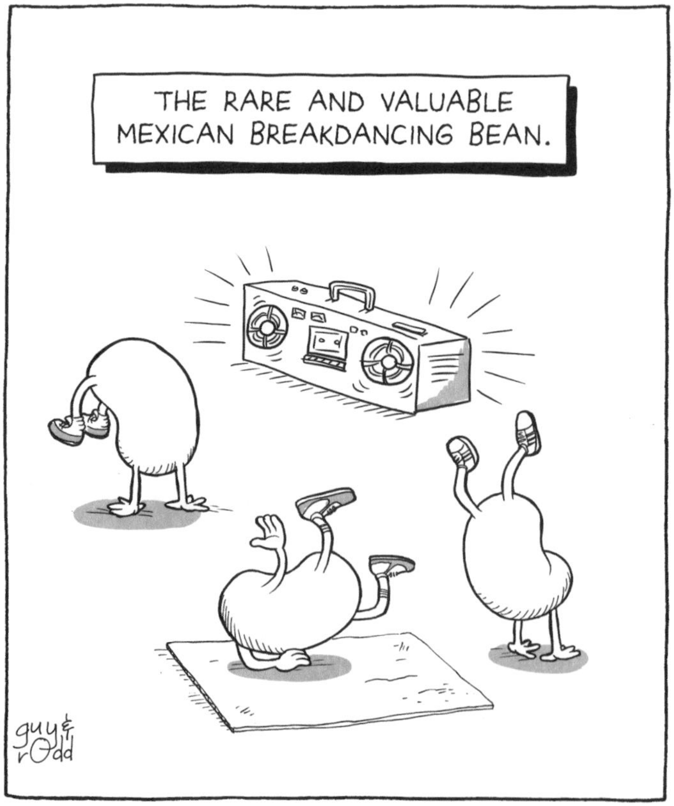
THE RARE AND VALUABLE MEXICAN BREAKDANCING BEAN.

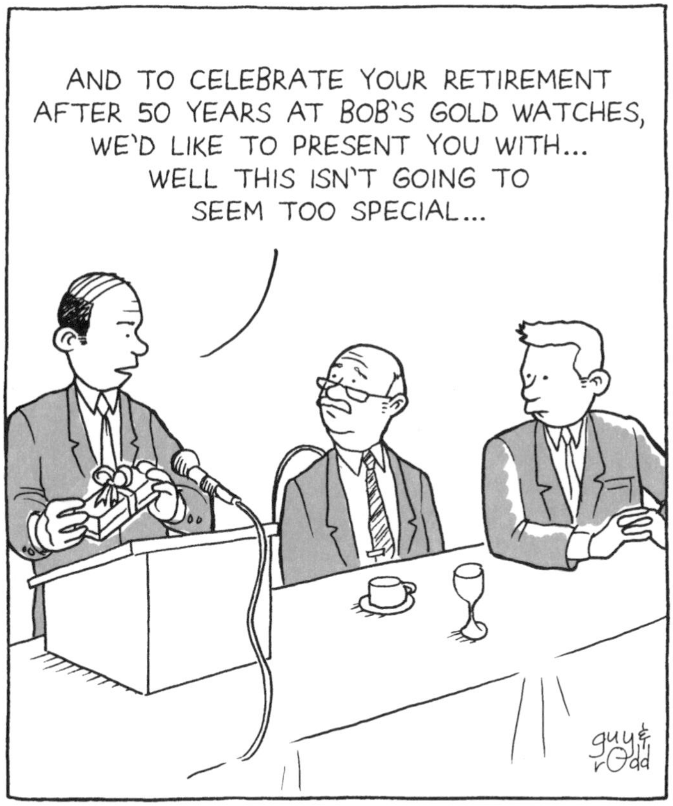
AND TO CELEBRATE YOUR RETIREMENT AFTER 50 YEARS AT BOB'S GOLD WATCHES, WE'D LIKE TO PRESENT YOU WITH... WELL THIS ISN'T GOING TO SEEM TOO SPECIAL...

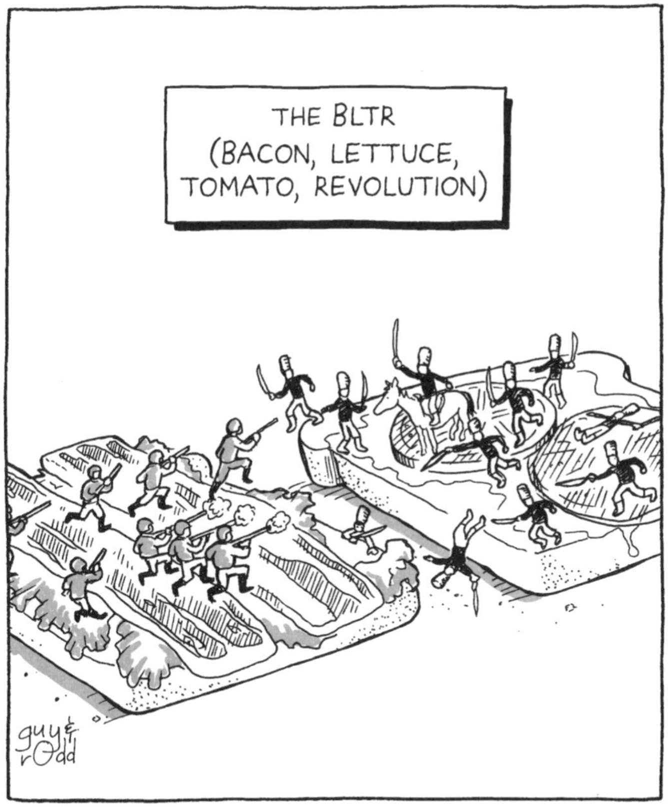
THE BLTR (BACON, LETTUCE, TOMATO, REVOLUTION)

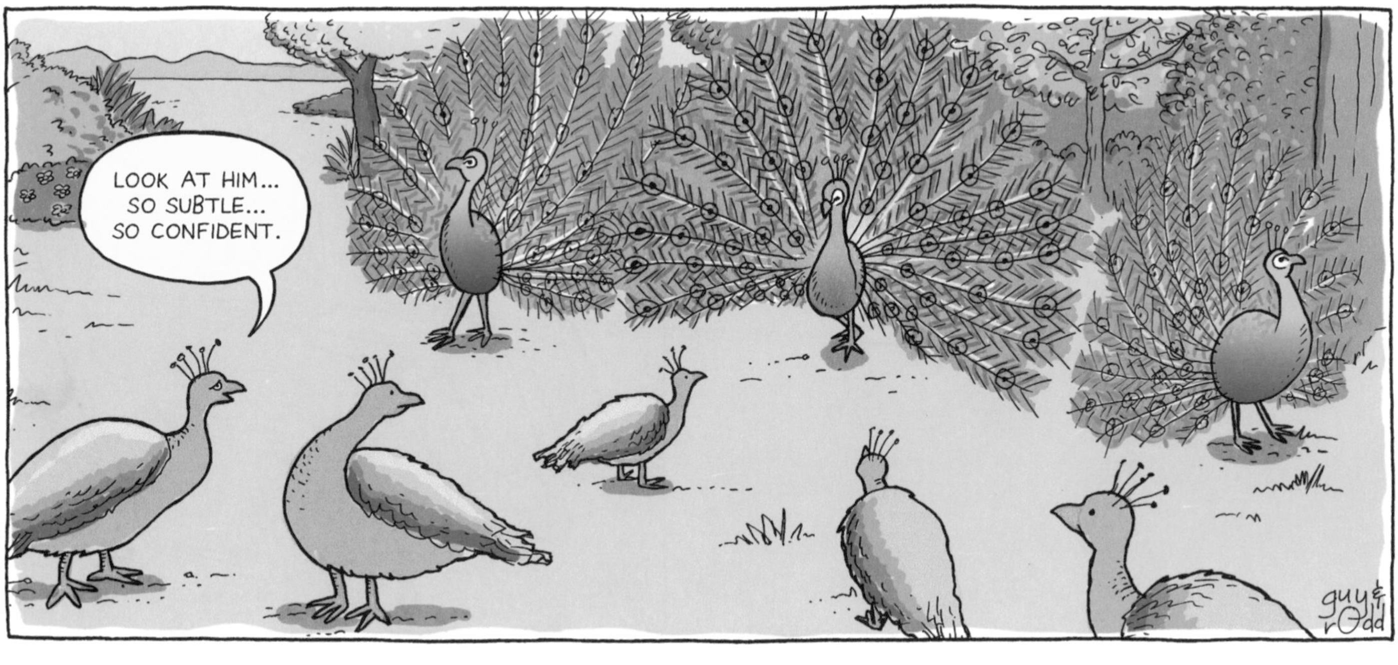
LOOK AT HIM... SO SUBTLE... SO CONFIDENT.

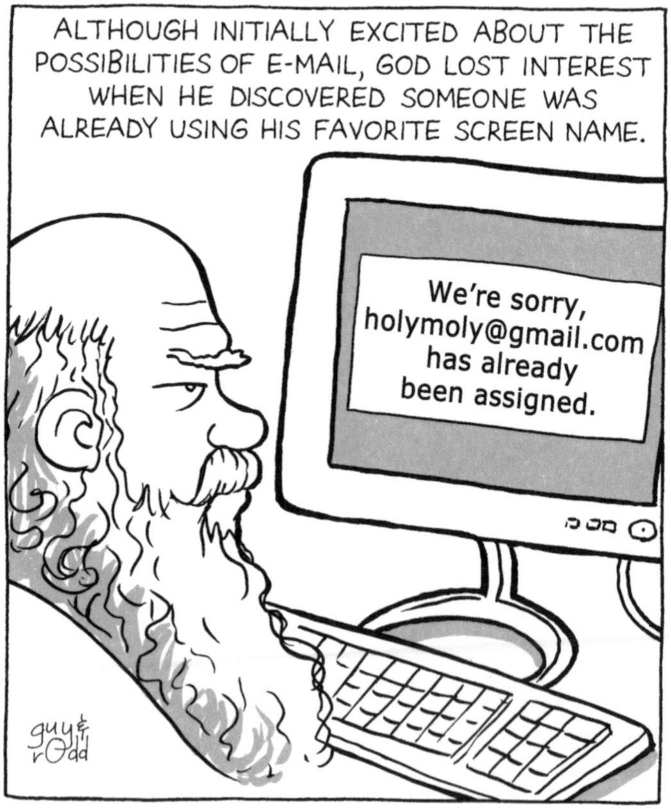
ALTHOUGH INITIALLY EXCITED ABOUT THE POSSIBILITIES OF E-MAIL, GOD LOST INTEREST WHEN HE DISCOVERED SOMEONE WAS ALREADY USING HIS FAVORITE SCREEN NAME.
We're sorry, holymoly@gmail.com has already been assigned.

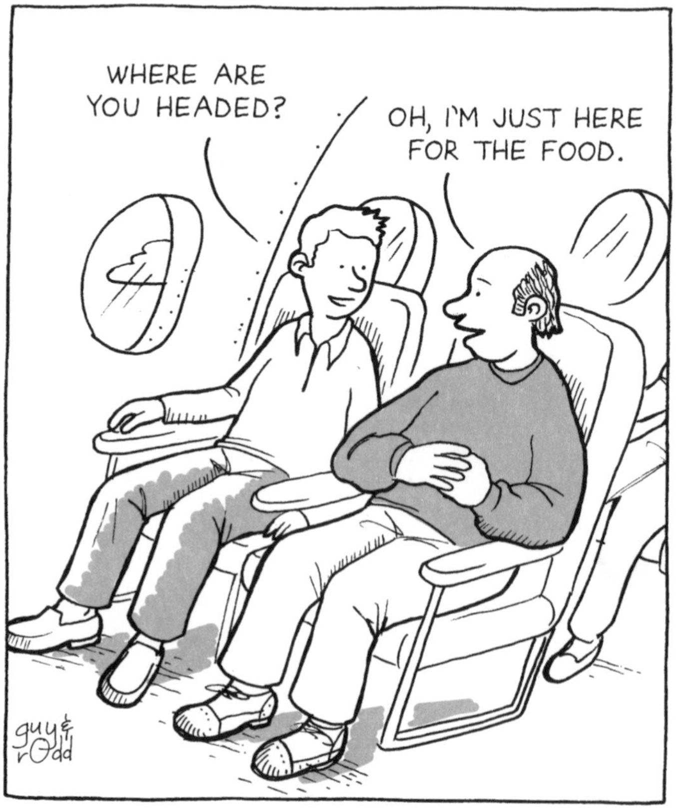
WHERE ARE YOU HEADED?
OH, I'M JUST HERE FOR THE FOOD.

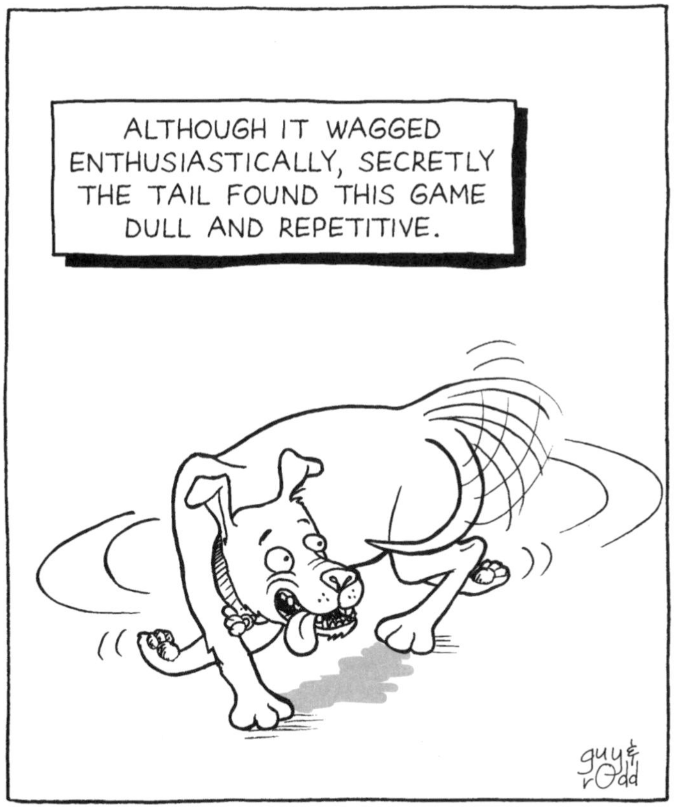
ALTHOUGH IT WAGGED ENTHUSIASTICALLY, SECRETLY THE TAIL FOUND THIS GAME DULL AND REPETITIVE.

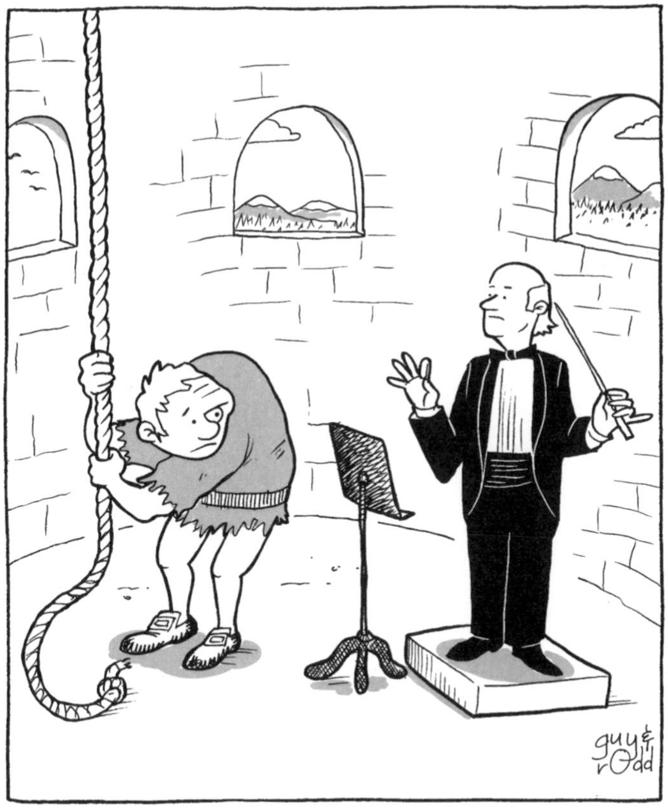

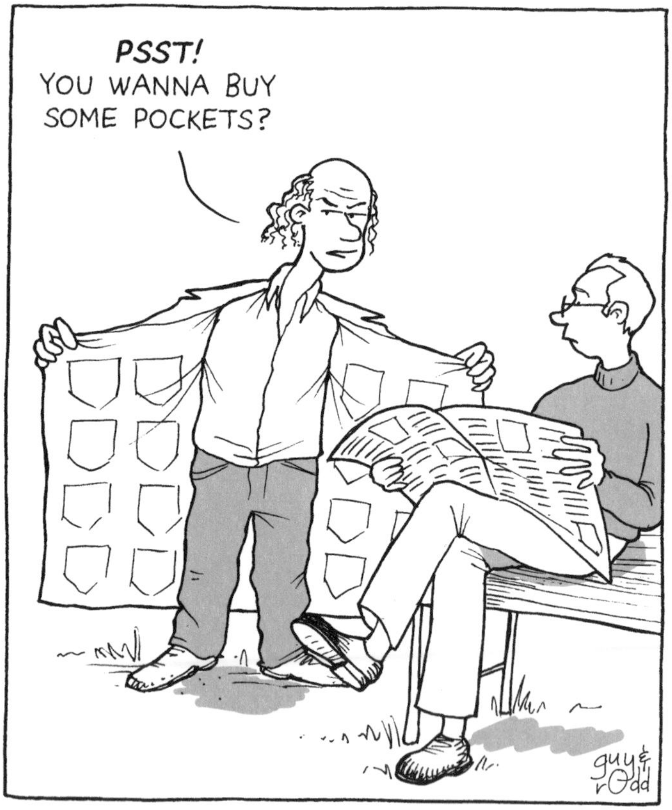
PSST!
YOU WANNA BUY SOME POCKETS?

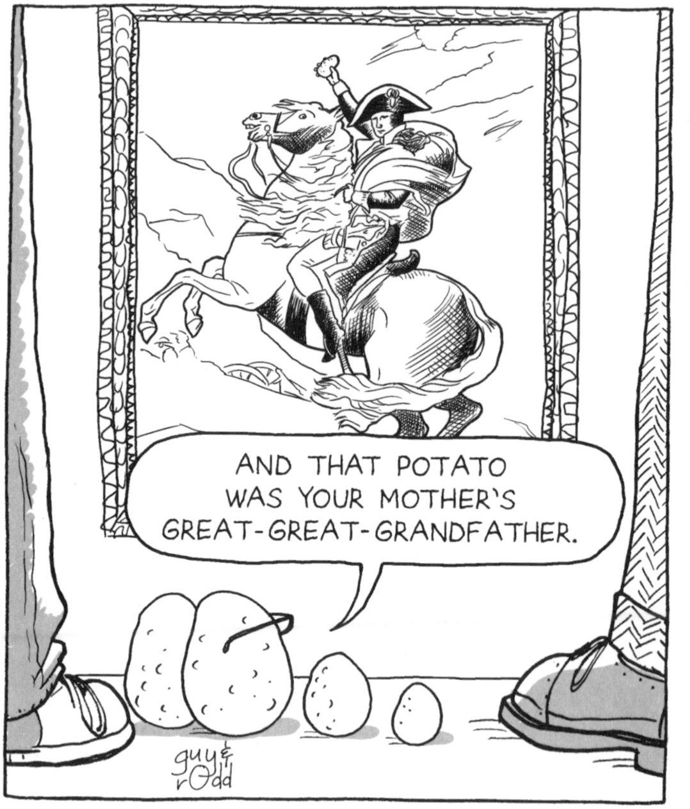
AND THAT POTATO WAS YOUR MOTHER'S GREAT-GREAT-GRANDFATHER.

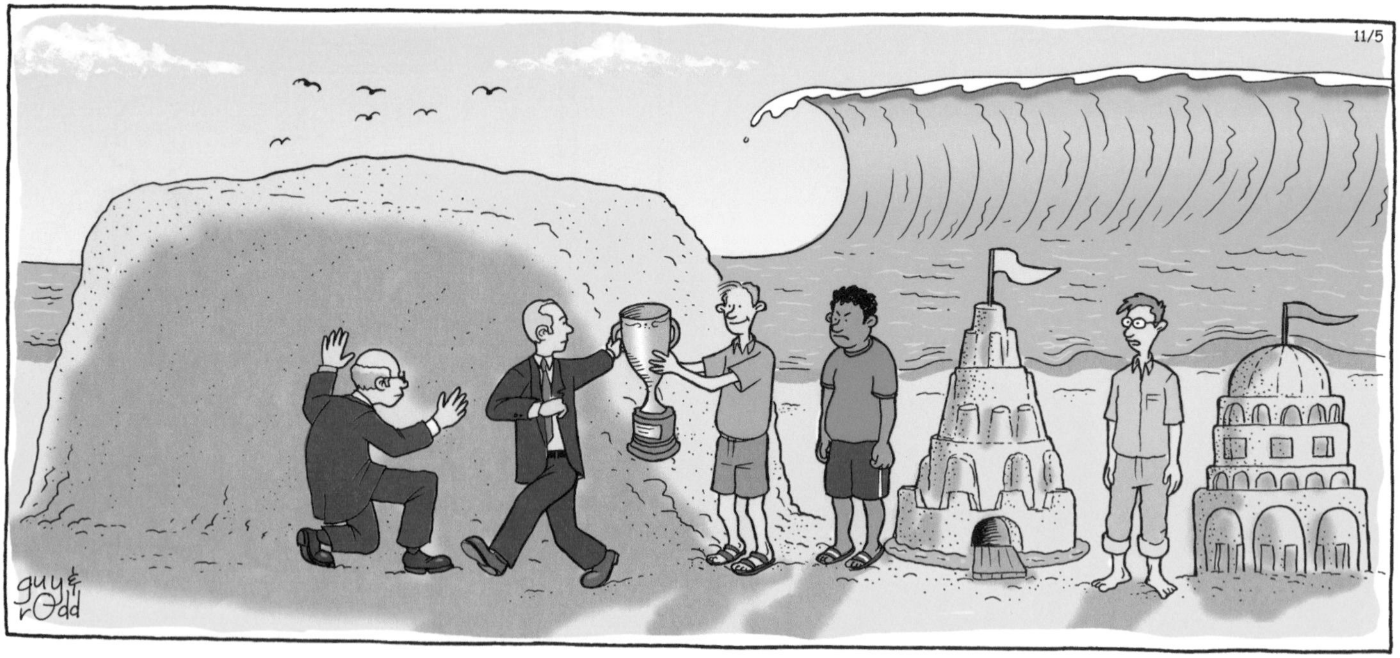

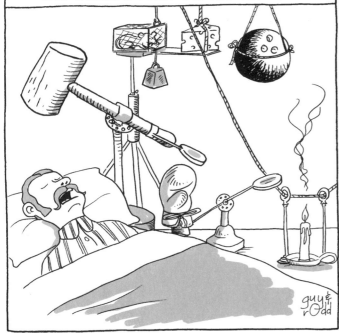

THOUGH THE R-331 WAS USED EXACTLY ONE TIME, IT IS STILL GENERALLY RECOGNIZED AS THE WORLD'S FIRST ALARM CLOCK.

WHAT, THEY'RE COMFORTABLE.

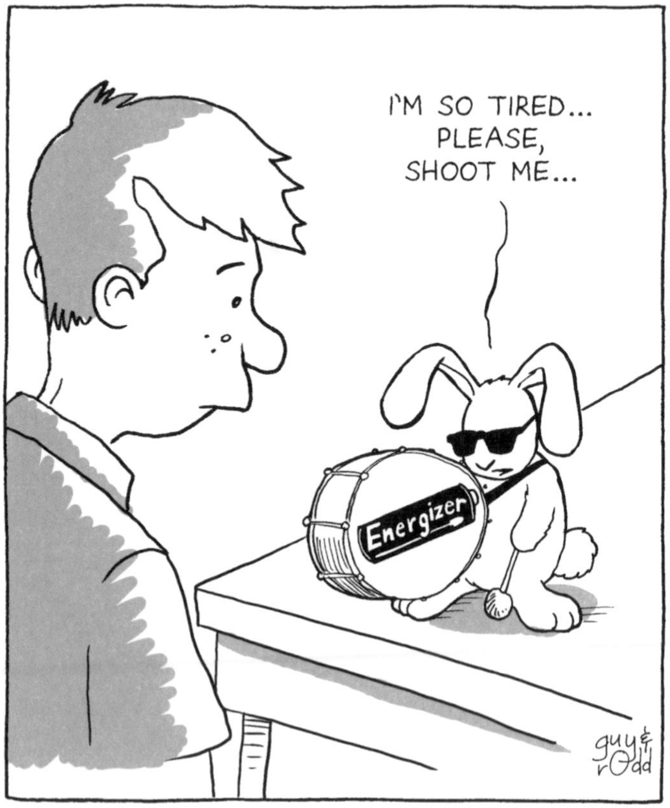
I'M SO TIRED... PLEASE, SHOOT ME...
Energizer

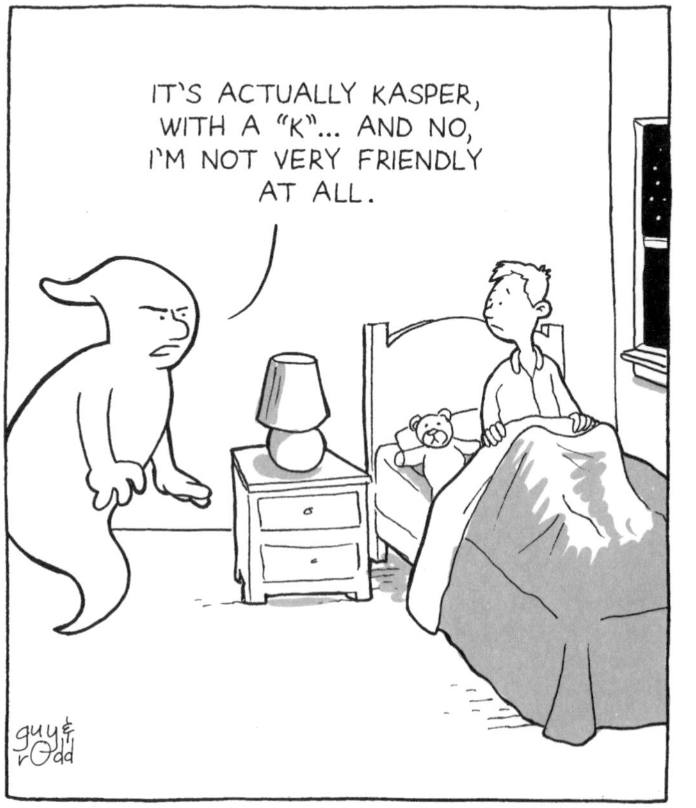
IT'S ACTUALLY KASPER, WITH A "K"... AND NO, I'M NOT VERY FRIENDLY AT ALL.

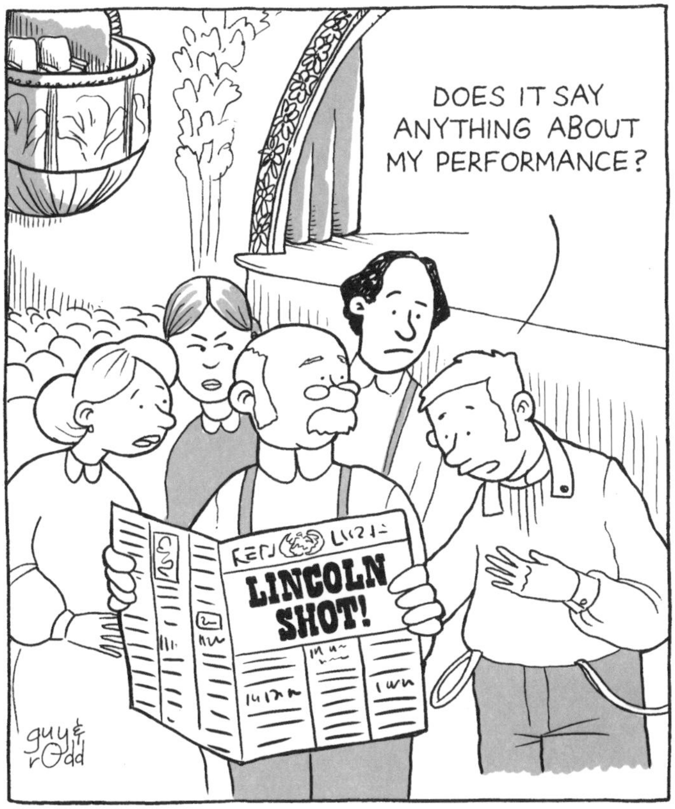
DOES IT SAY ANYTHING ABOUT MY PERFORMANCE?
LINCOLN SHOT!
guy & rOdd

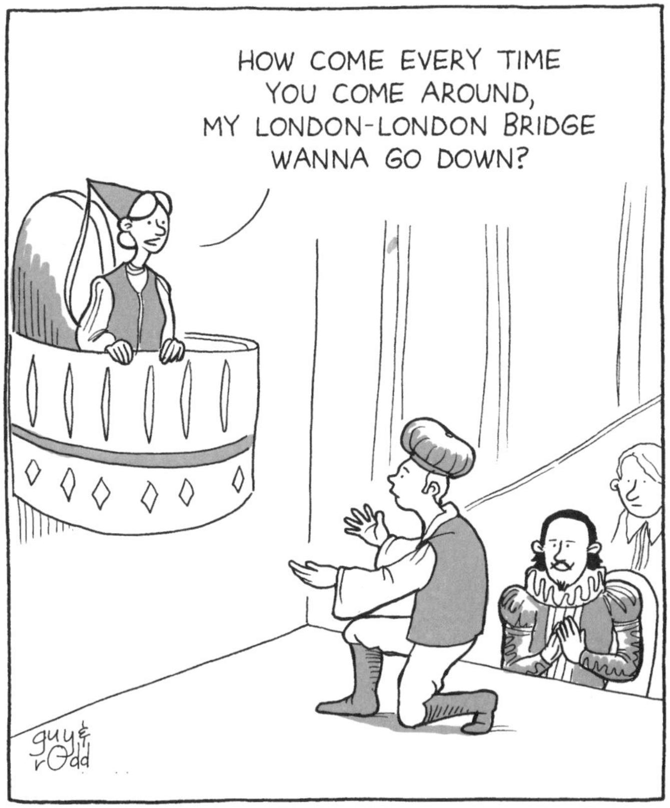
HOW COME EVERY TIME YOU COME AROUND, MY LONDON-LONDON BRIDGE WANNA GO DOWN?
guy & rOdd

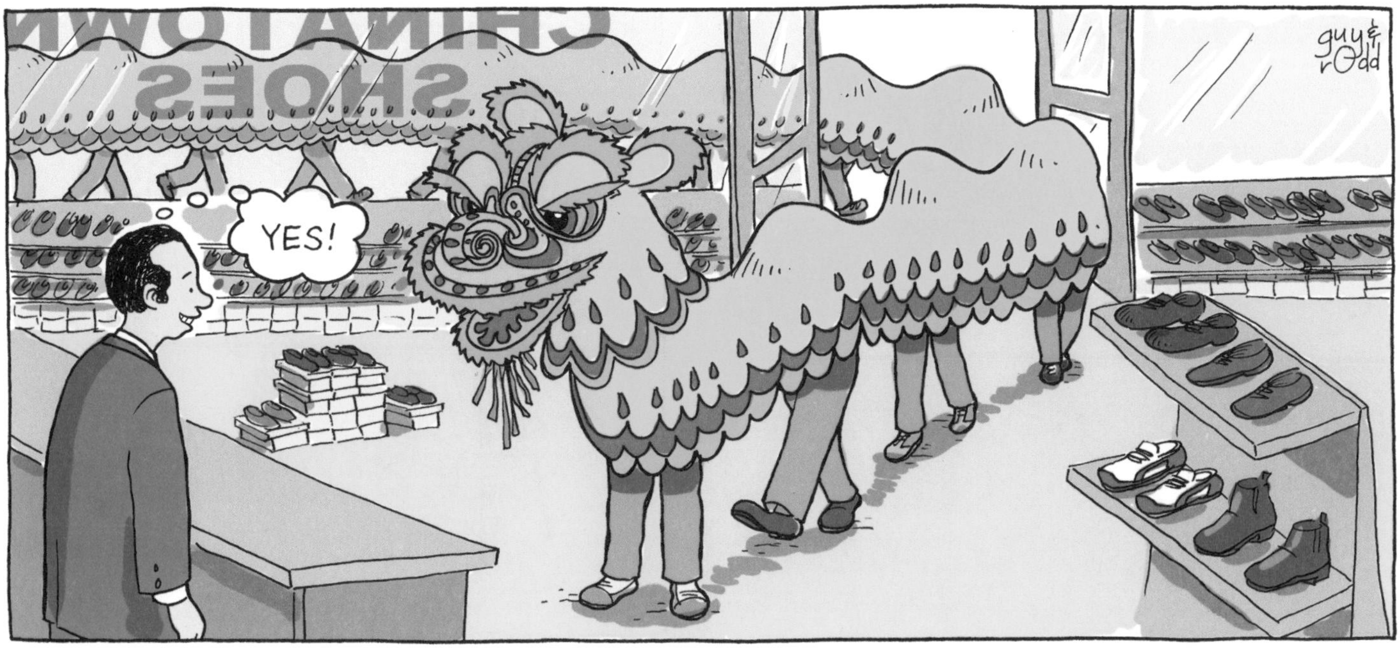
CHINATOWN SHOES
guy & rOdd
YES!

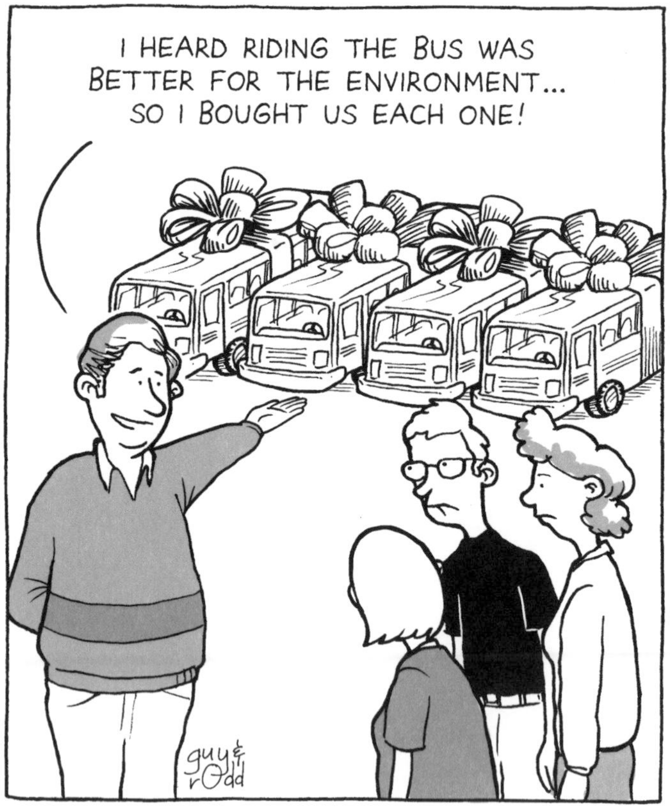
I HEARD RIDING THE BUS WAS BETTER FOR THE ENVIRONMENT... SO I BOUGHT US EACH ONE!

DEEP IN THE HEART OF THE RAND THINK TANK, THE WORLD'S GREAT SCIENTISTS WOULD GATHER TO BRAINSTORM BATMAN'S FIGHT SOUNDS.

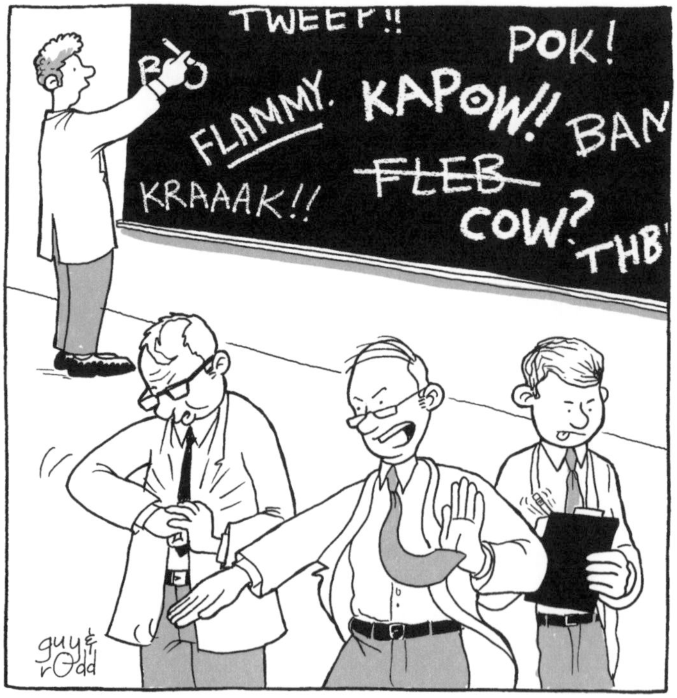
TWEEP!!
POK!
FLAMMY.
KAPOW!!
BAN
FLEB
KRAAAK!!
COW?
THB

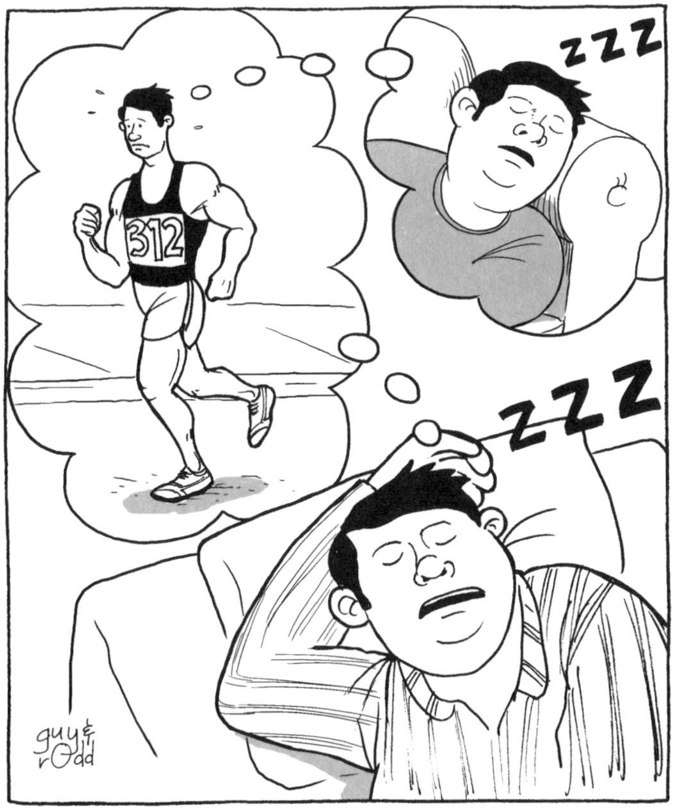
ZZZ
312
ZZZ
guy & rodd

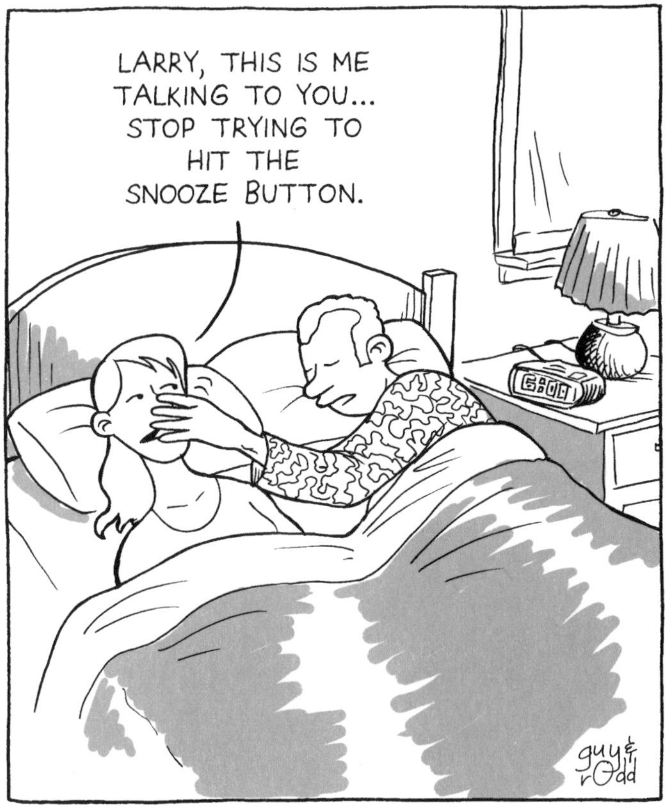
LARRY, THIS IS ME TALKING TO YOU... STOP TRYING TO HIT THE SNOOZE BUTTON.
guy & rodd

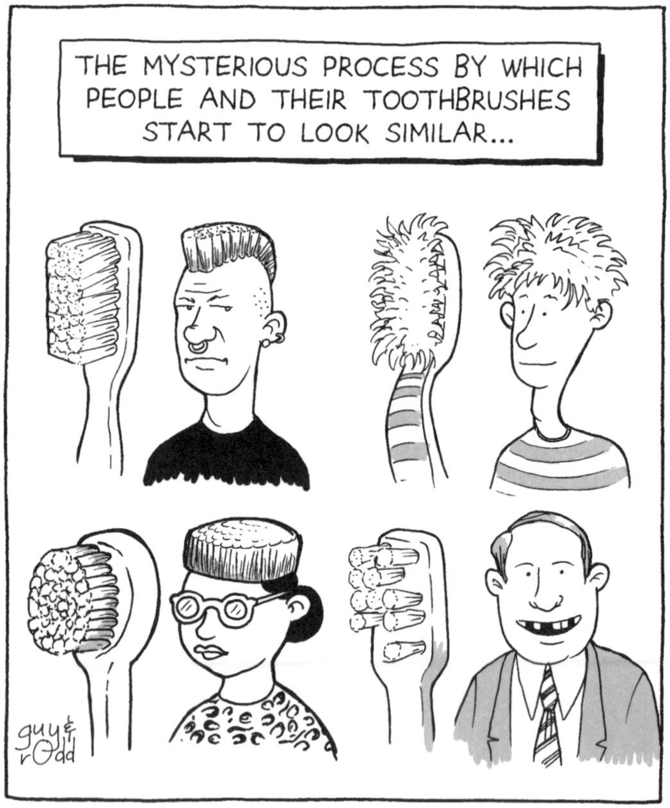
THE MYSTERIOUS PROCESS BY WHICH PEOPLE AND THEIR TOOTHBRUSHES START TO LOOK SIMILAR...

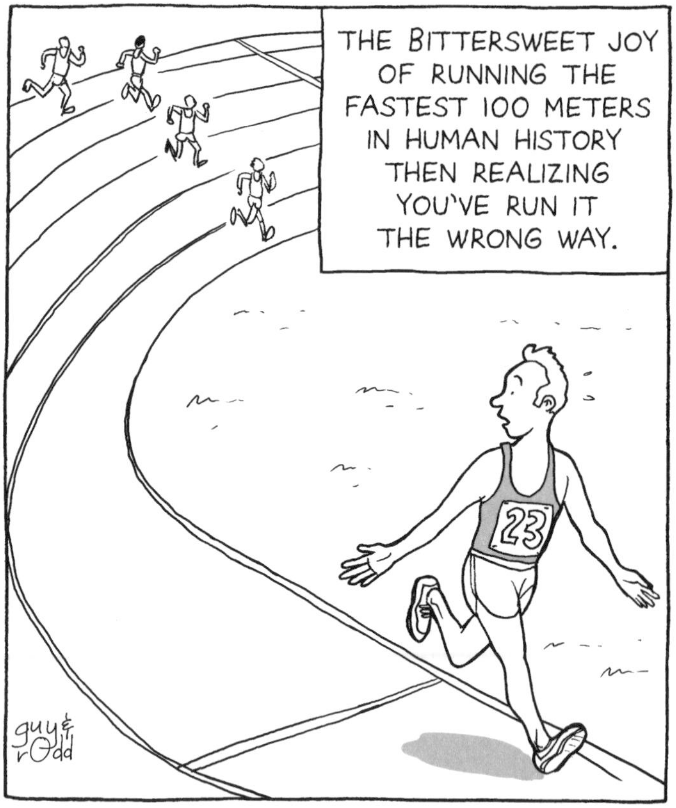
THE BITTERSWEET JOY OF RUNNING THE FASTEST 100 METERS IN HUMAN HISTORY THEN REALIZING YOU'VE RUN IT THE WRONG WAY.
23

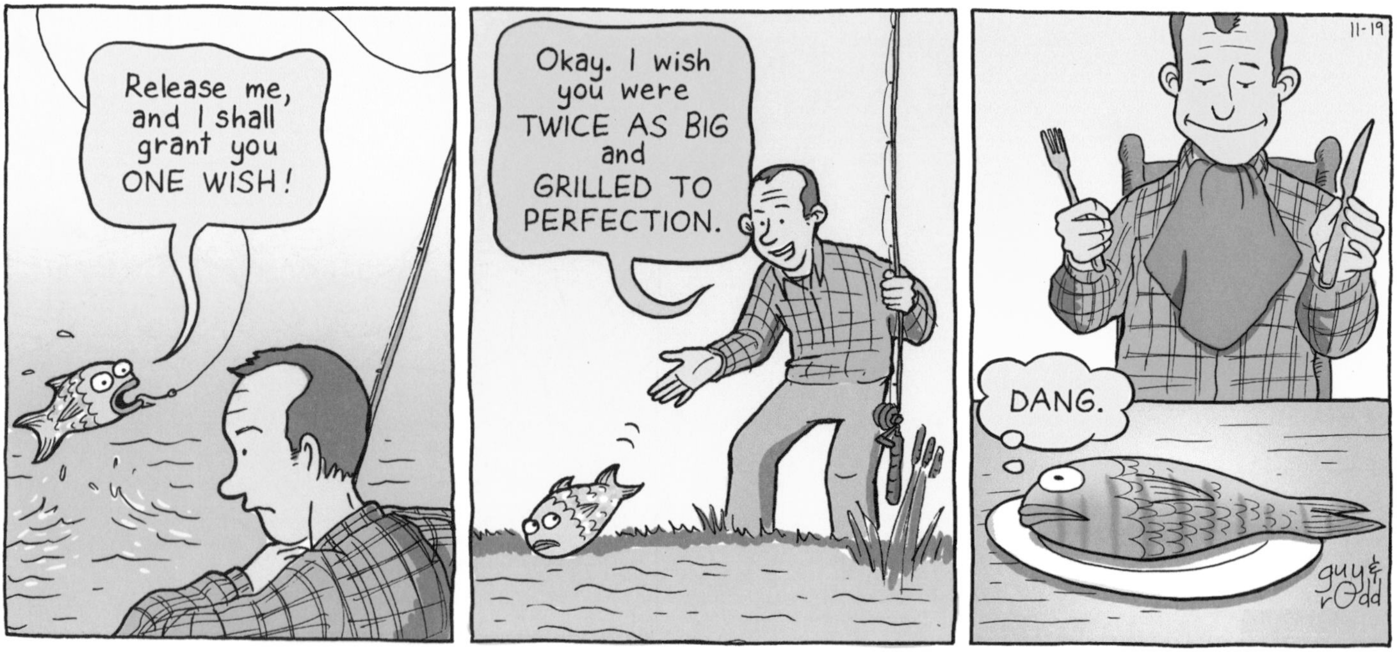
Release me, and I shall grant you ONE WISH!
Okay. I wish you were TWICE AS BIG and GRILLED TO PERFECTION.
11-19
DANG.

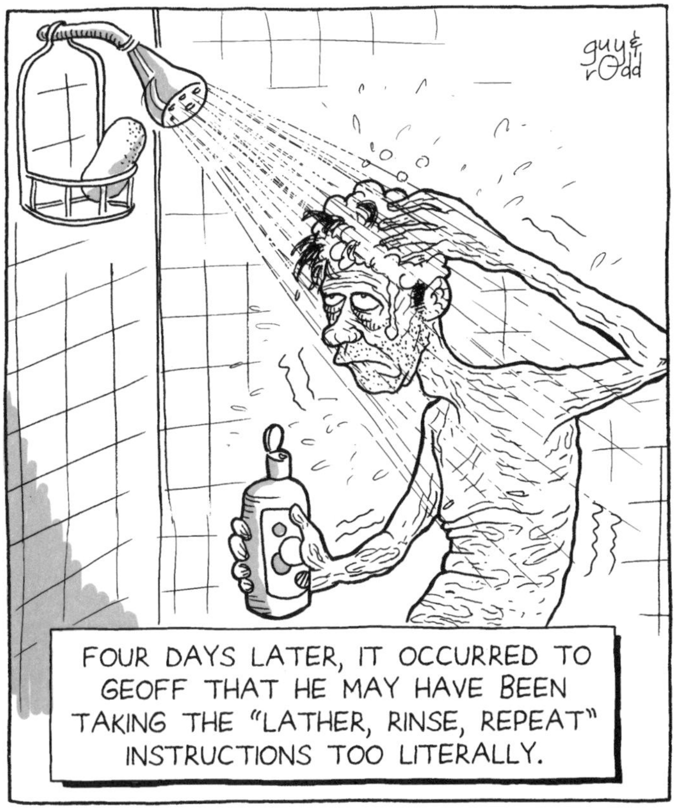
guy & rOdd
FOUR DAYS LATER, IT OCCURRED TO GEOFF THAT HE MAY HAVE BEEN TAKING THE "LATHER, RINSE, REPEAT" INSTRUCTIONS TOO LITERALLY.

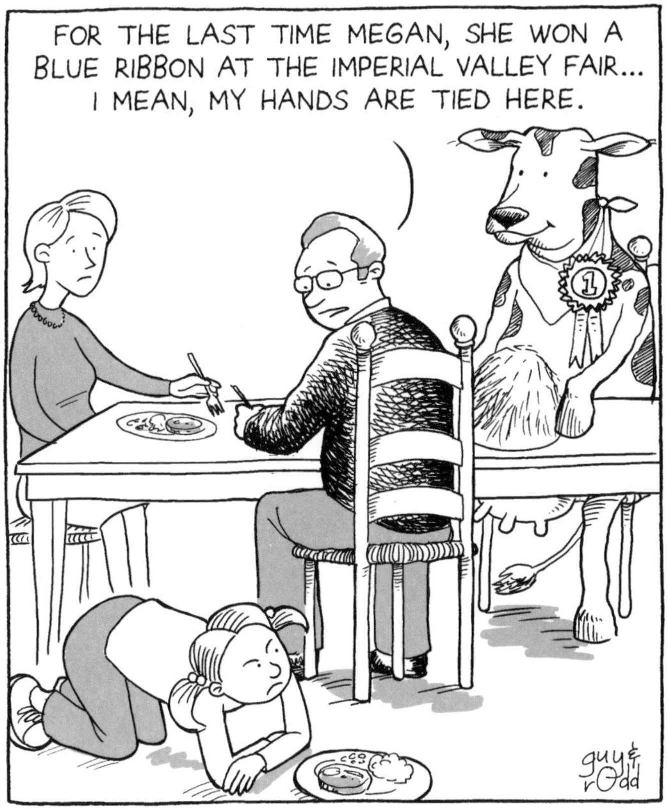
FOR THE LAST TIME MEGAN, SHE WON A BLUE RIBBON AT THE IMPERIAL VALLEY FAIR... I MEAN, MY HANDS ARE TIED HERE.
1
guy & rOdd

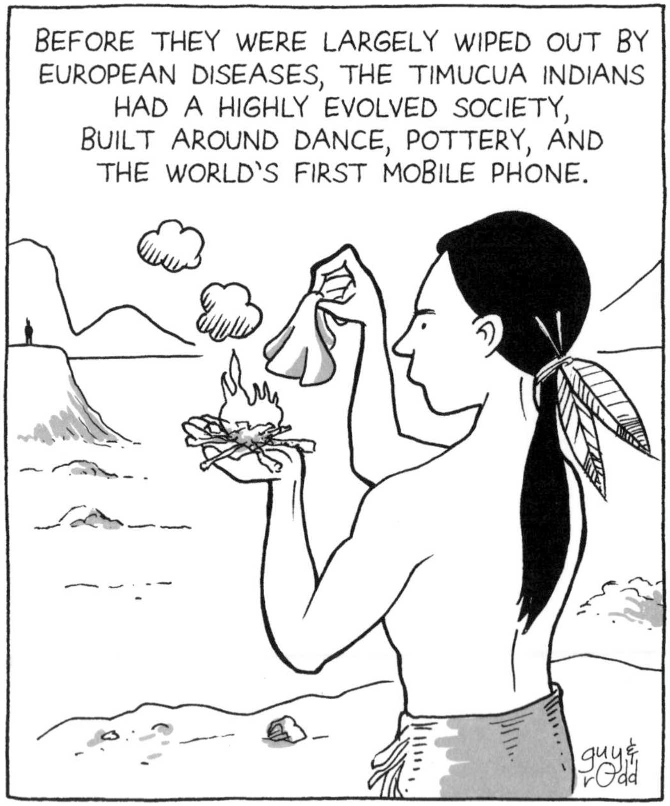
BEFORE THEY WERE LARGELY WIPED OUT BY EUROPEAN DISEASES, THE TIMUCUA INDIANS HAD A HIGHLY EVOLVED SOCIETY, BUILT AROUND DANCE, POTTERY, AND THE WORLD'S FIRST MOBILE PHONE.
guy & rOdd

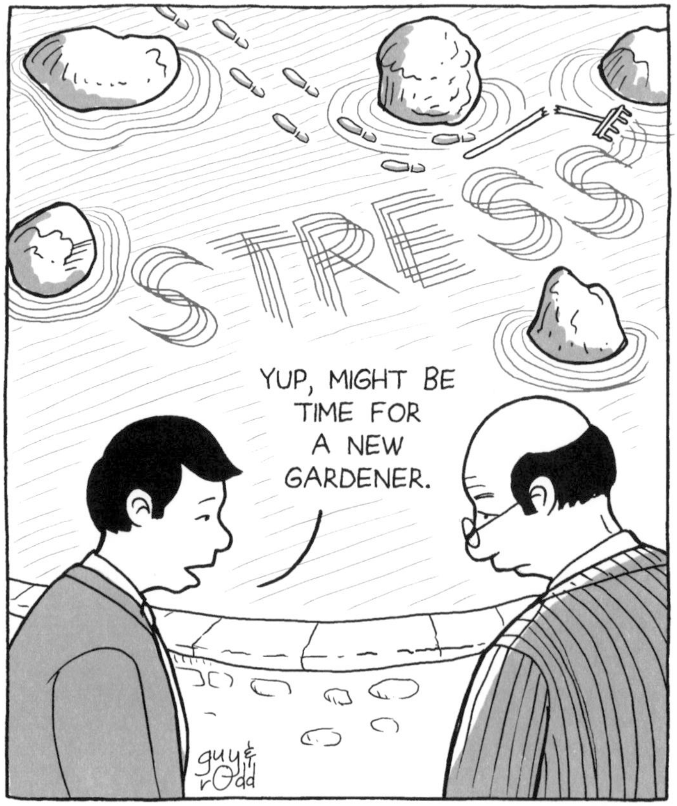
STRESS
YUP, MIGHT BE TIME FOR A NEW GARDENER.
guy & rOdd

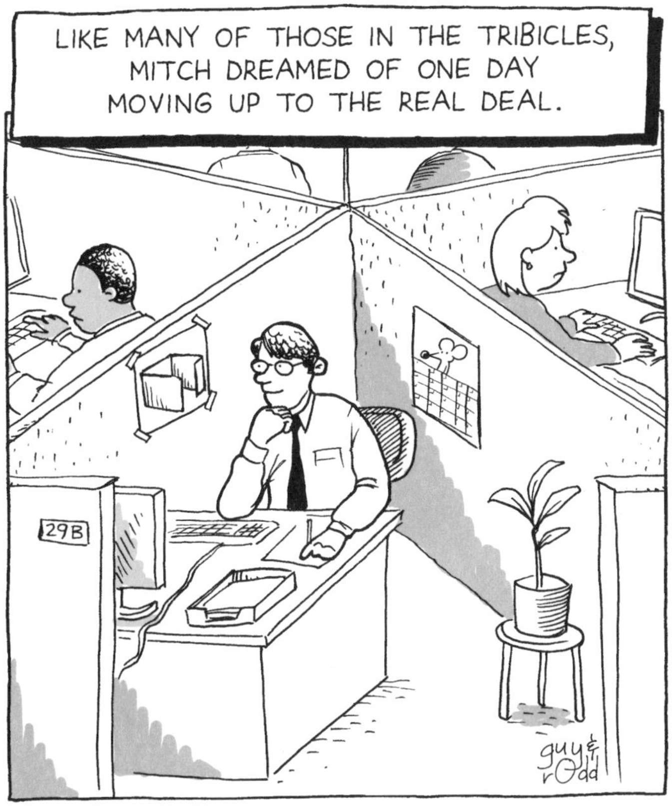
LIKE MANY OF THOSE IN THE TRIBICLES, MITCH DREAMED OF ONE DAY MOVING UP TO THE REAL DEAL.
29B

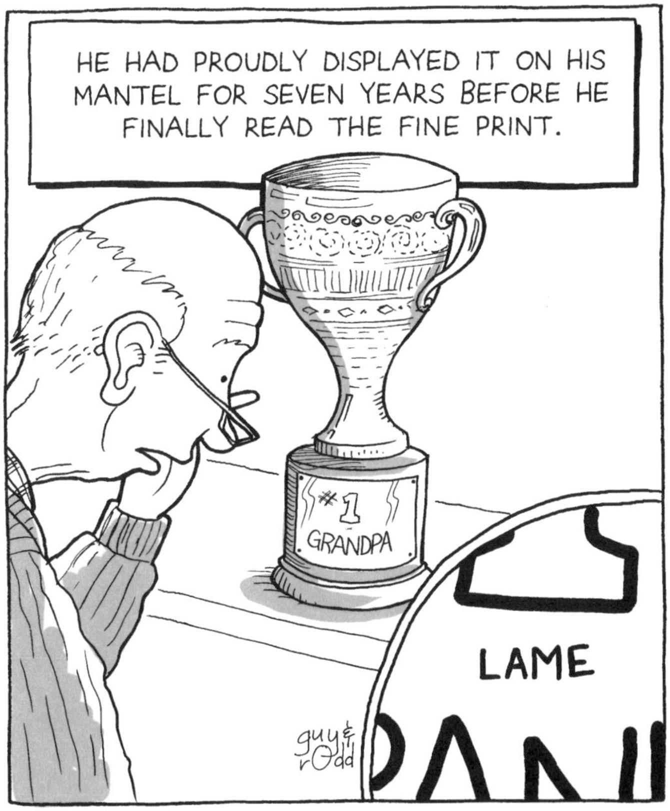
HE HAD PROUDLY DISPLAYED IT ON HIS MANTEL FOR SEVEN YEARS BEFORE HE FINALLY READ THE FINE PRINT.
#1
GRANDPA
LAME

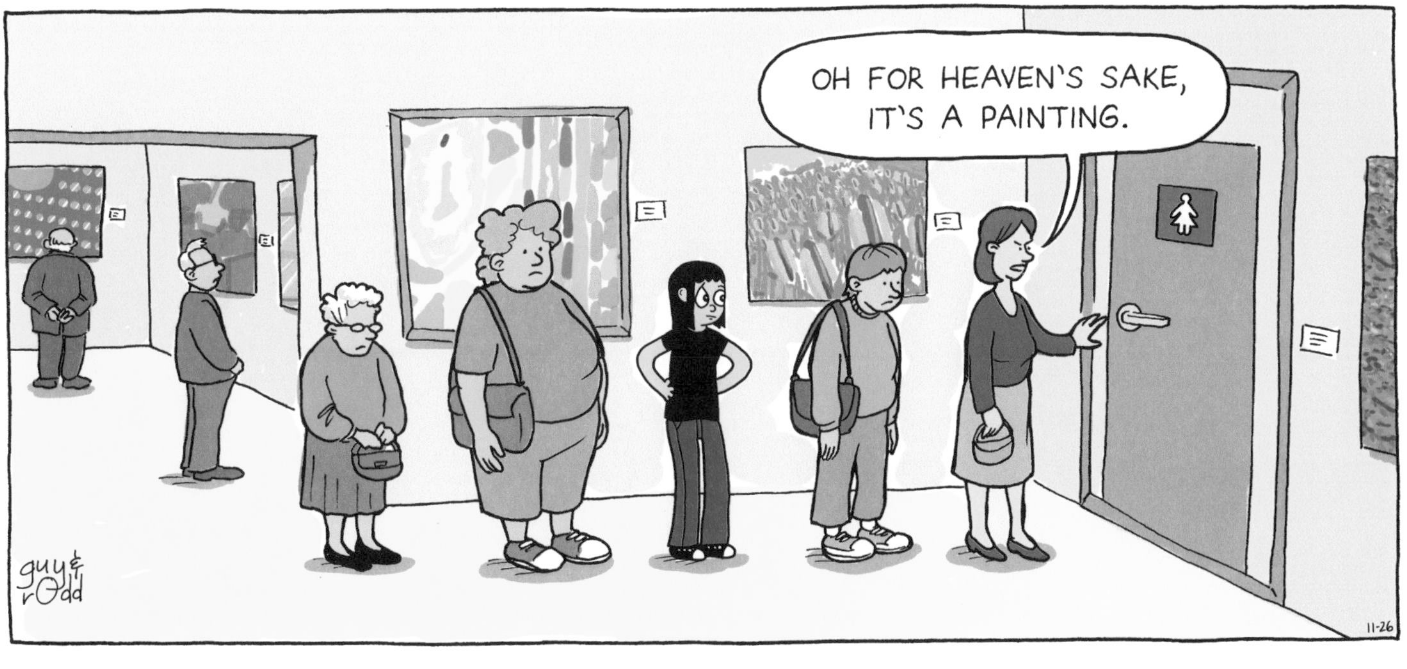
OH FOR HEAVEN'S SAKE, IT'S A PAINTING.

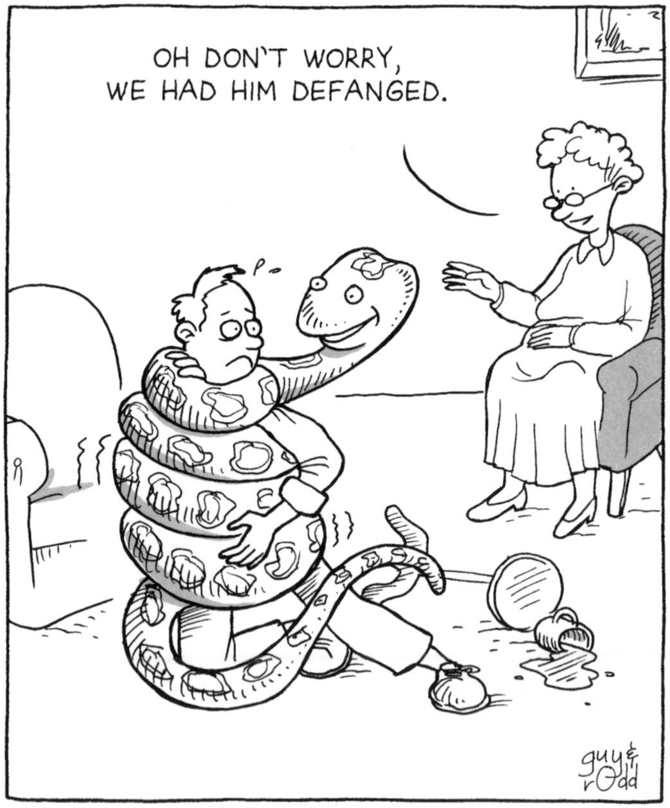
OH DON'T WORRY, WE HAD HIM DEFANGED.
guy & rOdd

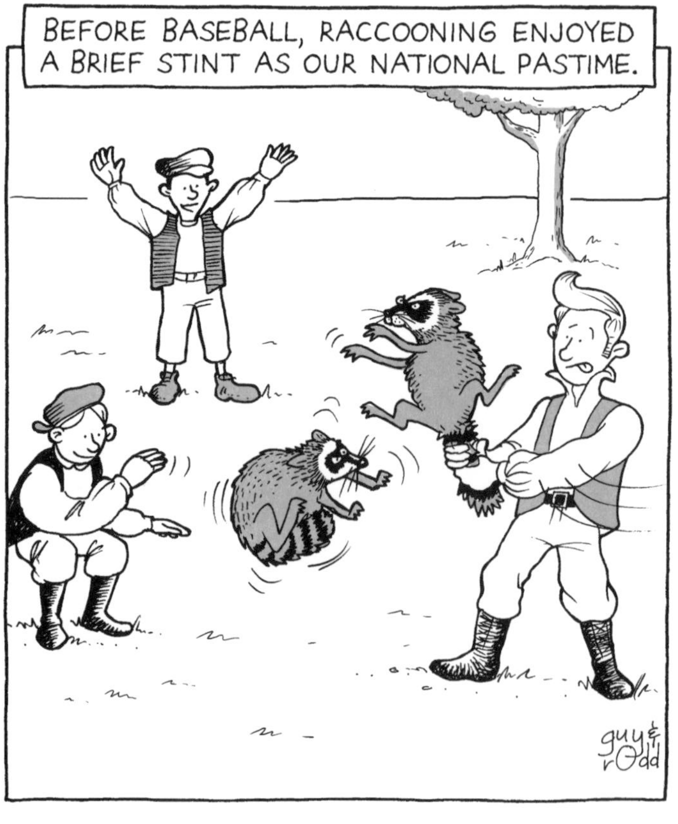
BEFORE BASEBALL, RACCOONING ENJOYED A BRIEF STINT AS OUR NATIONAL PASTIME.
guy & rOdd

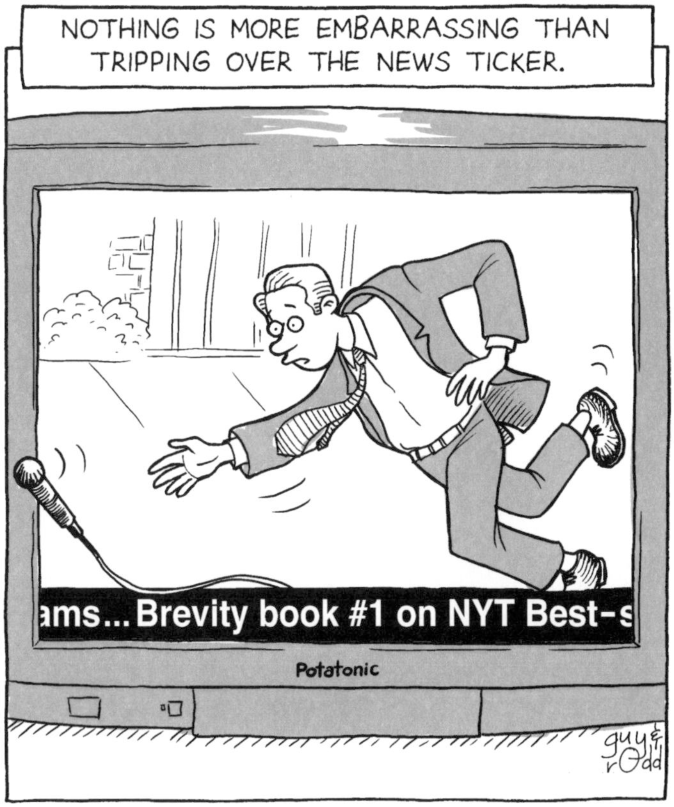
NOTHING IS MORE EMBARRASSING THAN TRIPPING OVER THE NEWS TICKER.
ams... Brevity book #1 on NYT Best-s
Potatonic
guy & rOdd

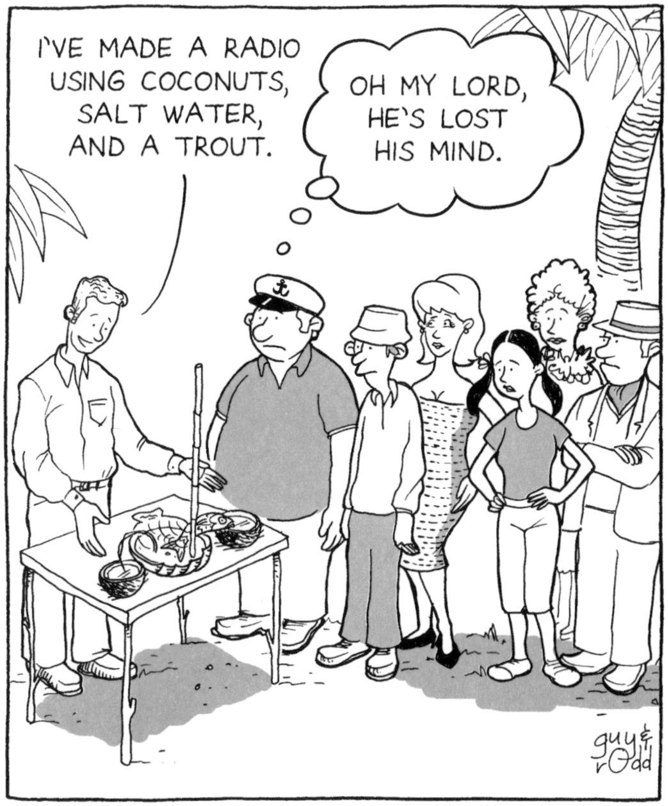
I'VE MADE A RADIO USING COCONUTS, SALT WATER, AND A TROUT.
OH MY LORD, HE'S LOST HIS MIND.
guy & rOdd

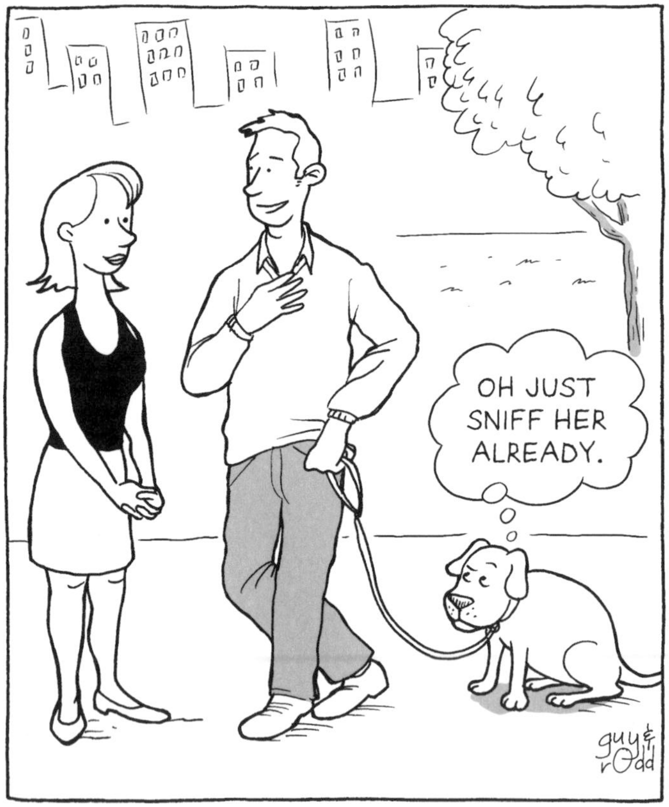
OH JUST SNIFF HER ALREADY.
guy & rOdd

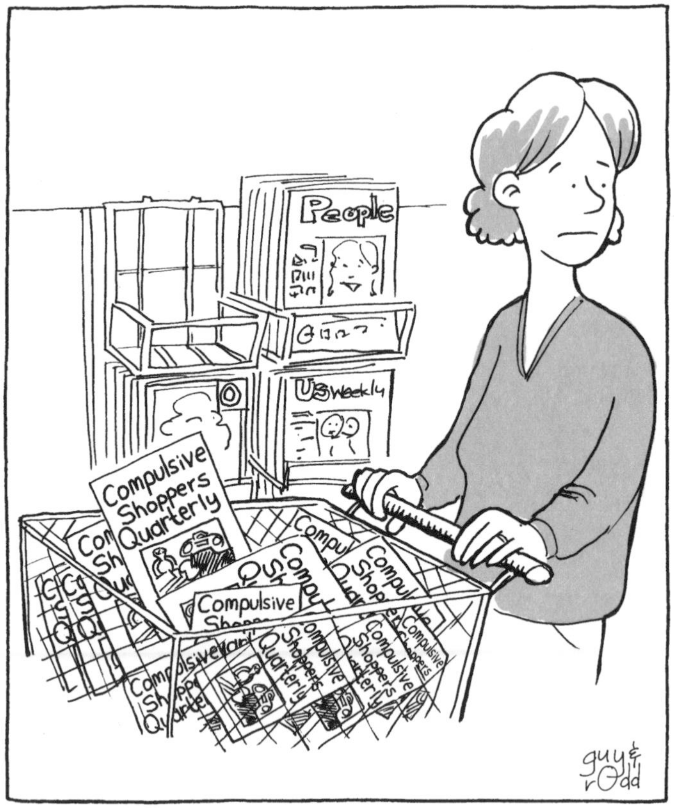
People
Us Weekly
Compulsive Shoppers Quarterly
guy & rOdd

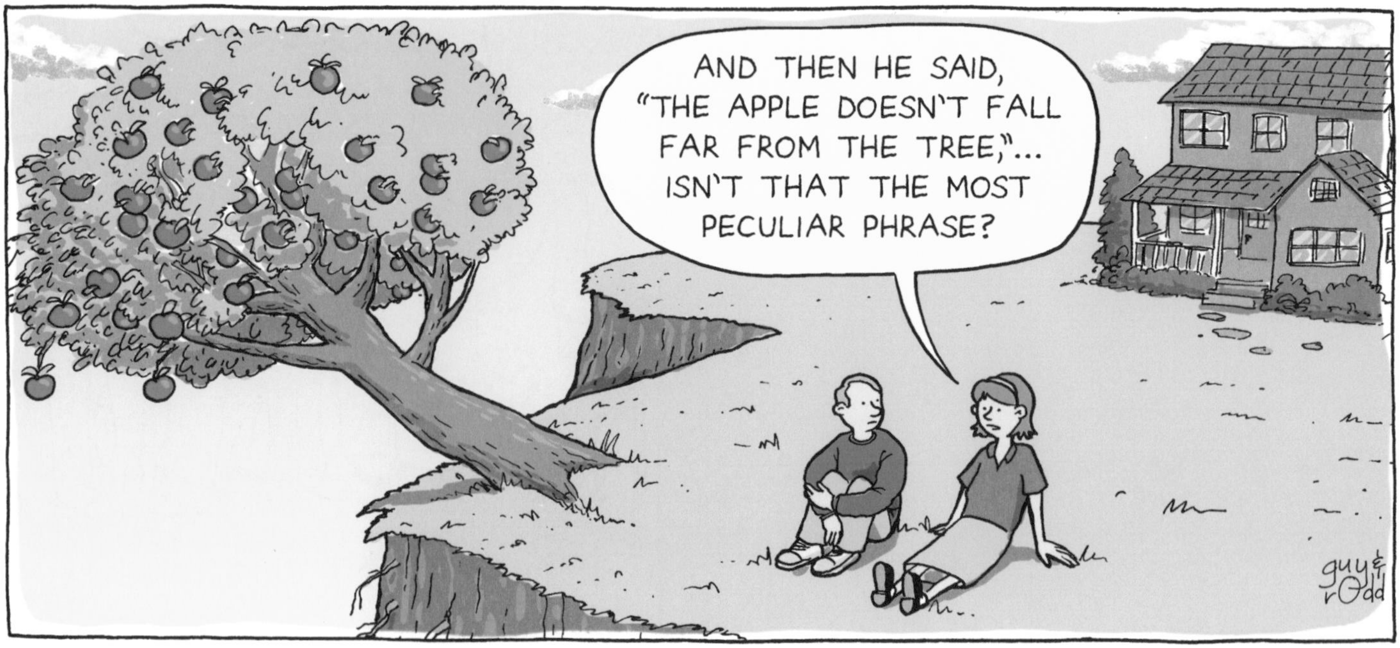
AND THEN HE SAID, "THE APPLE DOESN'T FALL FAR FROM THE TREE,"... ISN'T THAT THE MOST PECULIAR PHRASE?
guy & rOdd

800 YEARS, AND THIS IS HOW IT ALL ENDS... (SIGH).
guy & rodd

...AND OLD MAN COLLIGAN HERE HAS BEEN WITH US FOR THIRTY YEARS... ORDERED UNICORN FOR HIS LAST MEAL... KINDA CAUGHT US ON A TECHNICALITY.
guy & rodd

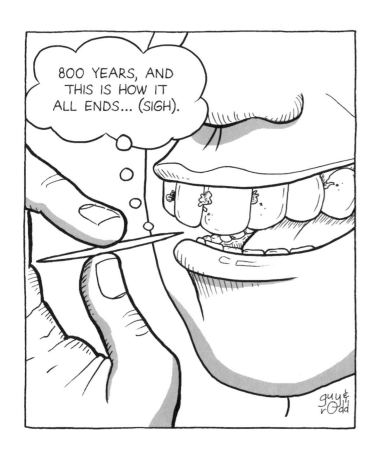

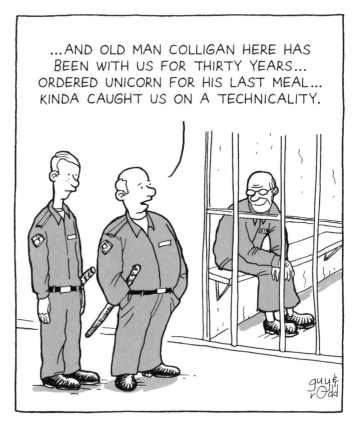

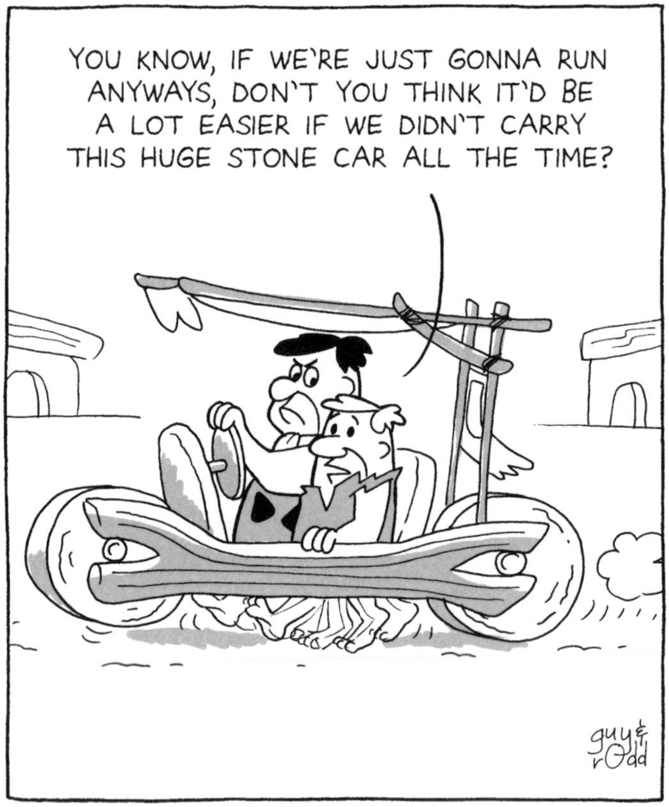
YOU KNOW, IF WE'RE JUST GONNA RUN ANYWAYS, DON'T YOU THINK IT'D BE A LOT EASIER IF WE DIDN'T CARRY THIS HUGE STONE CAR ALL THE TIME?
guy & rOdd

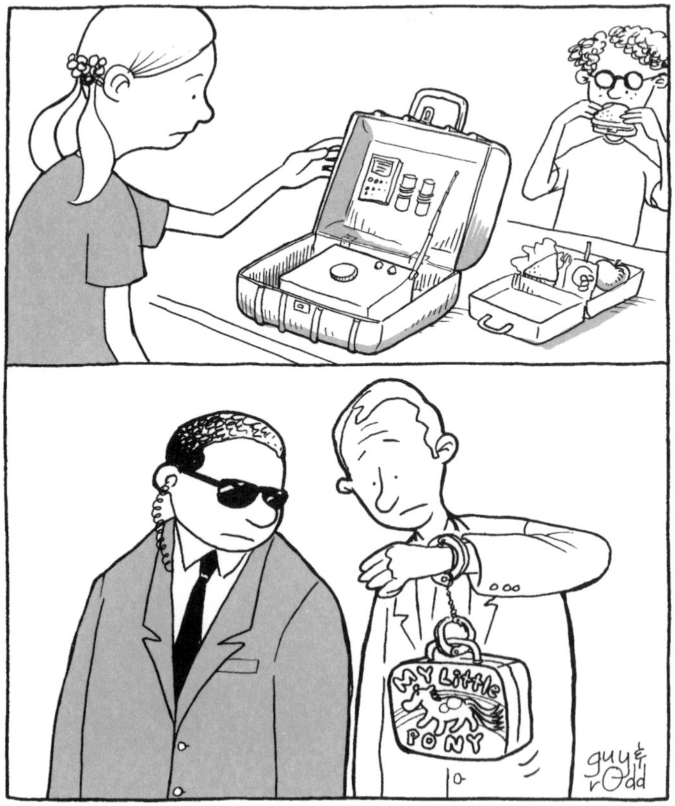
MY Little PONY
guy & rOdd

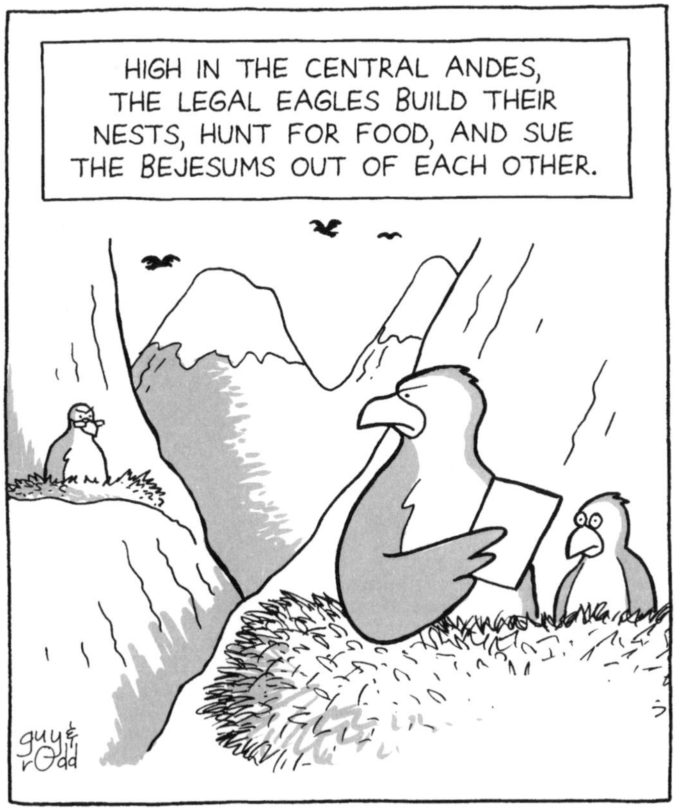
HIGH IN THE CENTRAL ANDES, THE LEGAL EAGLES BUILD THEIR NESTS, HUNT FOR FOOD, AND SUE THE BEJESUMS OUT OF EACH OTHER.

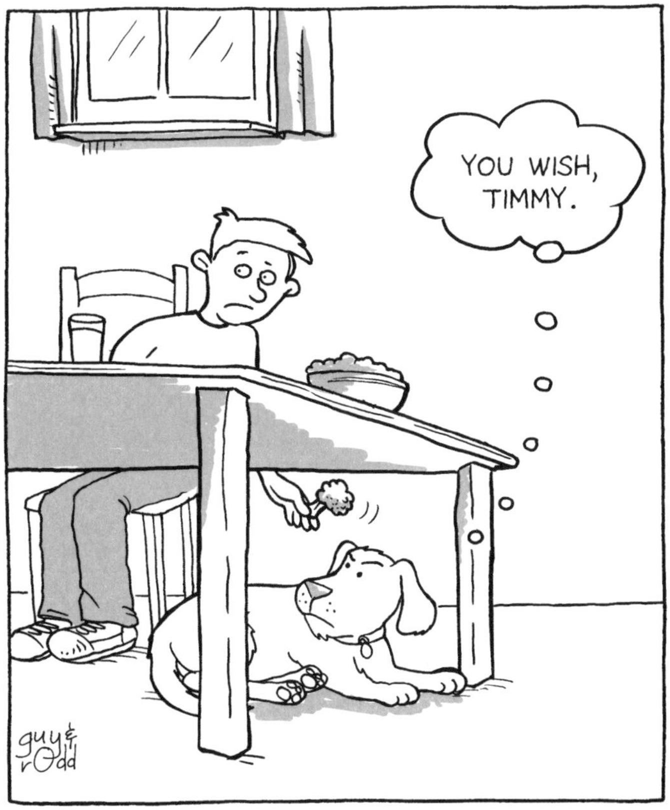
YOU WISH, TIMMY.

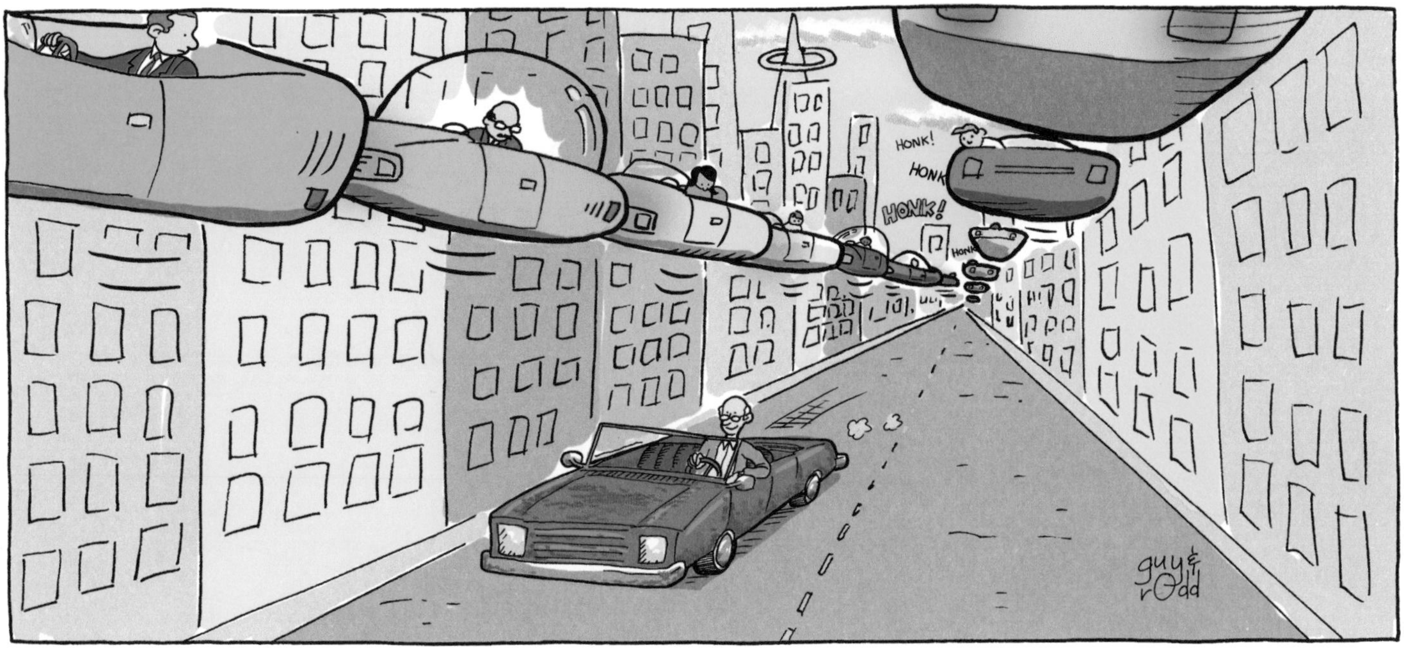
HONK!
HONK
HONK!

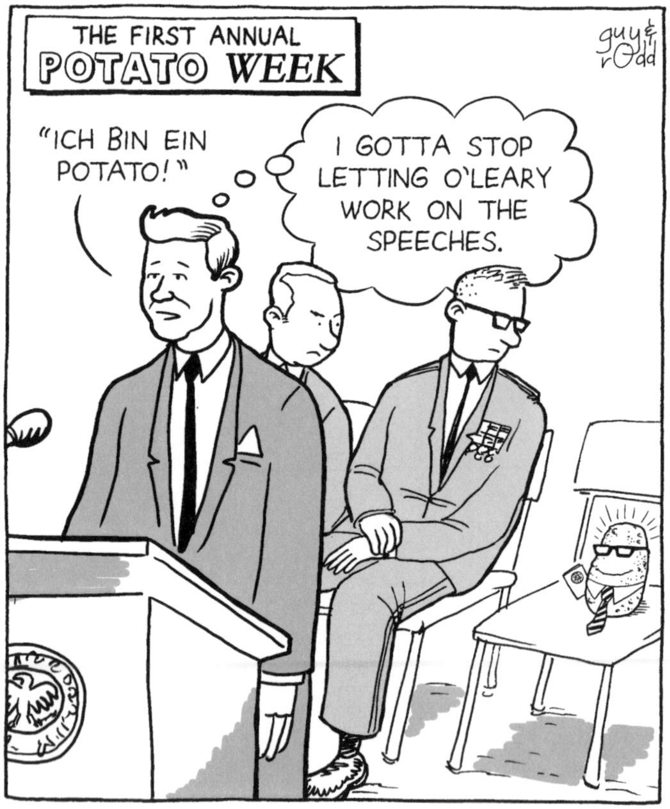
THE FIRST ANNUAL
POTATO WEEK
guy & rOdd
"ICH BIN EIN POTATO!"
I GOTTA STOP LETTING O'LEARY WORK ON THE SPEECHES.

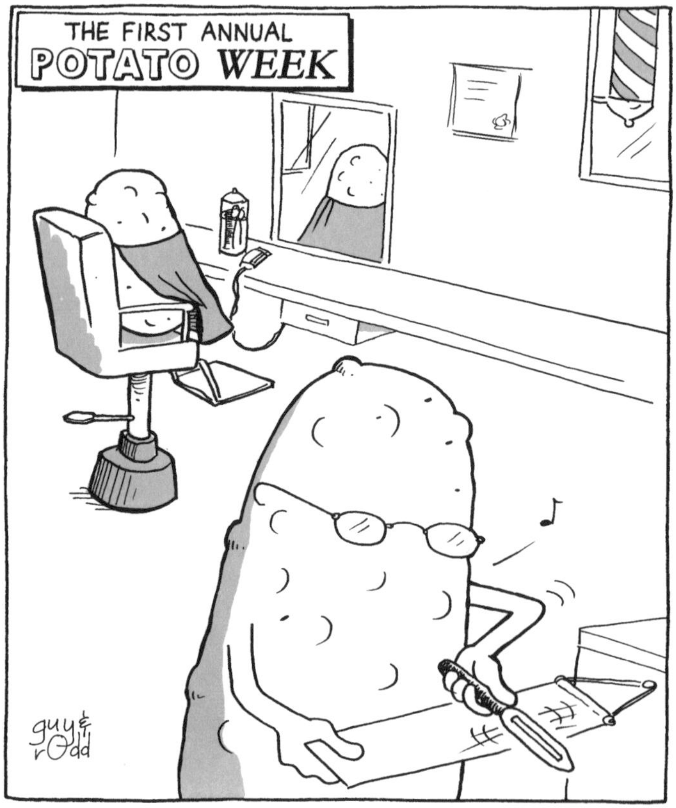
THE FIRST ANNUAL
POTATO WEEK
guy & rOdd

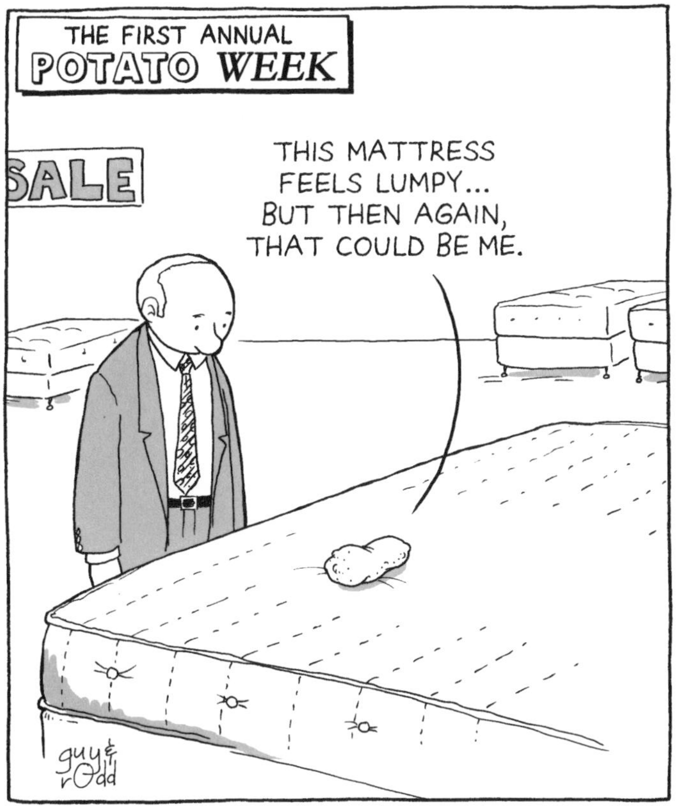
THE FIRST ANNUAL
POTATO WEEK
SALE
THIS MATTRESS FEELS LUMPY... BUT THEN AGAIN, THAT COULD BE ME.

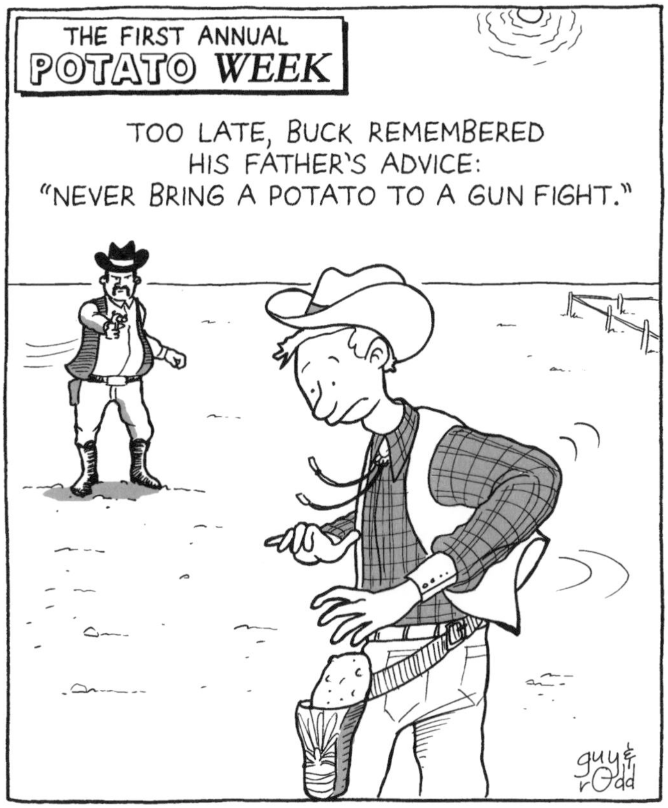
THE FIRST ANNUAL
POTATO WEEK
TOO LATE, BUCK REMEMBERED HIS FATHER'S ADVICE: "NEVER BRING A POTATO TO A GUN FIGHT."

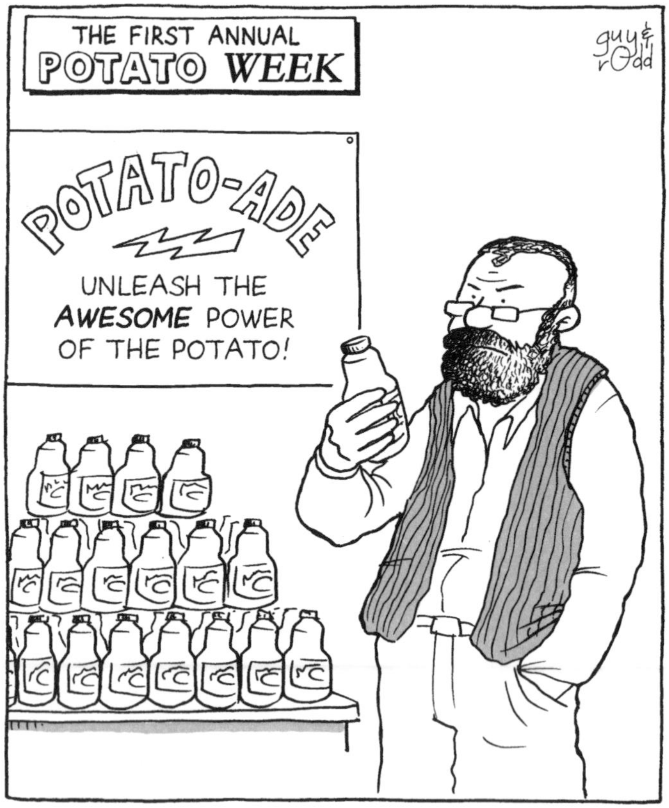
THE FIRST ANNUAL
POTATO WEEK
POTATO-ADE
UNLEASH THE **AWESOME** POWER OF THE POTATO!
guy & rOdd

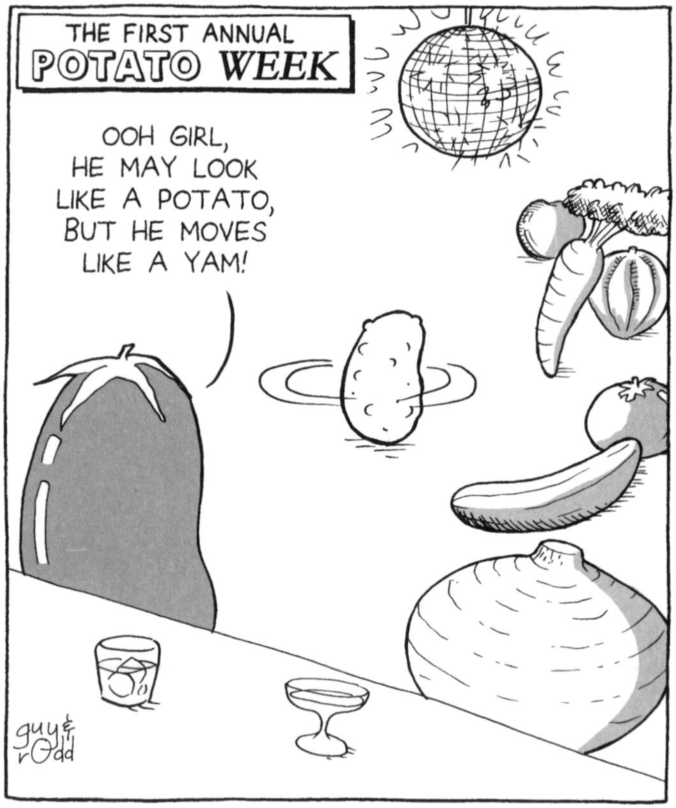
THE FIRST ANNUAL
POTATO WEEK
OOH GIRL, HE MAY LOOK LIKE A POTATO, BUT HE MOVES LIKE A YAM!
guy & rOdd

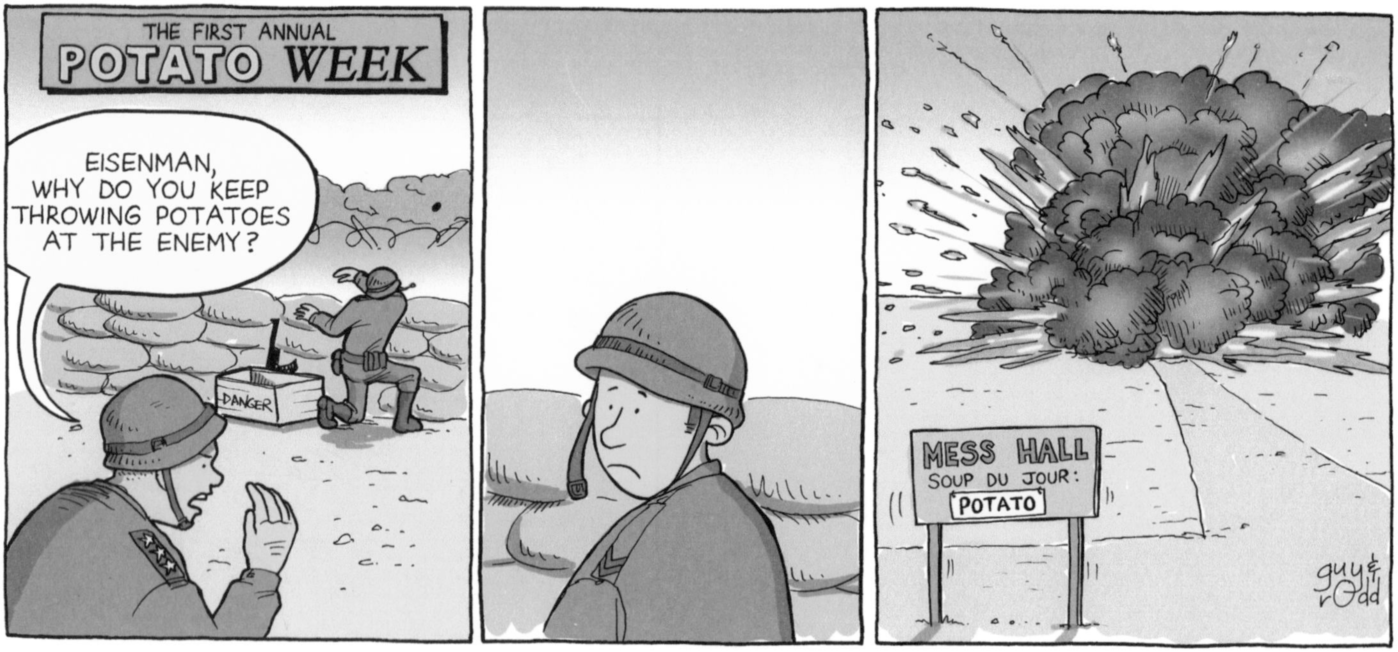
THE FIRST ANNUAL
POTATO WEEK
EISENMAN, WHY DO YOU KEEP THROWING POTATOES AT THE ENEMY?
DANGER
MESS HALL
SOUP DU JOUR:
POTATO
guy & rOdd

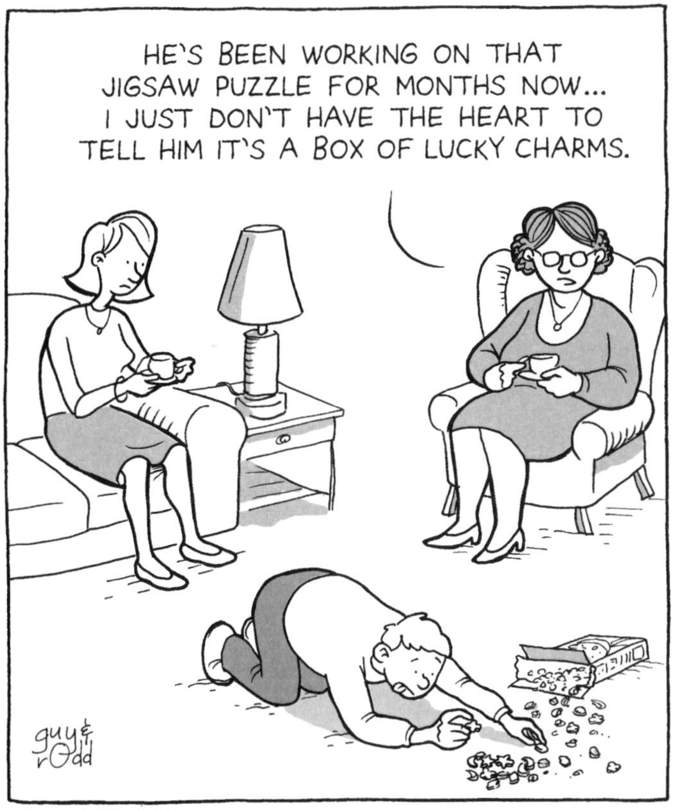
HE'S BEEN WORKING ON THAT JIGSAW PUZZLE FOR MONTHS NOW... I JUST DON'T HAVE THE HEART TO TELL HIM IT'S A BOX OF LUCKY CHARMS.

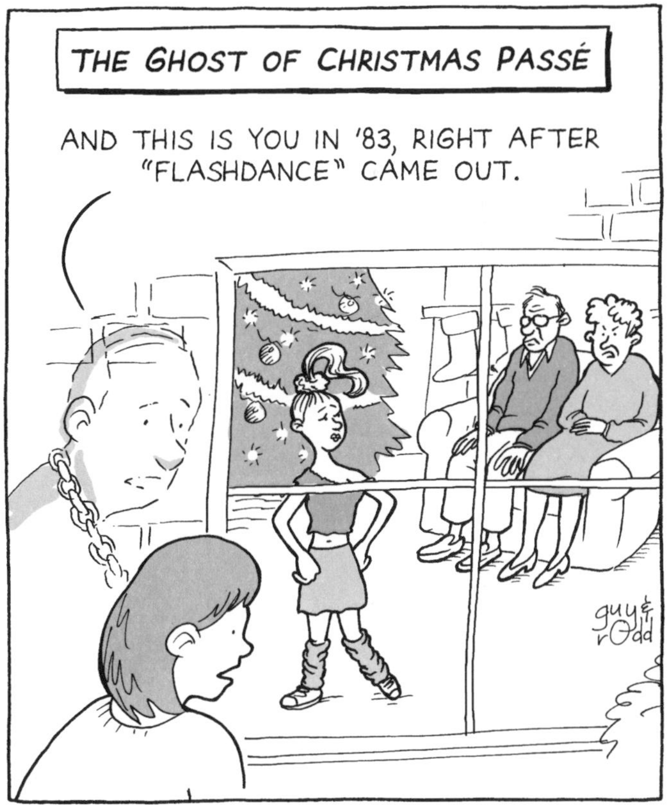
THE GHOST OF CHRISTMAS PASSÉ
AND THIS IS YOU IN '83, RIGHT AFTER "FLASHDANCE" CAME OUT.

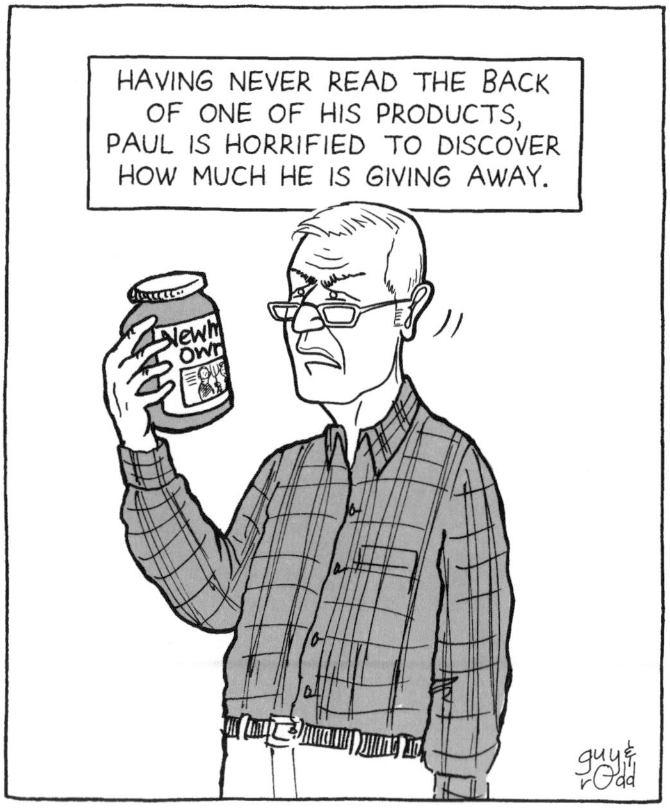
HAVING NEVER READ THE BACK OF ONE OF HIS PRODUCTS, PAUL IS HORRIFIED TO DISCOVER HOW MUCH HE IS GIVING AWAY.
guy & rOdd

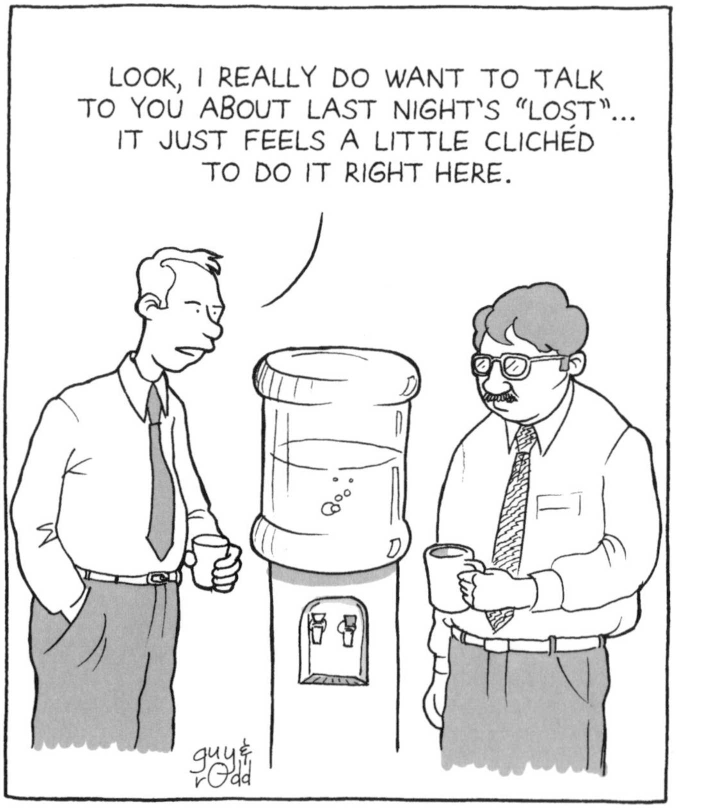
LOOK, I REALLY DO WANT TO TALK TO YOU ABOUT LAST NIGHT'S "LOST"... IT JUST FEELS A LITTLE CLICHÉD TO DO IT RIGHT HERE.
guy & rOdd

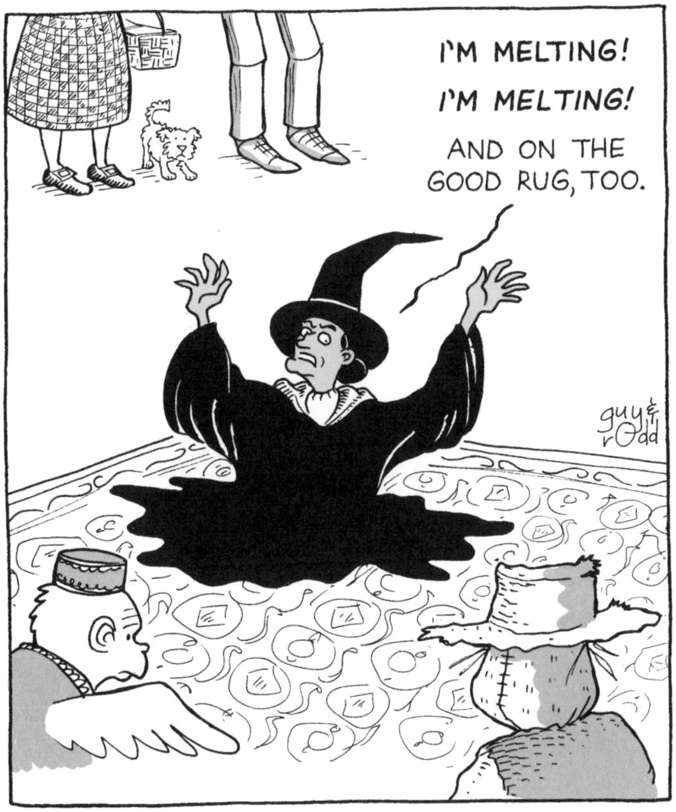
I'M MELTING!
I'M MELTING!
AND ON THE GOOD RUG, TOO.

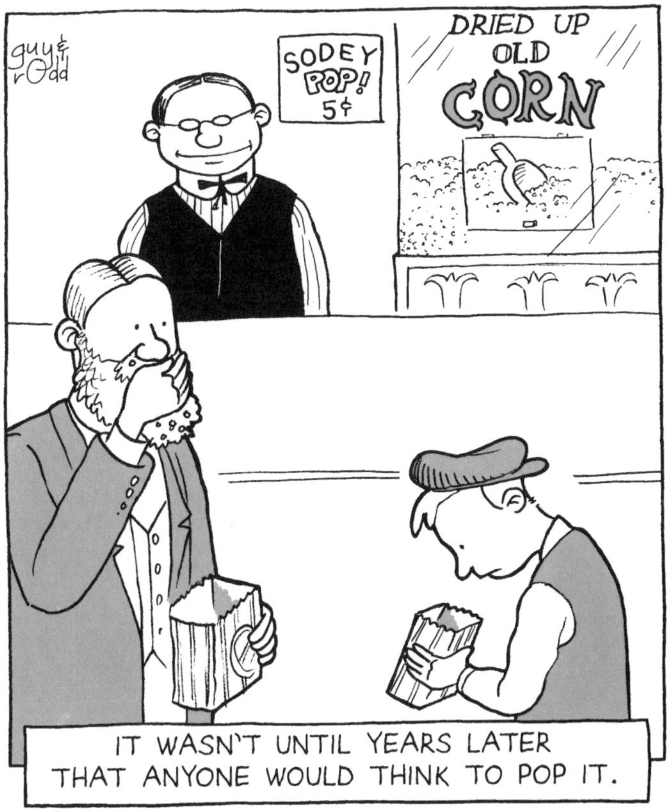
SODEY POP! 5¢
DRIED UP OLD CORN
IT WASN'T UNTIL YEARS LATER THAT ANYONE WOULD THINK TO POP IT.

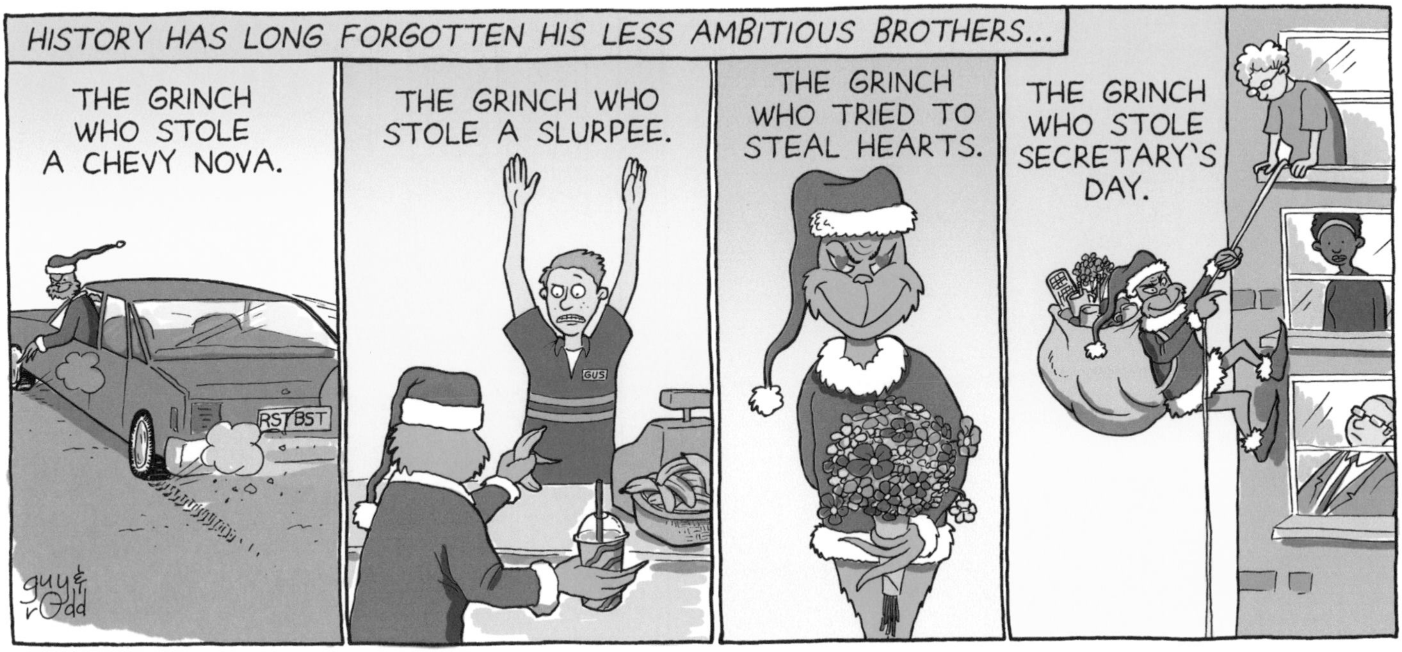
HISTORY HAS LONG FORGOTTEN HIS LESS AMBITIOUS BROTHERS...
THE GRINCH WHO STOLE A CHEVY NOVA.
RST BST
THE GRINCH WHO STOLE A SLURPEE.
GUS
THE GRINCH WHO TRIED TO STEAL HEARTS.
THE GRINCH WHO STOLE SECRETARY'S DAY.

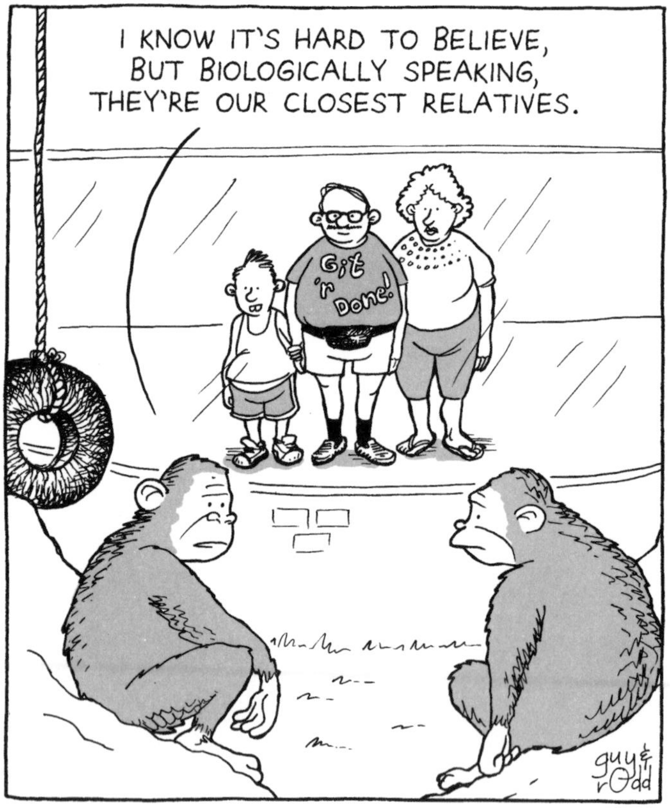
I KNOW IT'S HARD TO BELIEVE, BUT BIOLOGICALLY SPEAKING, THEY'RE OUR CLOSEST RELATIVES.
Git 'r Done!
guy & rOdd

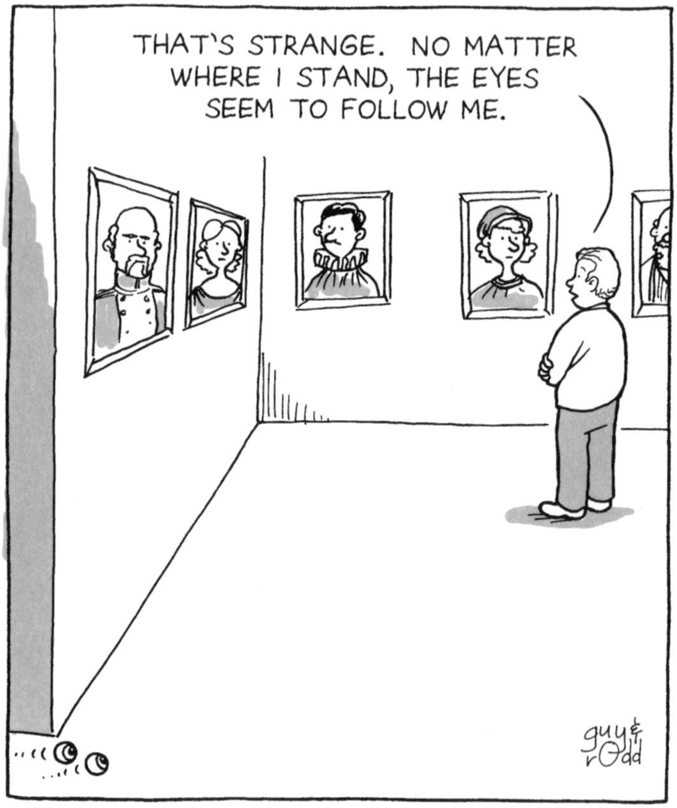
THAT'S STRANGE. NO MATTER WHERE I STAND, THE EYES SEEM TO FOLLOW ME.
guy & rOdd

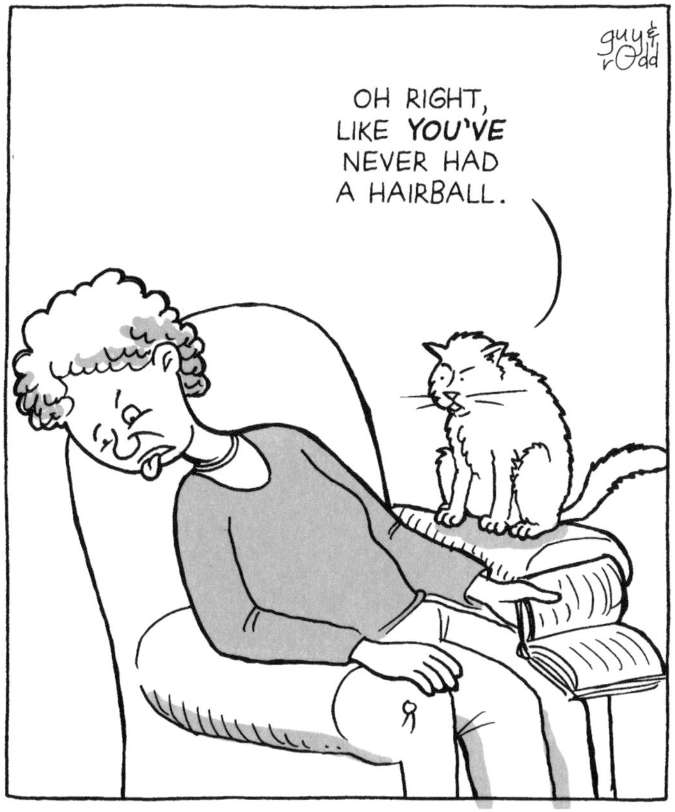
guy & rOdd
OH RIGHT, LIKE **YOU'VE** NEVER HAD A HAIRBALL.

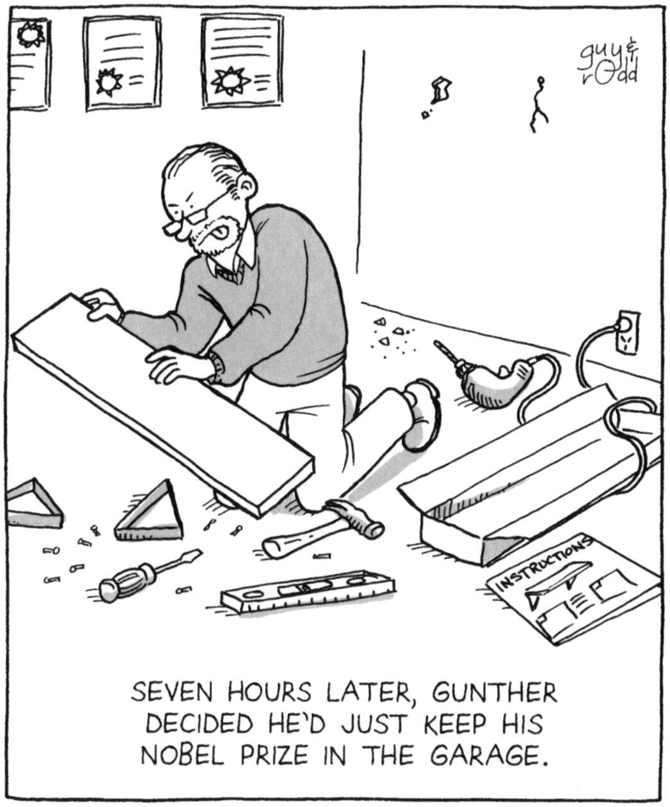
guy & rOdd
INSTRUCTIONS
SEVEN HOURS LATER, GUNTHER DECIDED HE'D JUST KEEP HIS NOBEL PRIZE IN THE GARAGE.

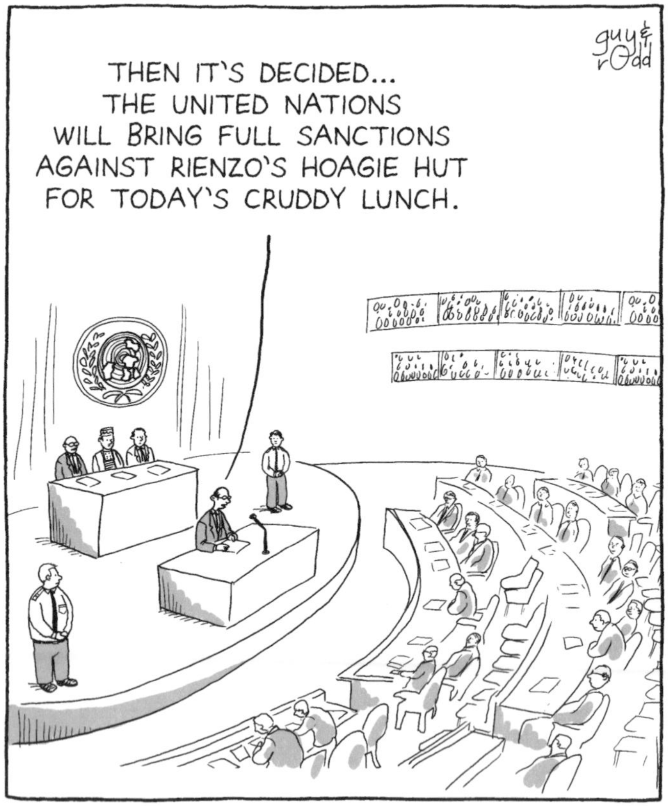
THEN IT'S DECIDED... THE UNITED NATIONS WILL BRING FULL SANCTIONS AGAINST RIENZO'S HOAGIE HUT FOR TODAY'S CRUDDY LUNCH.

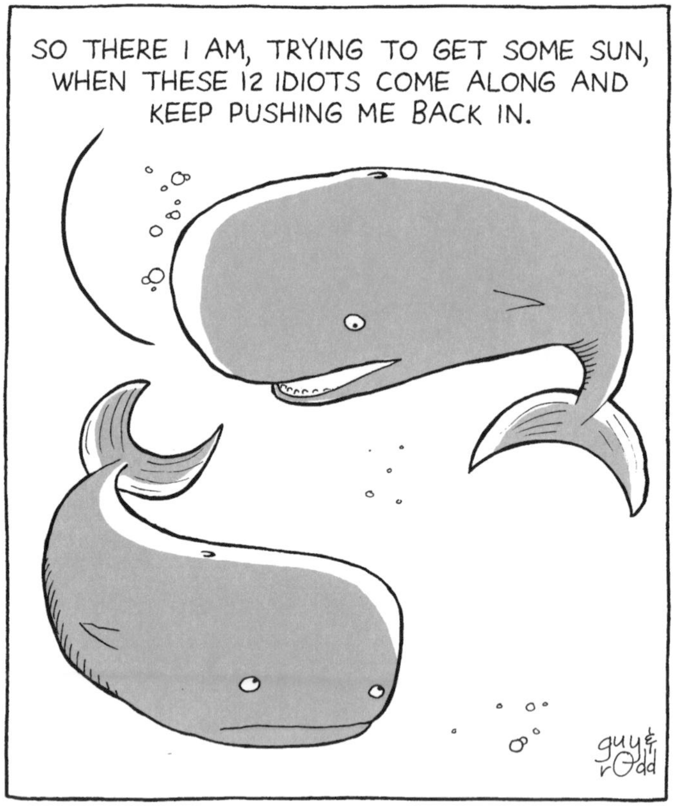
SO THERE I AM, TRYING TO GET SOME SUN, WHEN THESE 12 IDIOTS COME ALONG AND KEEP PUSHING ME BACK IN.

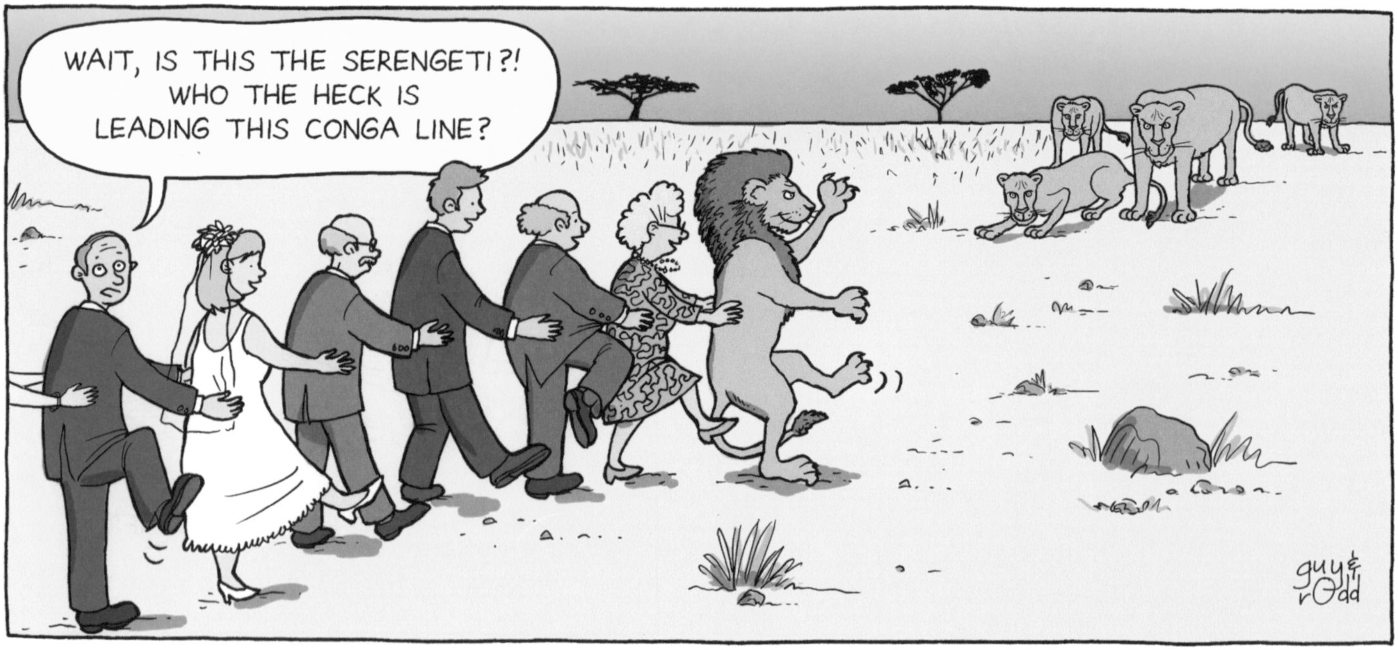
WAIT, IS THIS THE SERENGETI?! WHO THE HECK IS LEADING THIS CONGA LINE?

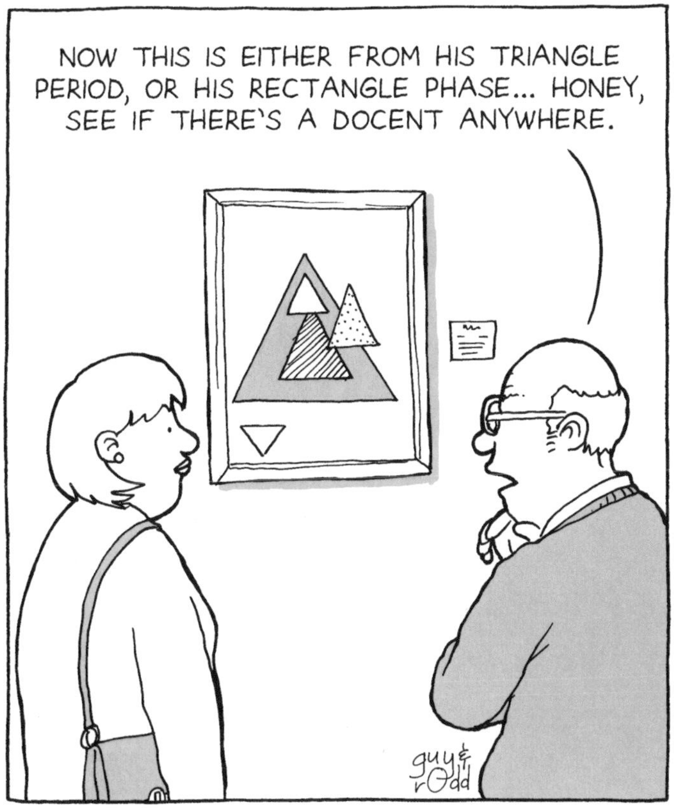
NOW THIS IS EITHER FROM HIS TRIANGLE PERIOD, OR HIS RECTANGLE PHASE... HONEY, SEE IF THERE'S A DOCENT ANYWHERE.
guy & rodd

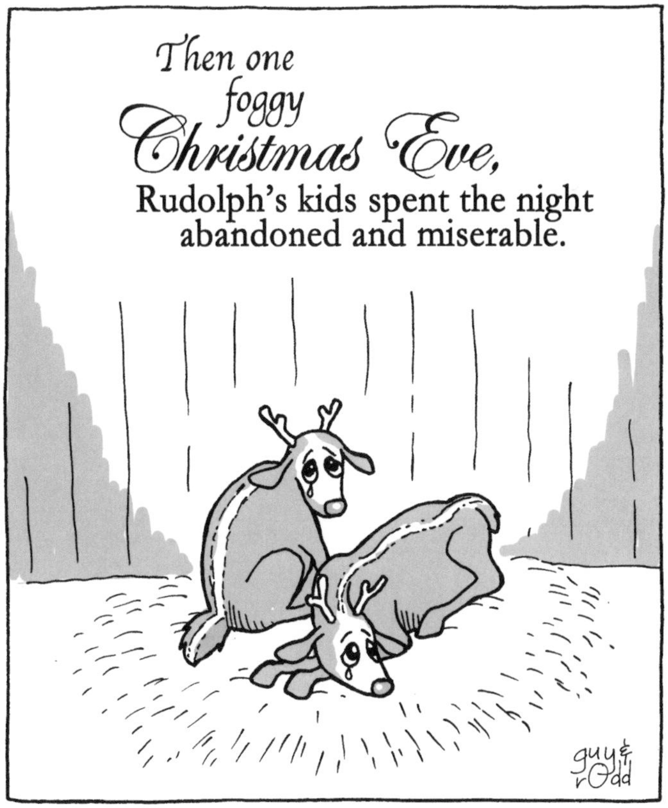
Then one foggy Christmas Eve,
Rudolph's kids spent the night abandoned and miserable.
guy & rodd

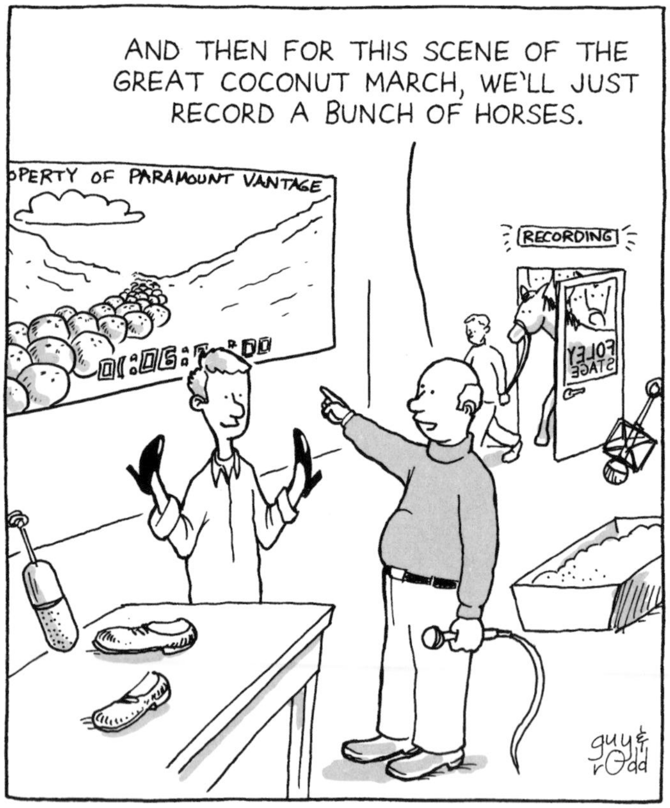
AND THEN FOR THIS SCENE OF THE GREAT COCONUT MARCH, WE'LL JUST RECORD A BUNCH OF HORSES.
PROPERTY OF PARAMOUNT VANTAGE
RECORDING
FOLEY STAGE
guy & rOdd

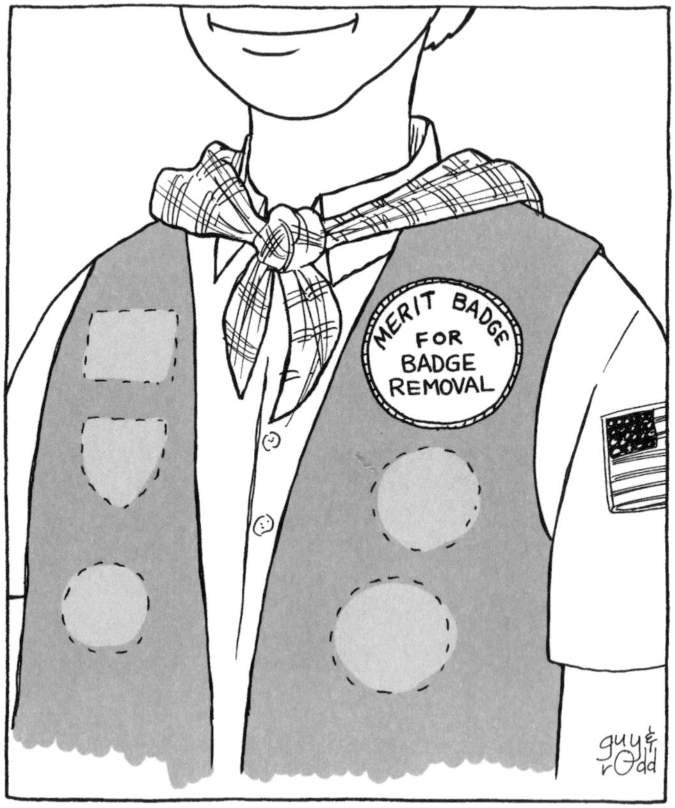
MERIT BADGE FOR BADGE REMOVAL
guy & rOdd

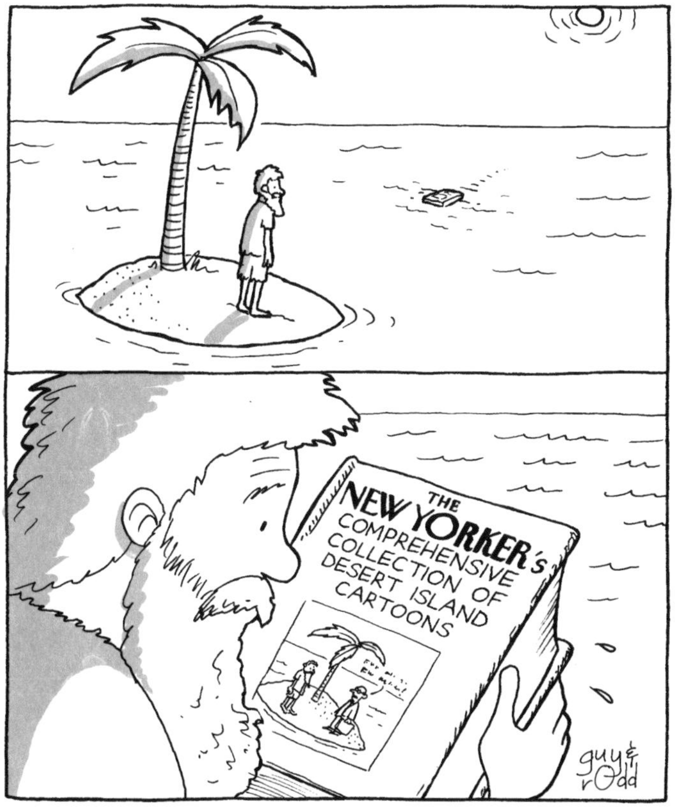
THE NEW YORKER's
COMPREHENSIVE
COLLECTION OF
DESERT ISLAND
CARTOONS

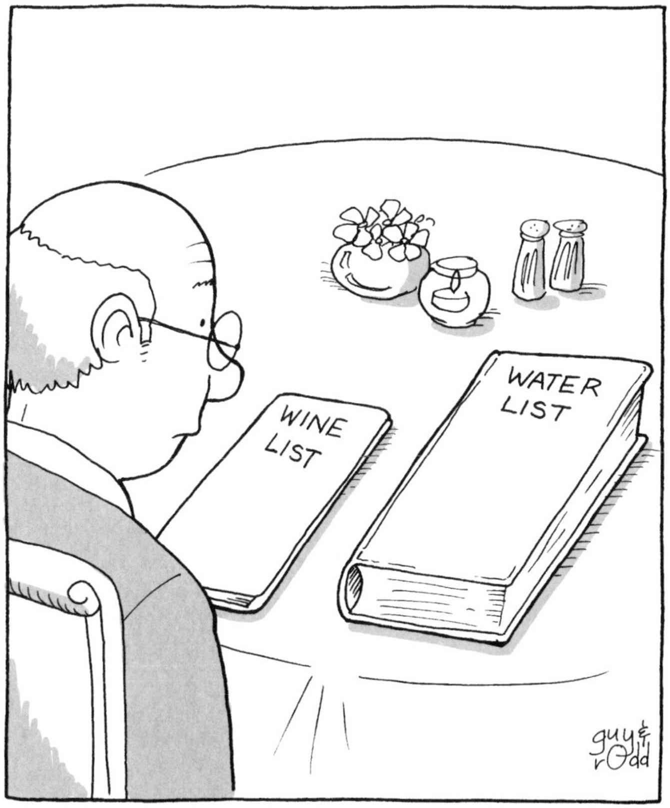
WINE LIST
WATER LIST

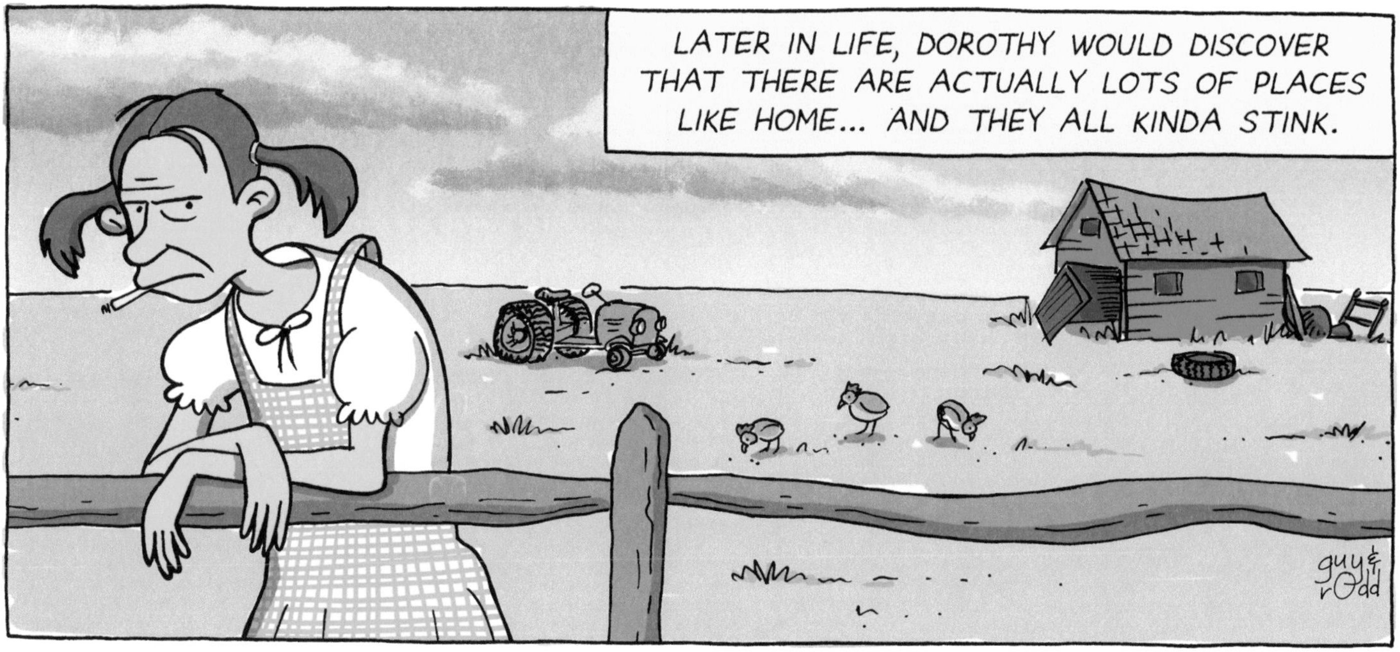
LATER IN LIFE, DOROTHY WOULD DISCOVER THAT THERE ARE ACTUALLY LOTS OF PLACES LIKE HOME... AND THEY ALL KINDA STINK.

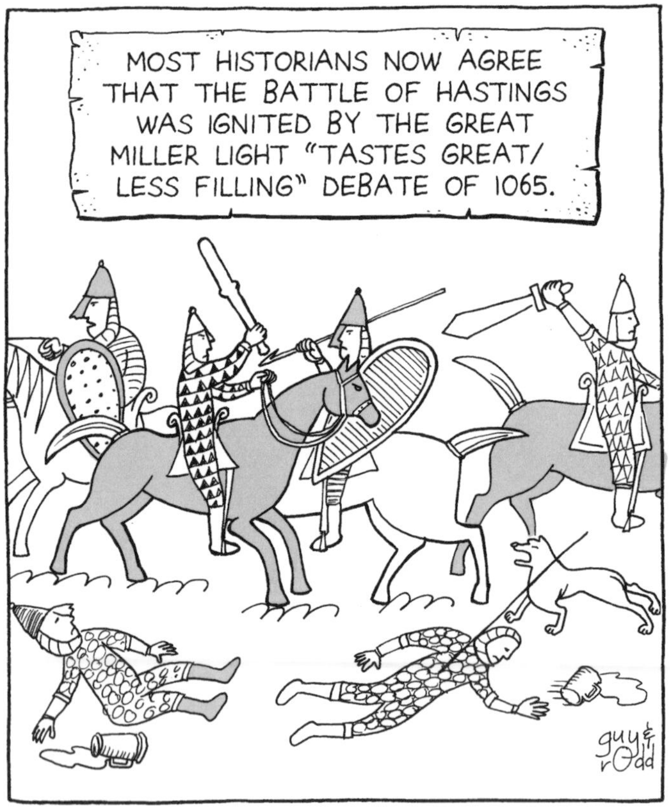
MOST HISTORIANS NOW AGREE THAT THE BATTLE OF HASTINGS WAS IGNITED BY THE GREAT MILLER LIGHT "TASTES GREAT/ LESS FILLING" DEBATE OF 1065.
guy & rodd

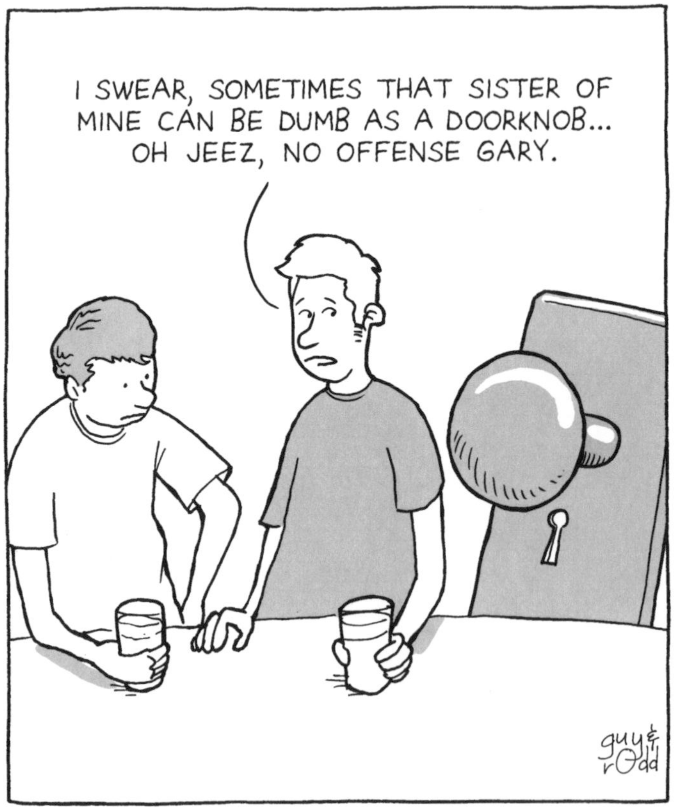
I SWEAR, SOMETIMES THAT SISTER OF MINE CAN BE DUMB AS A DOORKNOB... OH JEEZ, NO OFFENSE GARY.
guy & rodd

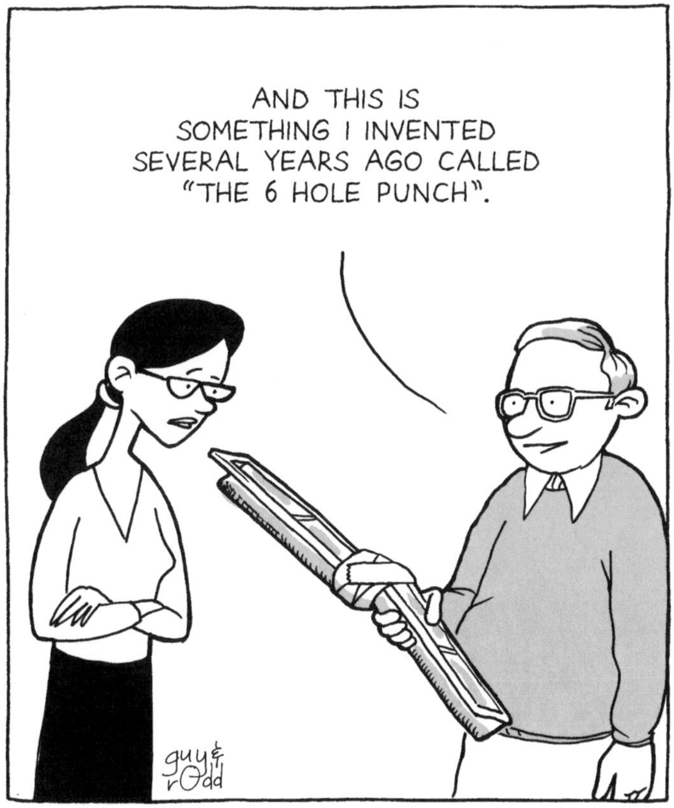
AND THIS IS SOMETHING I INVENTED SEVERAL YEARS AGO CALLED "THE 6 HOLE PUNCH".

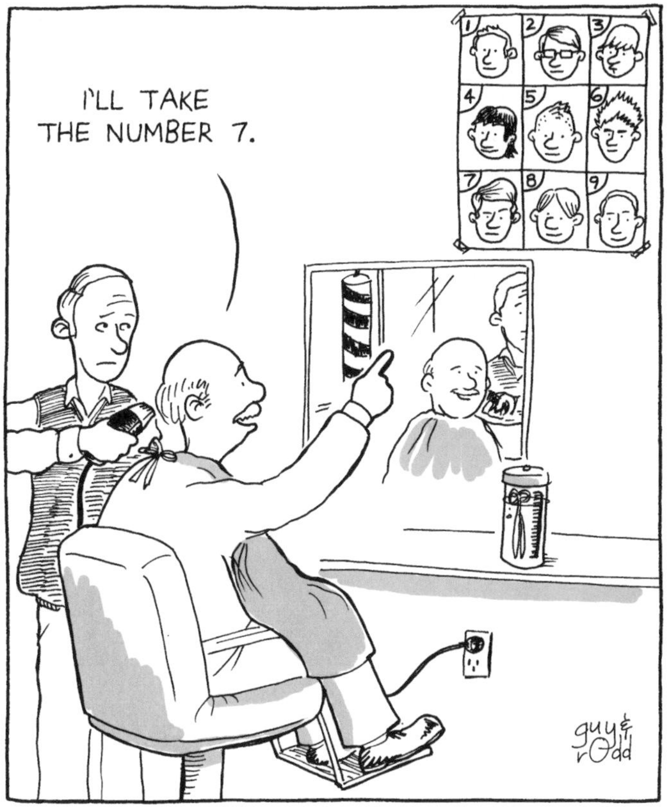
I'LL TAKE THE NUMBER 7.

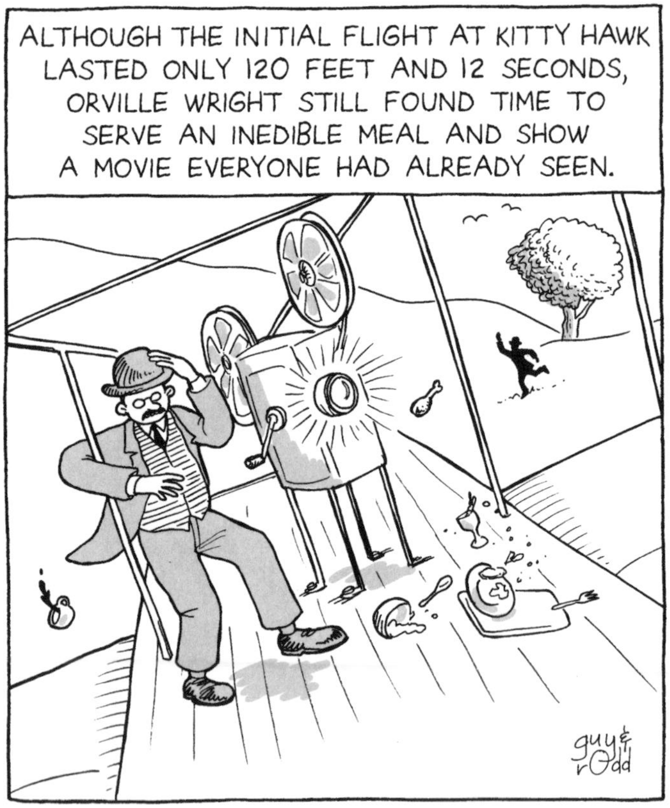
ALTHOUGH THE INITIAL FLIGHT AT KITTY HAWK LASTED ONLY 120 FEET AND 12 SECONDS, ORVILLE WRIGHT STILL FOUND TIME TO SERVE AN INEDIBLE MEAL AND SHOW A MOVIE EVERYONE HAD ALREADY SEEN.

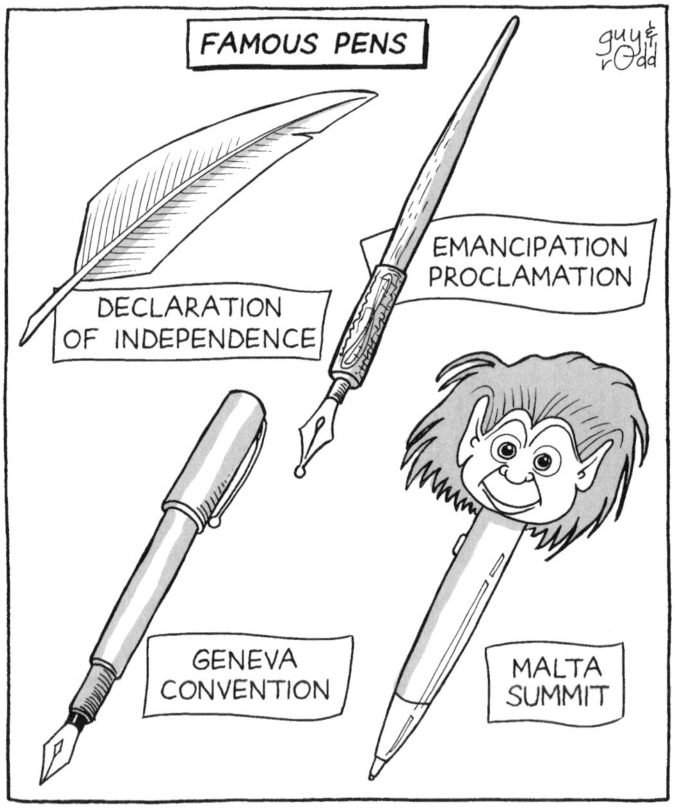
FAMOUS PENS
DECLARATION OF INDEPENDENCE
EMANCIPATION PROCLAMATION
GENEVA CONVENTION
MALTA SUMMIT

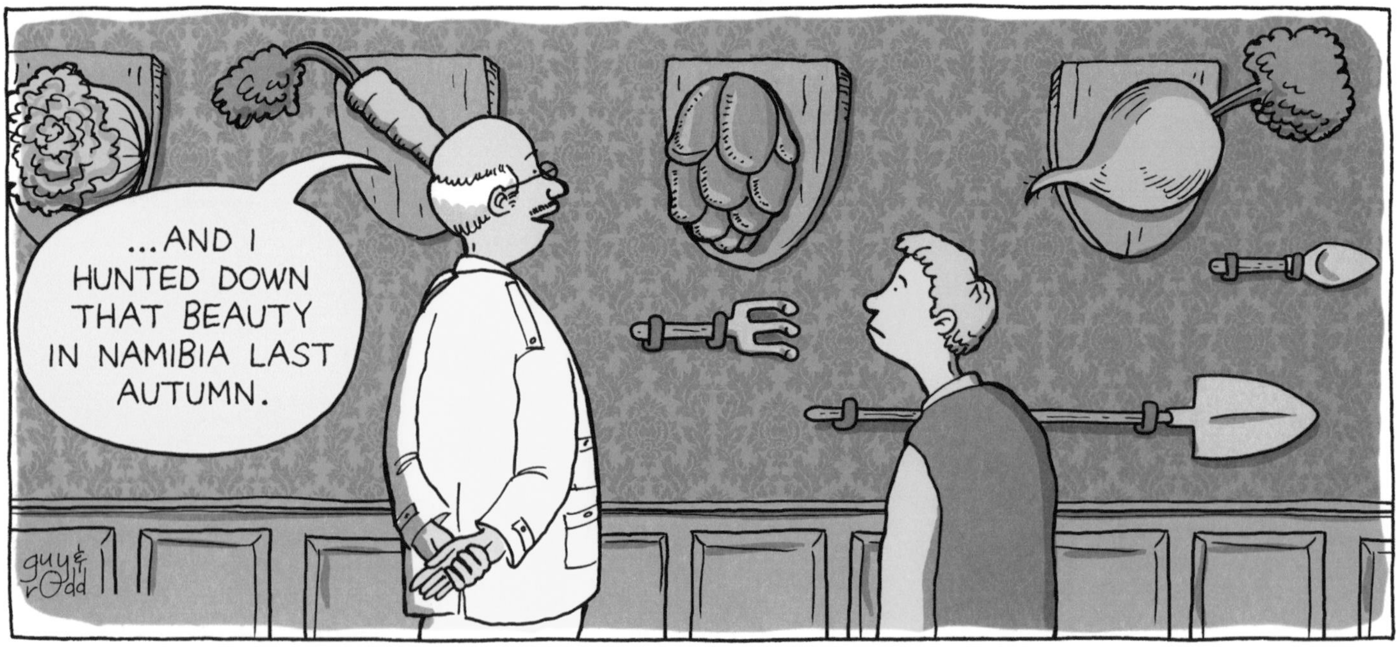
...AND I HUNTED DOWN THAT BEAUTY IN NAMIBIA LAST AUTUMN.

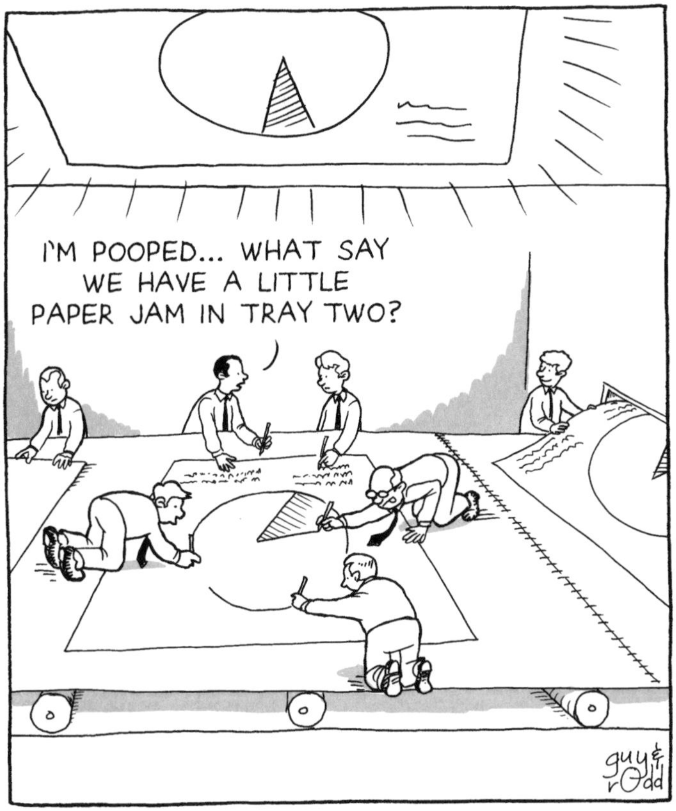
I'M POOPED... WHAT SAY WE HAVE A LITTLE PAPER JAM IN TRAY TWO?

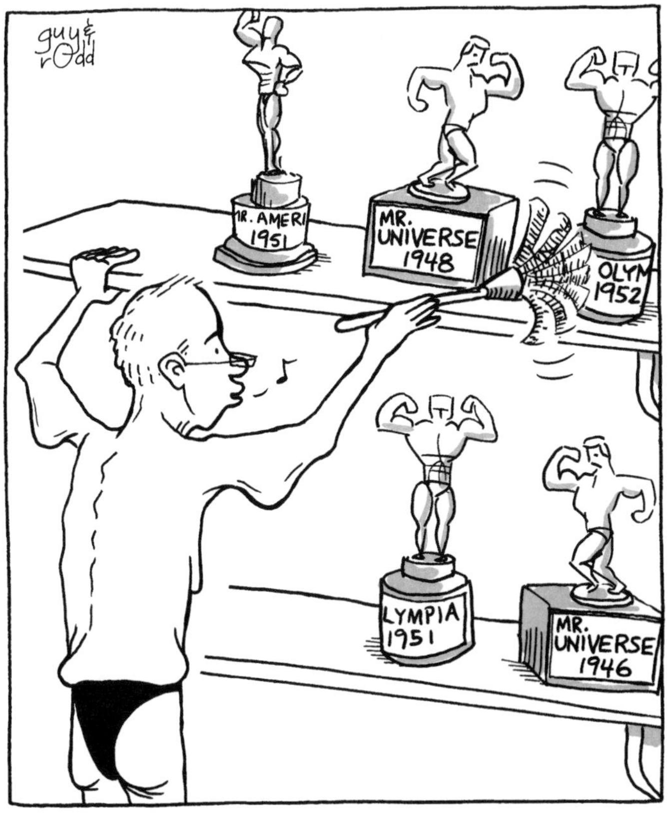
R. AMERI 1951
MR. UNIVERSE 1948
OLYM 1952
LYMPIA 1951
MR. UNIVERSE 1946

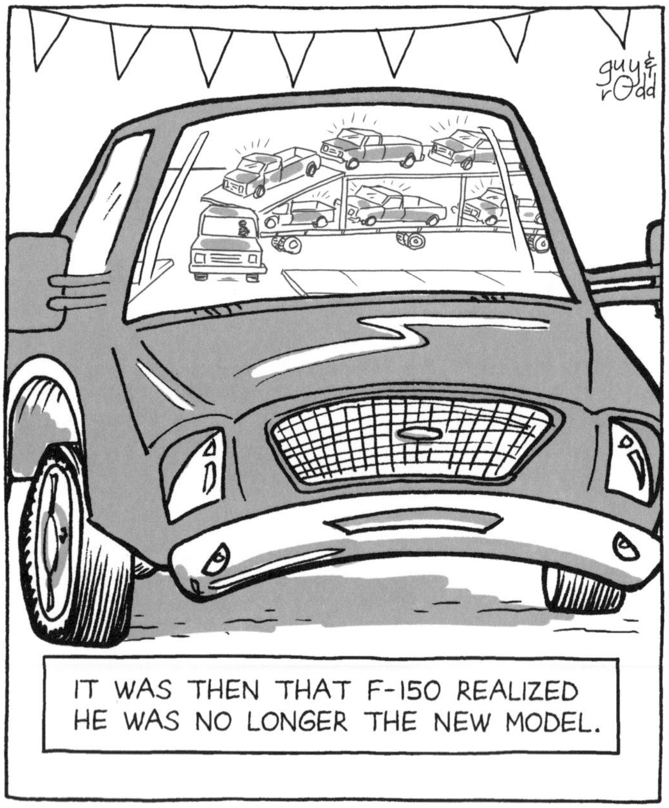
IT WAS THEN THAT F-150 REALIZED HE WAS NO LONGER THE NEW MODEL.

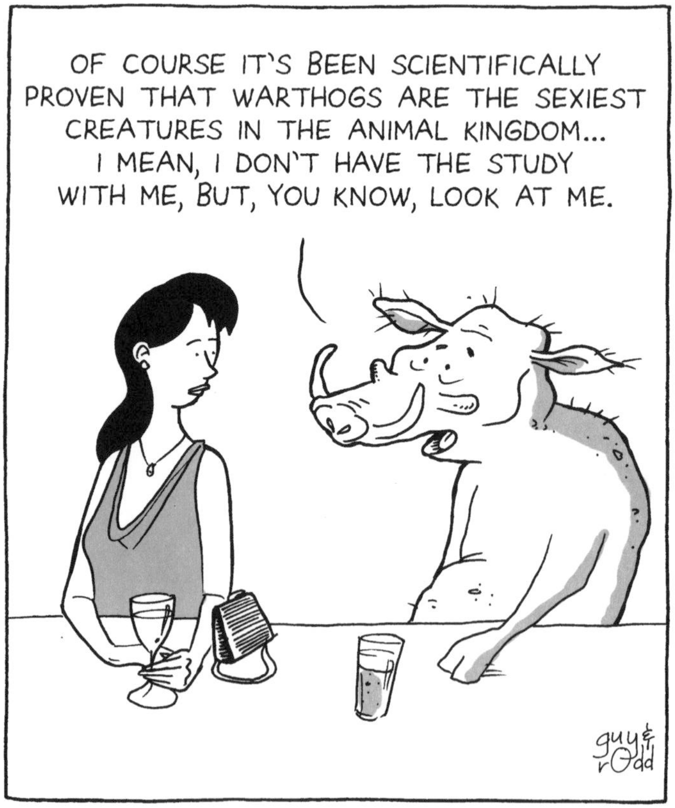
OF COURSE IT'S BEEN SCIENTIFICALLY PROVEN THAT WARTHOGS ARE THE SEXIEST CREATURES IN THE ANIMAL KINGDOM... I MEAN, I DON'T HAVE THE STUDY WITH ME, BUT, YOU KNOW, LOOK AT ME.

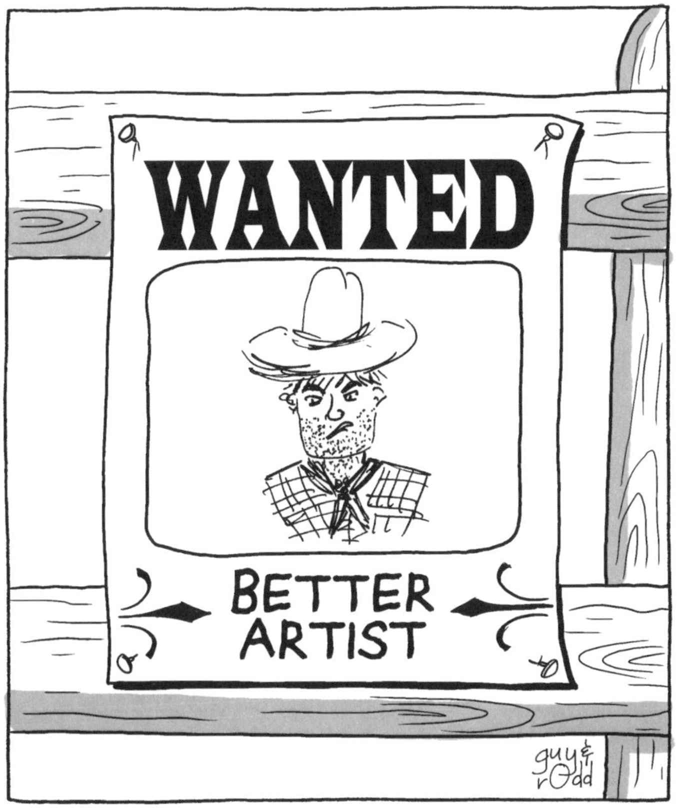
WANTED
BETTER ARTIST

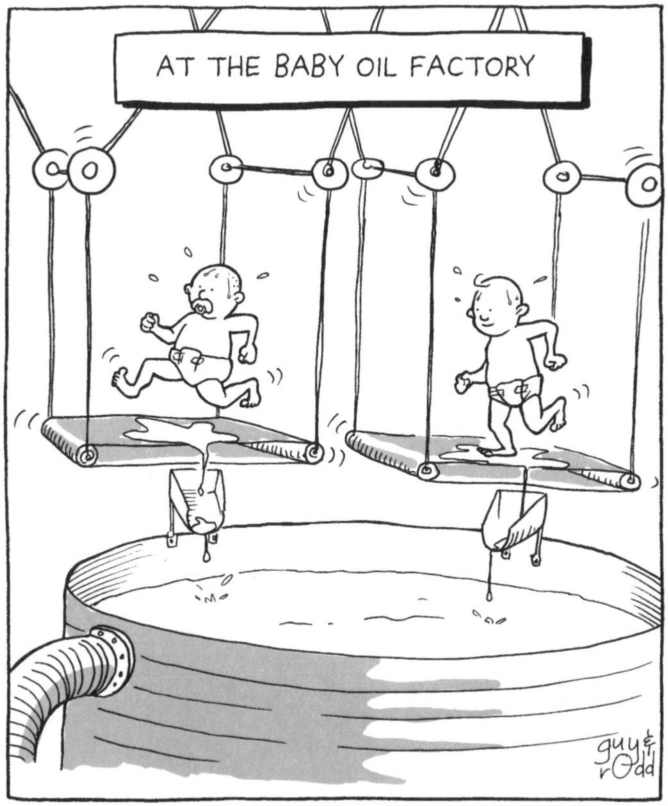
AT THE BABY OIL FACTORY

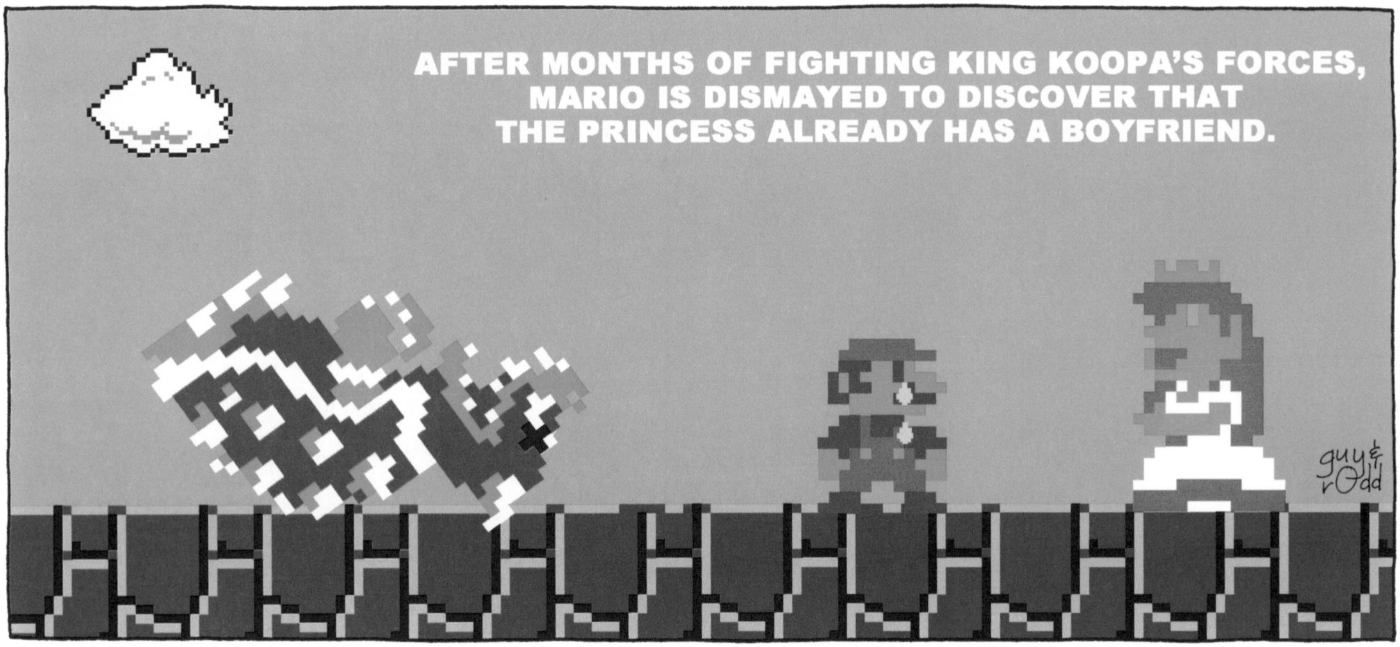
AFTER MONTHS OF FIGHTING KING KOOPA'S FORCES, MARIO IS DISMAYED TO DISCOVER THAT THE PRINCESS ALREADY HAS A BOYFRIEND.

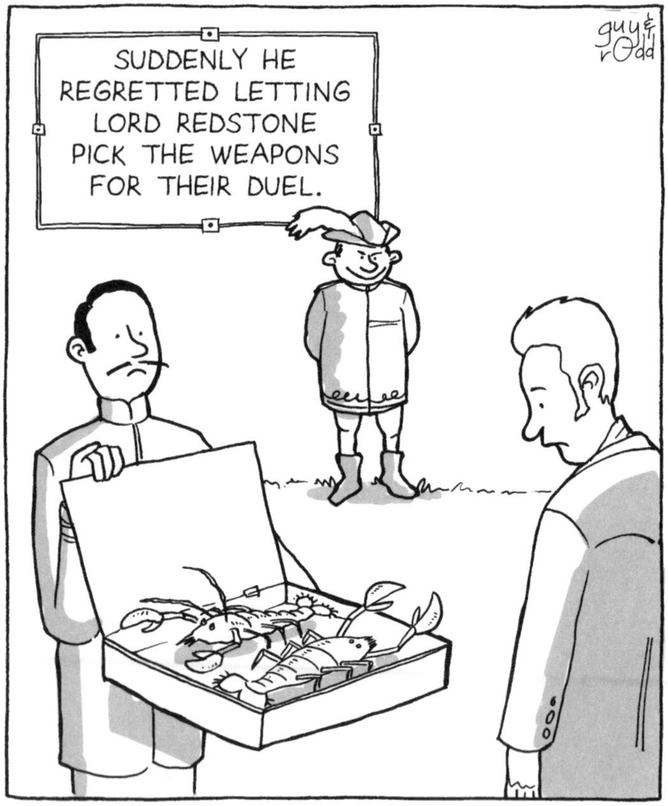
SUDDENLY HE REGRETTED LETTING LORD REDSTONE PICK THE WEAPONS FOR THEIR DUEL.
guy & rOdd

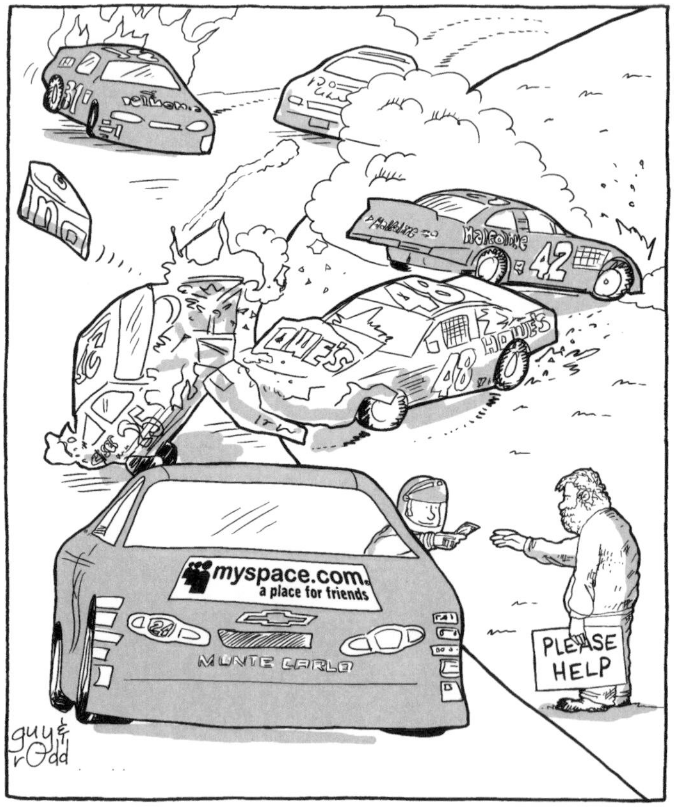
myspace.com
a place for friends
MONTE CARLO
PLEASE HELP
48
42
guy & rOdd

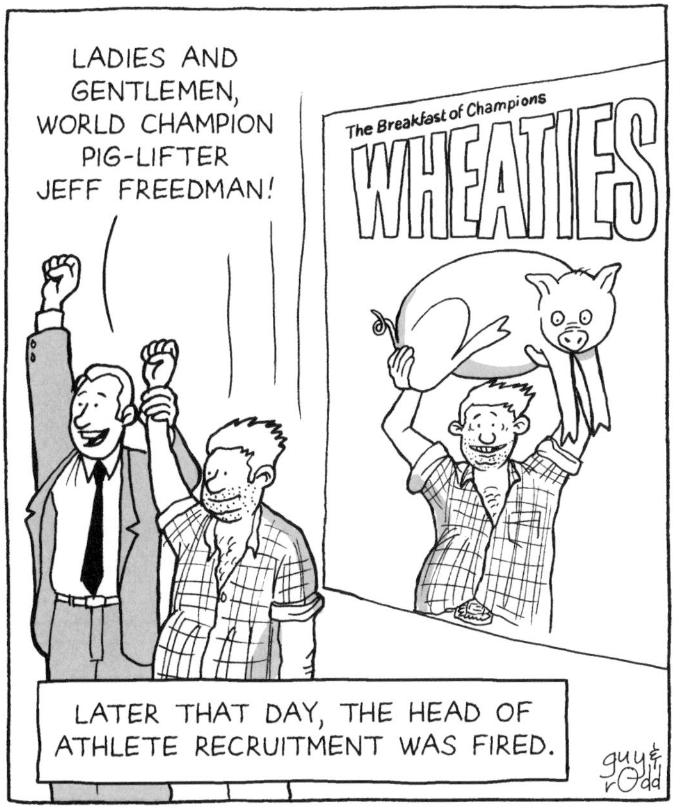
LADIES AND GENTLEMEN, WORLD CHAMPION PIG-LIFTER JEFF FREEDMAN!
The Breakfast of Champions
WHEATIES
LATER THAT DAY, THE HEAD OF ATHLETE RECRUITMENT WAS FIRED.

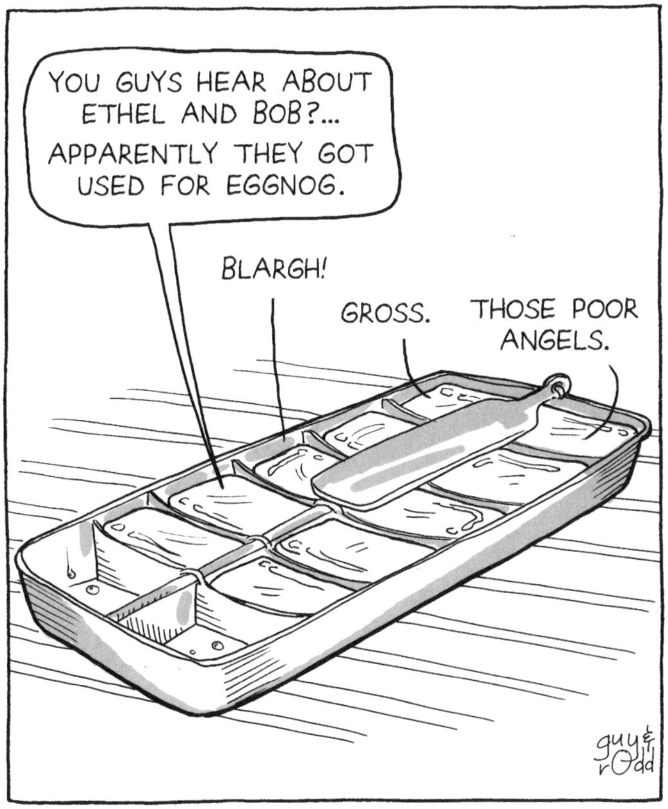
YOU GUYS HEAR ABOUT ETHEL AND BOB?... APPARENTLY THEY GOT USED FOR EGGNOG.
BLARGH!
GROSS.
THOSE POOR ANGELS.

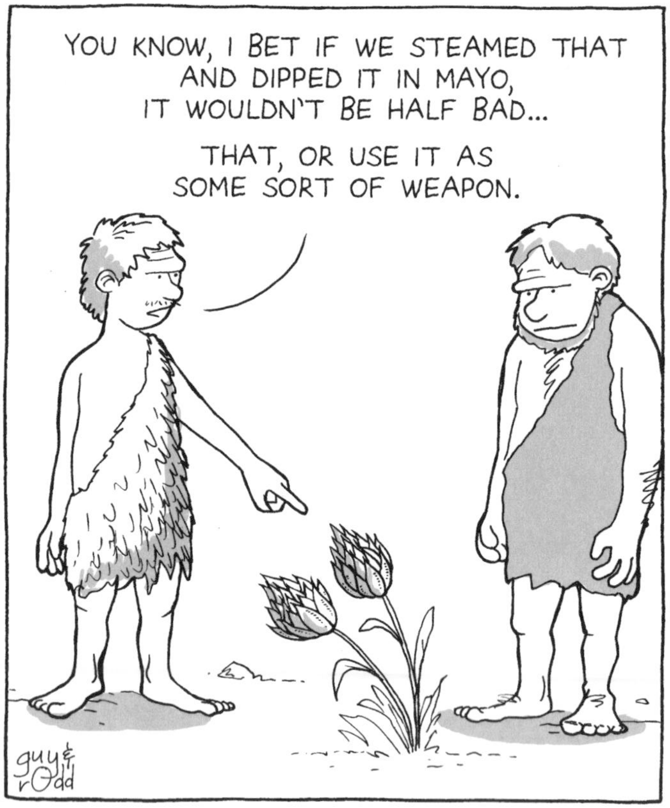
YOU KNOW, I BET IF WE STEAMED THAT AND DIPPED IT IN MAYO, IT WOULDN'T BE HALF BAD...
THAT, OR USE IT AS SOME SORT OF WEAPON.

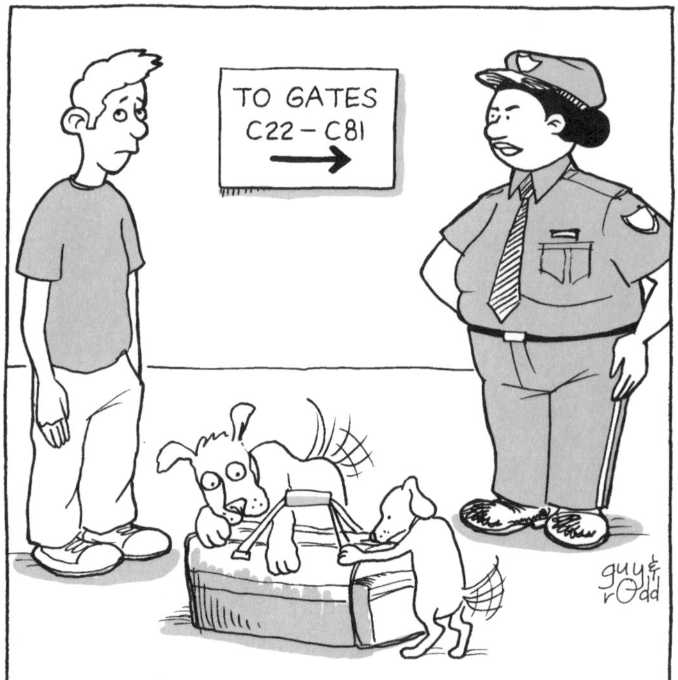
TO GATES C22 – C81

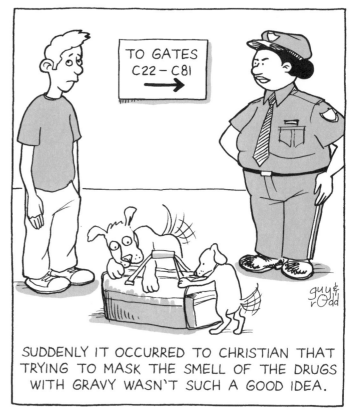

SUDDENLY IT OCCURRED TO CHRISTIAN THAT TRYING TO MASK THE SMELL OF THE DRUGS WITH GRAVY WASN'T SUCH A GOOD IDEA.

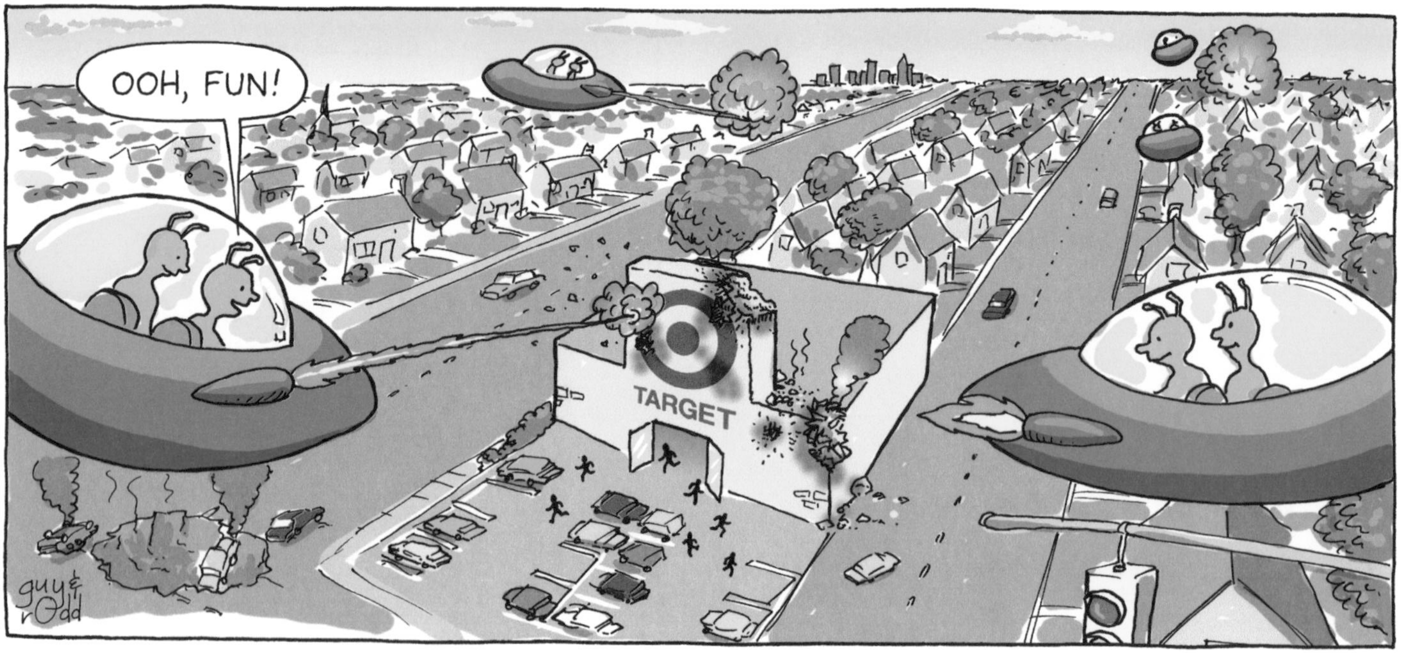
OOH, FUN!
TARGET

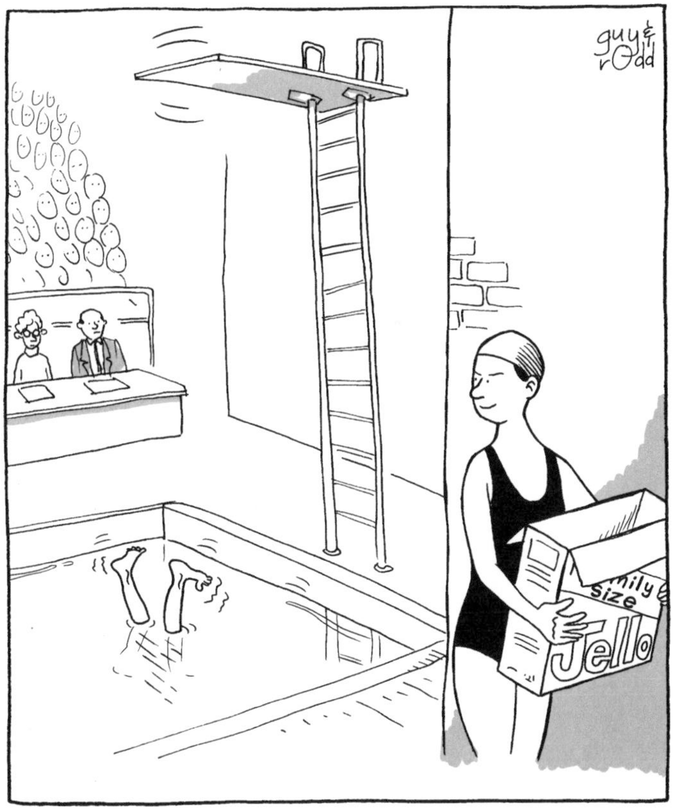
guy & rOdd
Family size
Jello

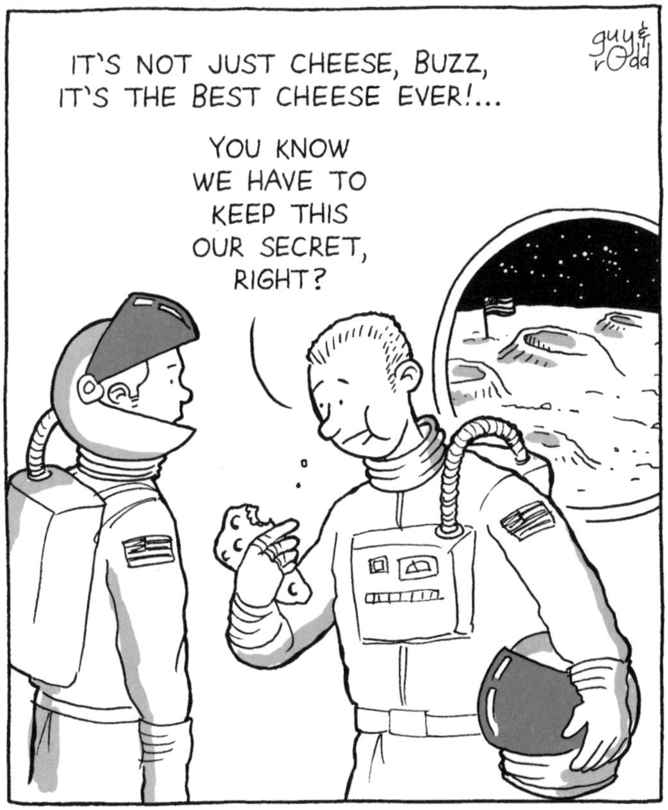
guy & rOdd
IT'S NOT JUST CHEESE, BUZZ, IT'S THE BEST CHEESE EVER!...
YOU KNOW WE HAVE TO KEEP THIS OUR SECRET, RIGHT?

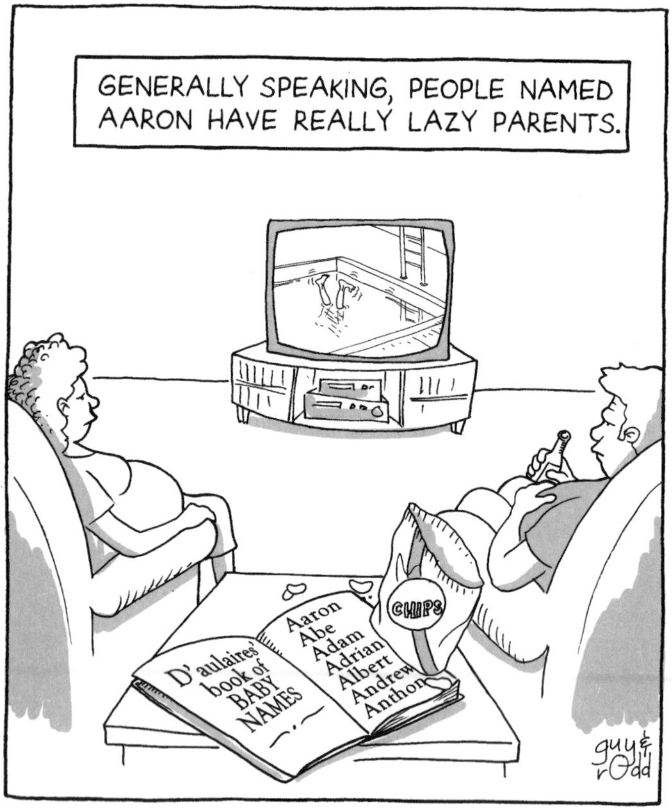
GENERALLY SPEAKING, PEOPLE NAMED AARON HAVE REALLY LAZY PARENTS.
D'aulaires' book of BABY NAMES
Aaron
Abe
Adam
Adrian
Albert
Andrew
Anthon
CHIPS
guy & rOdd

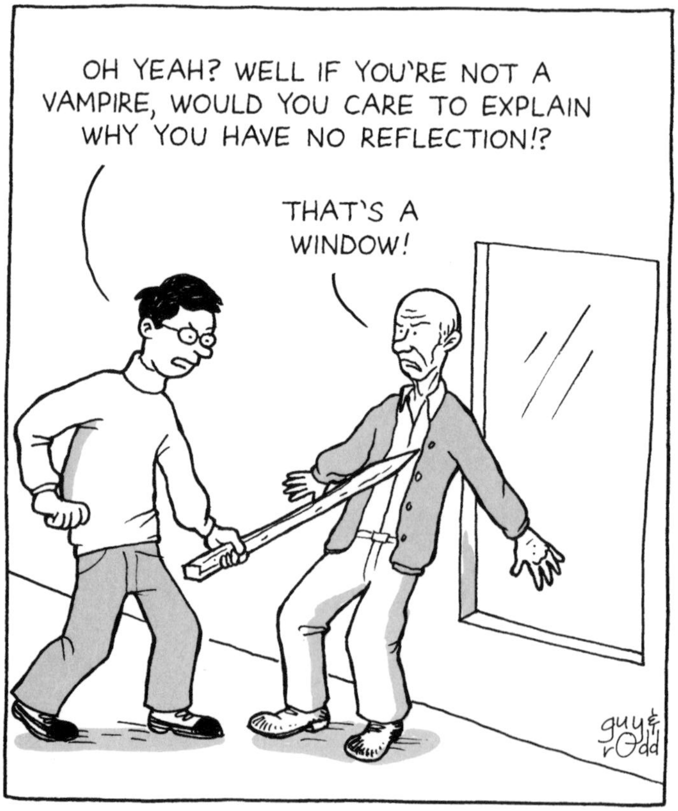
OH YEAH? WELL IF YOU'RE NOT A VAMPIRE, WOULD YOU CARE TO EXPLAIN WHY YOU HAVE NO REFLECTION!?
THAT'S A WINDOW!
guy & rOdd

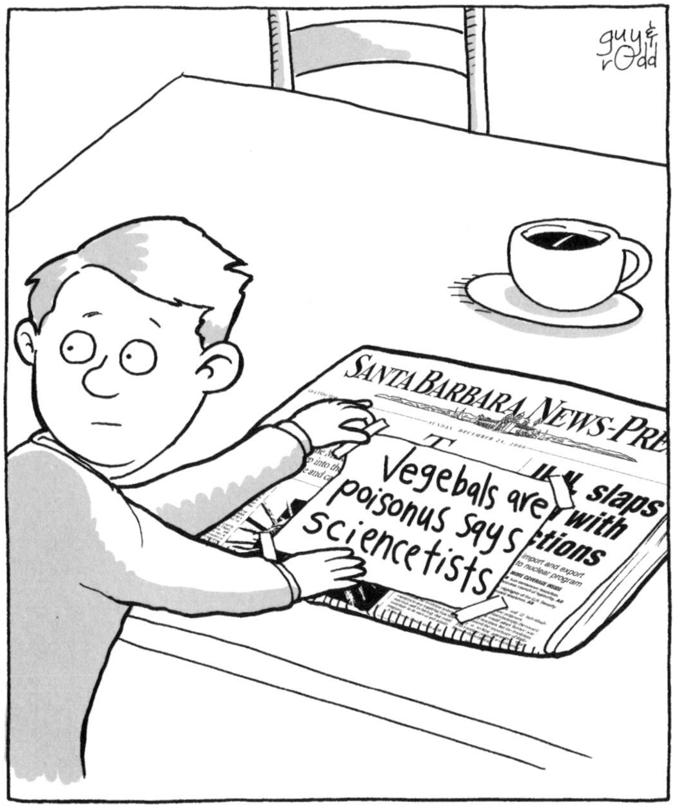
guy & rOdd
Santa Barbara News-Press
Vegebals are poisonus says sciencetists
slaps
with
tions
import and export
to nuclear program

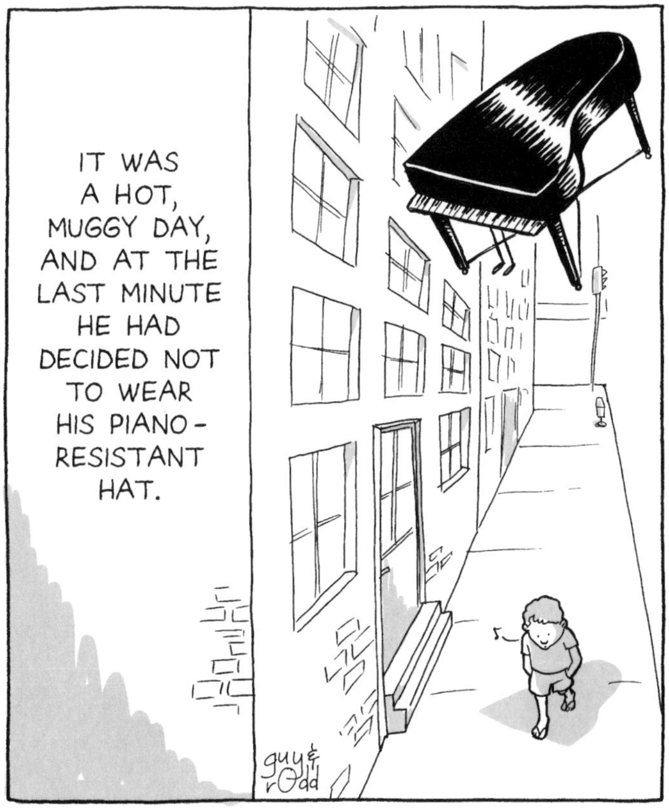
IT WAS A HOT, MUGGY DAY, AND AT THE LAST MINUTE HE HAD DECIDED NOT TO WEAR HIS PIANO-RESISTANT HAT.
guy & rOdd

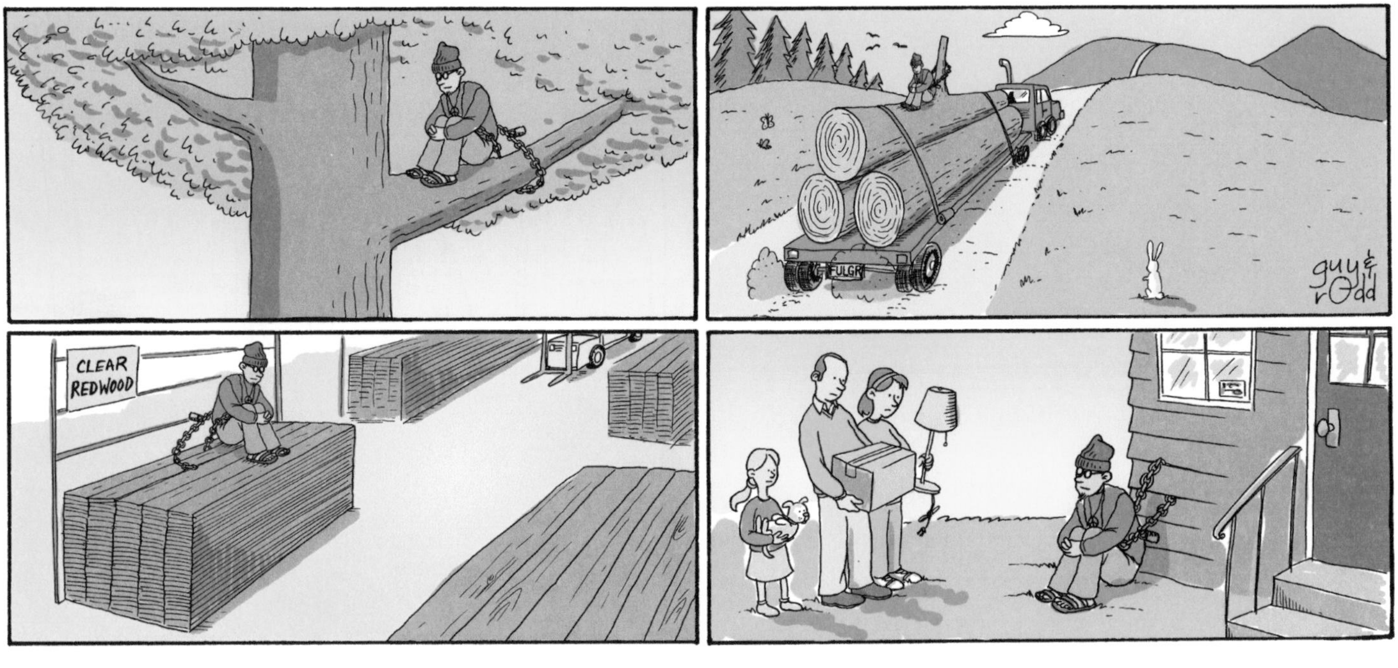
FULGR
guy & rOdd
CLEAR REDWOOD

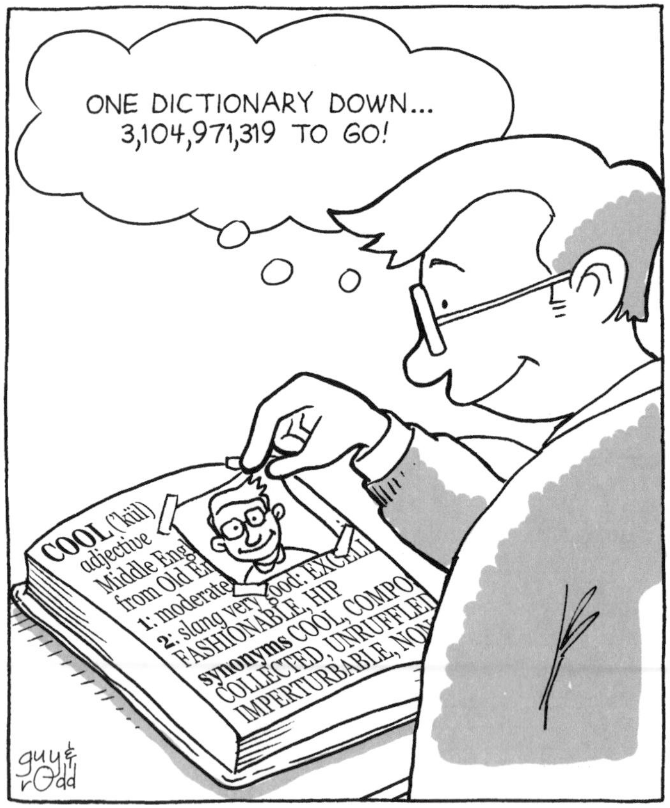
ONE DICTIONARY DOWN... 3,104,971,319 TO GO!

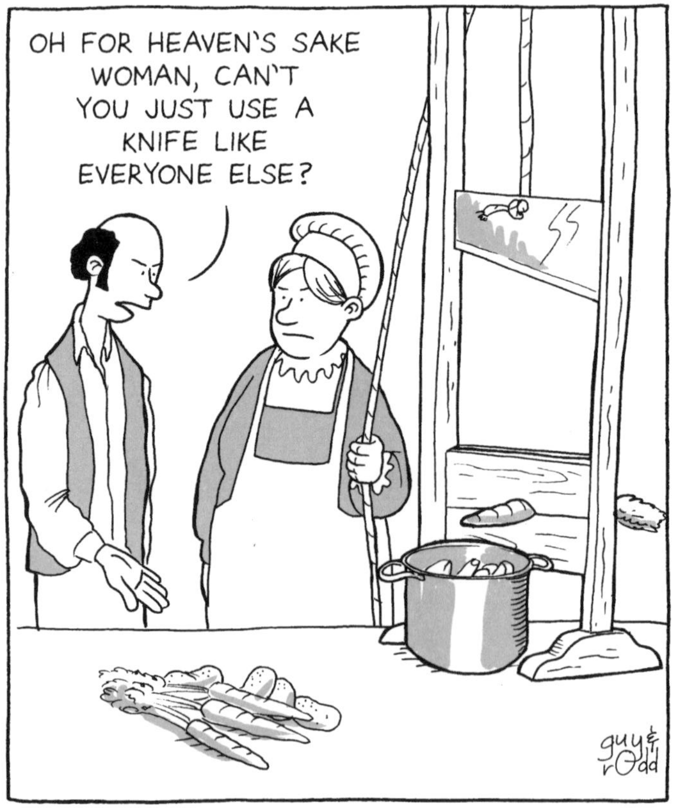
OH FOR HEAVEN'S SAKE WOMAN, CAN'T YOU JUST USE A KNIFE LIKE EVERYONE ELSE?

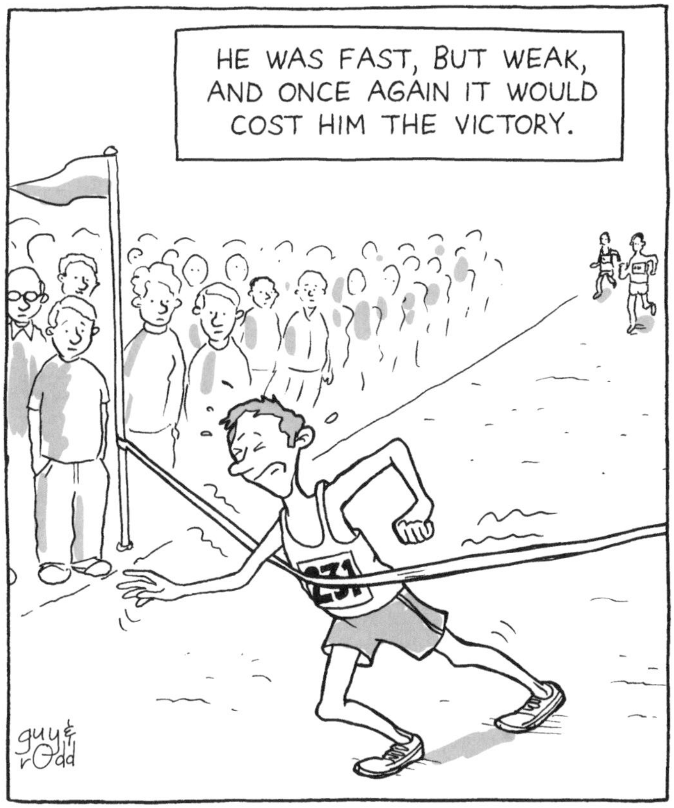
HE WAS FAST, BUT WEAK, AND ONCE AGAIN IT WOULD COST HIM THE VICTORY.

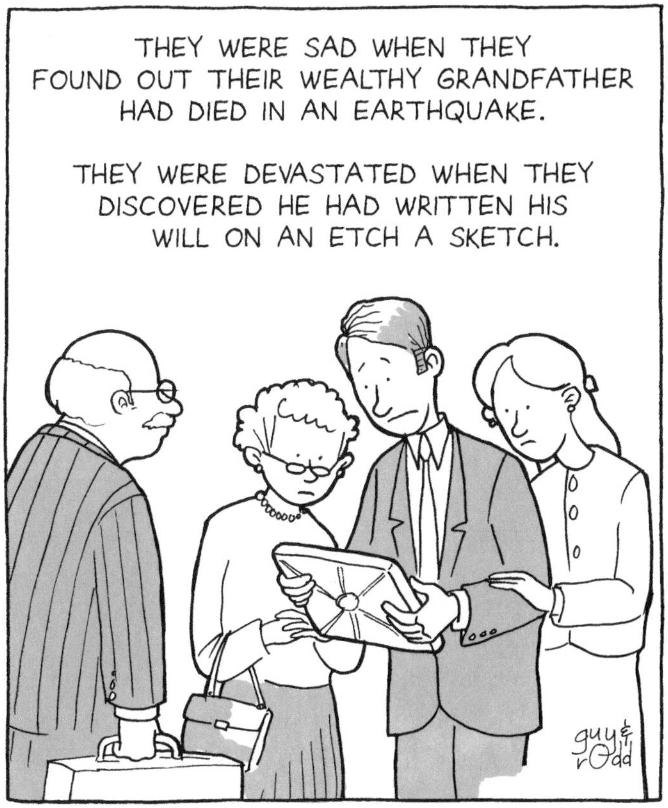
THEY WERE SAD WHEN THEY FOUND OUT THEIR WEALTHY GRANDFATHER HAD DIED IN AN EARTHQUAKE.
THEY WERE DEVASTATED WHEN THEY DISCOVERED HE HAD WRITTEN HIS WILL ON AN ETCH A SKETCH.

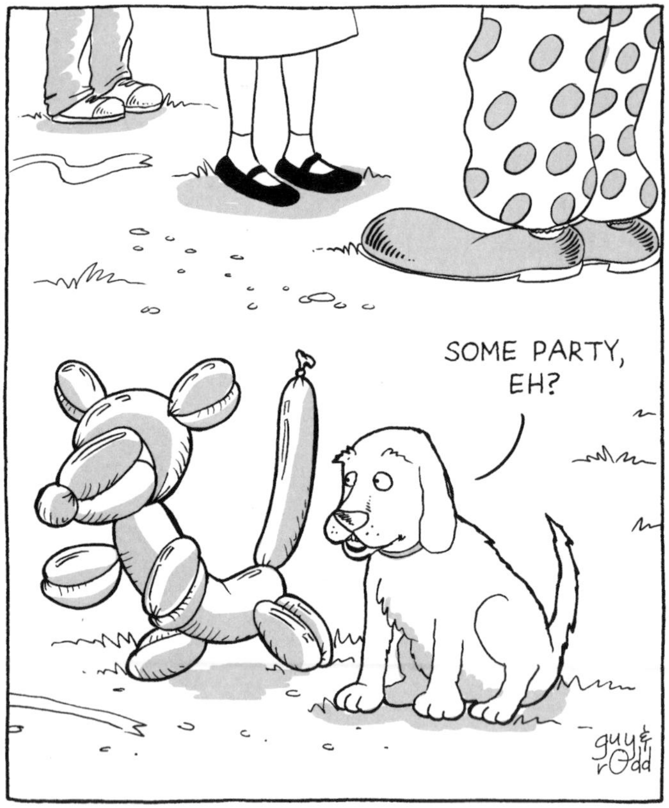
SOME PARTY, EH?

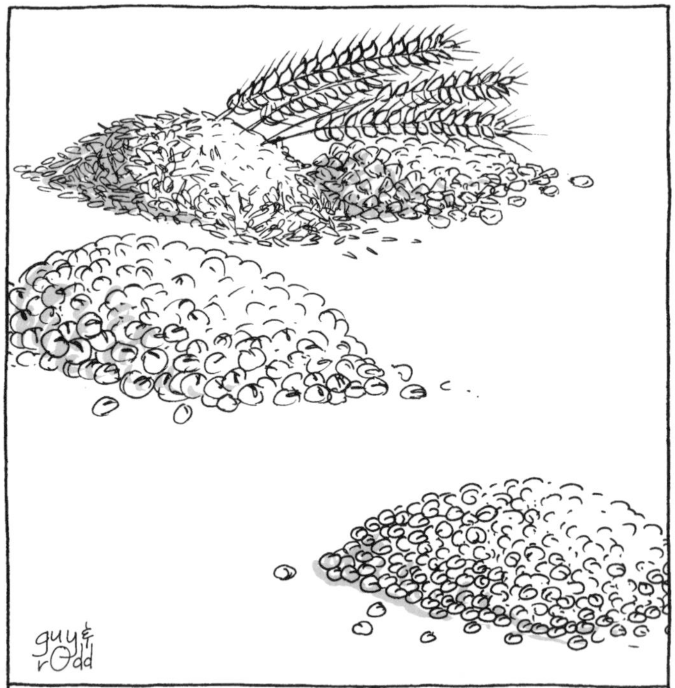

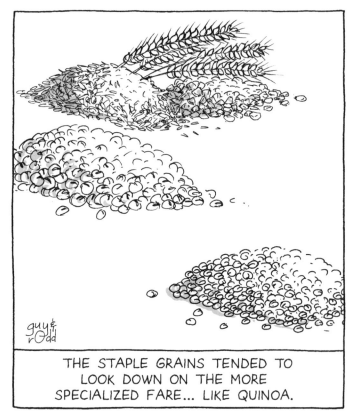

THE STAPLE GRAINS TENDED TO LOOK DOWN ON THE MORE SPECIALIZED FARE... LIKE QUINOA.

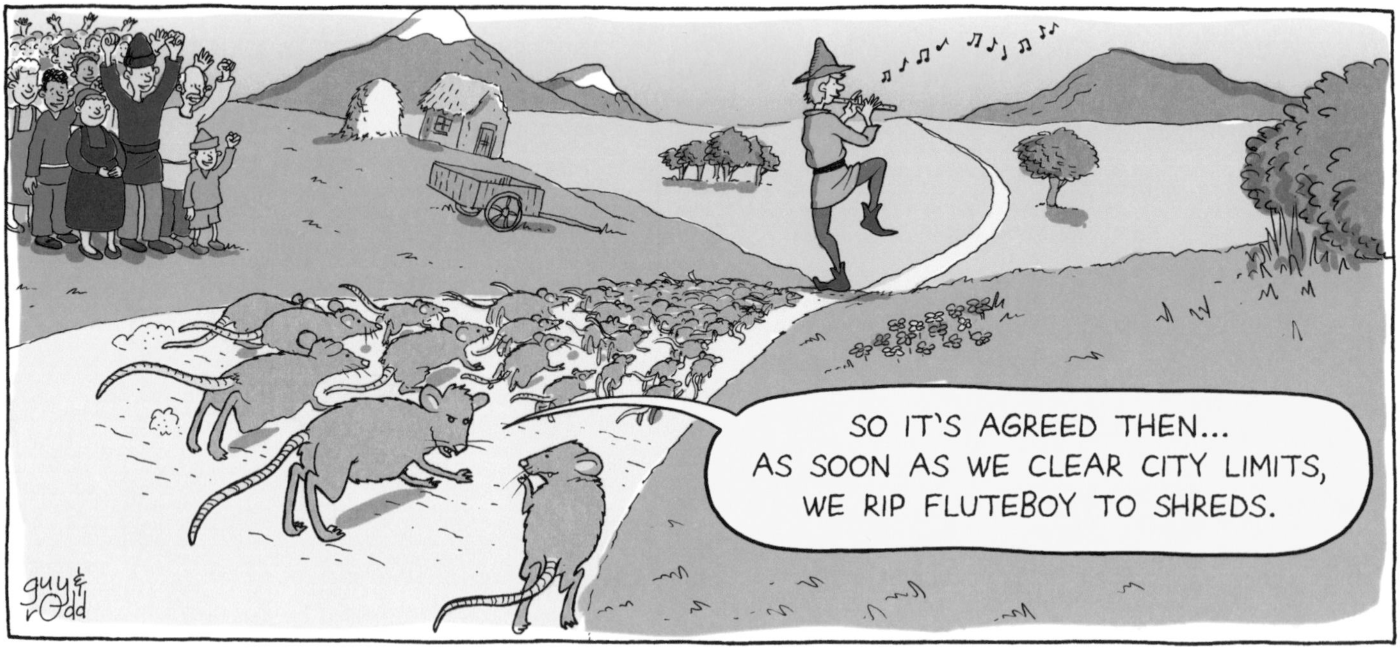
SO IT'S AGREED THEN... AS SOON AS WE CLEAR CITY LIMITS, WE RIP FLUTEBOY TO SHREDS.

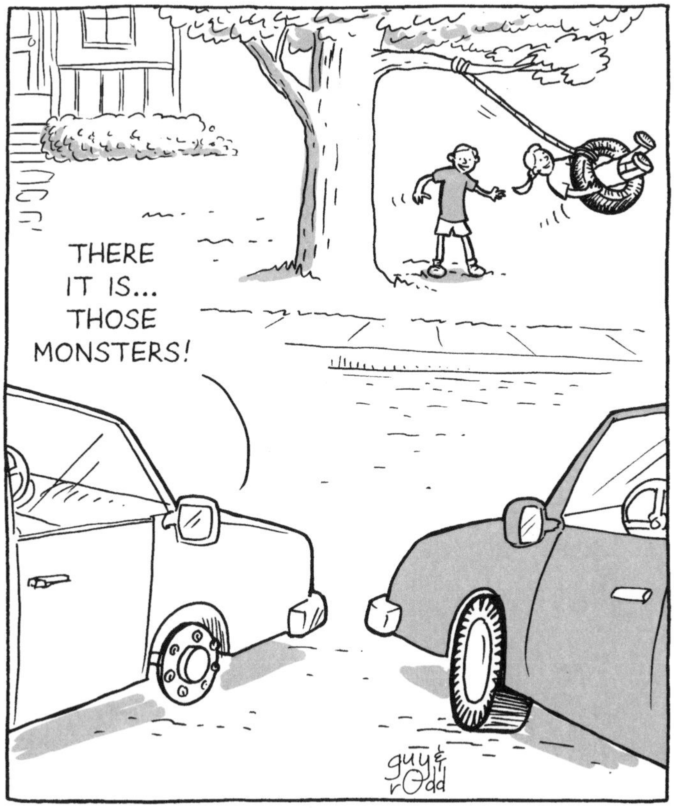
THERE IT IS... THOSE MONSTERS!

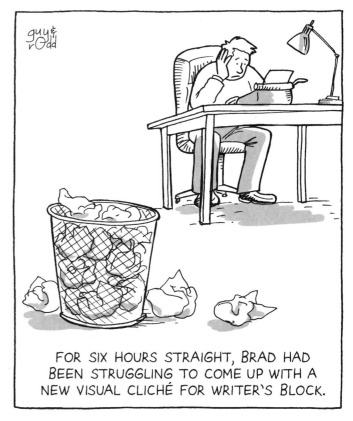

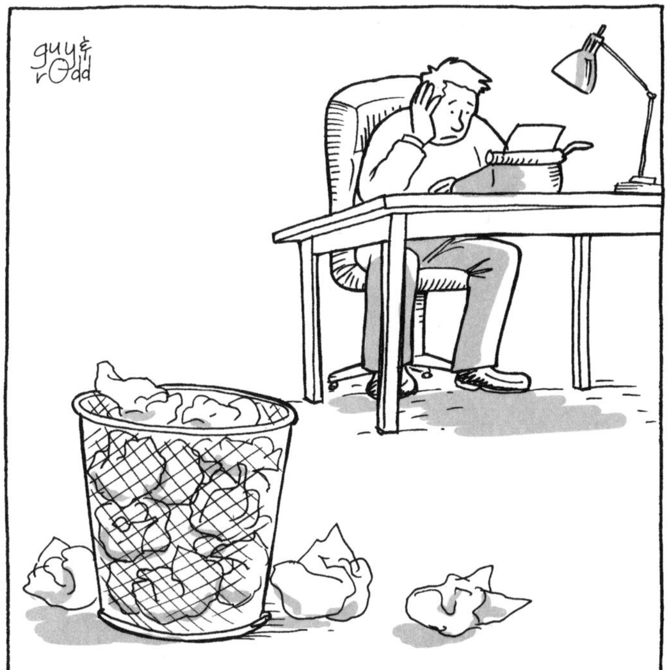
FOR SIX HOURS STRAIGHT, BRAD HAD BEEN STRUGGLING TO COME UP WITH A NEW VISUAL CLICHÉ FOR WRITER'S BLOCK.

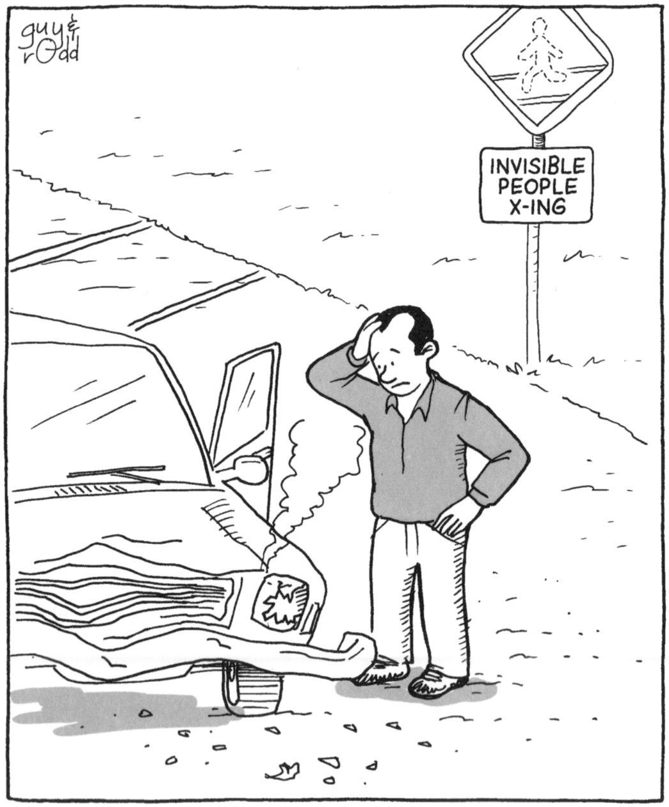
guy & rOdd
INVISIBLE PEOPLE X-ING

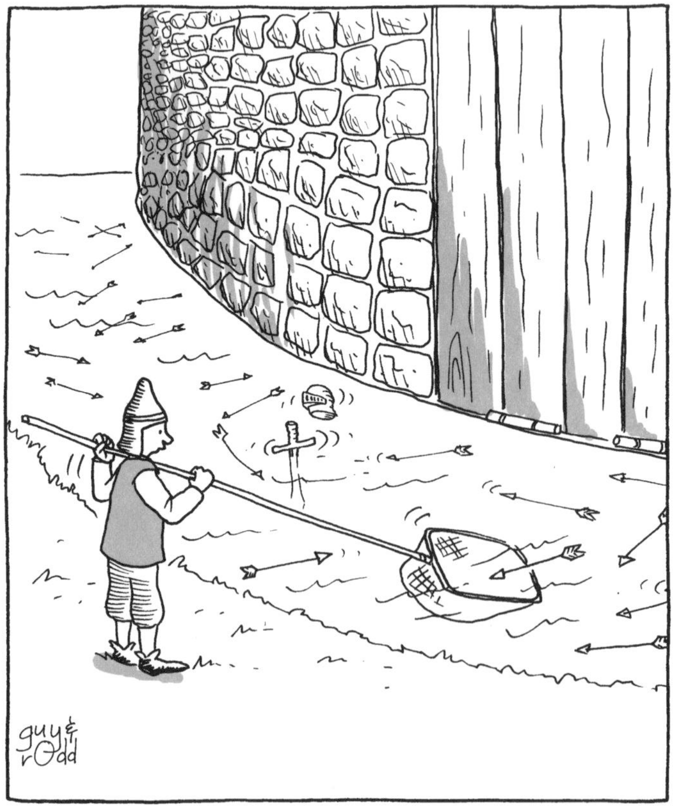
guy & rOdd

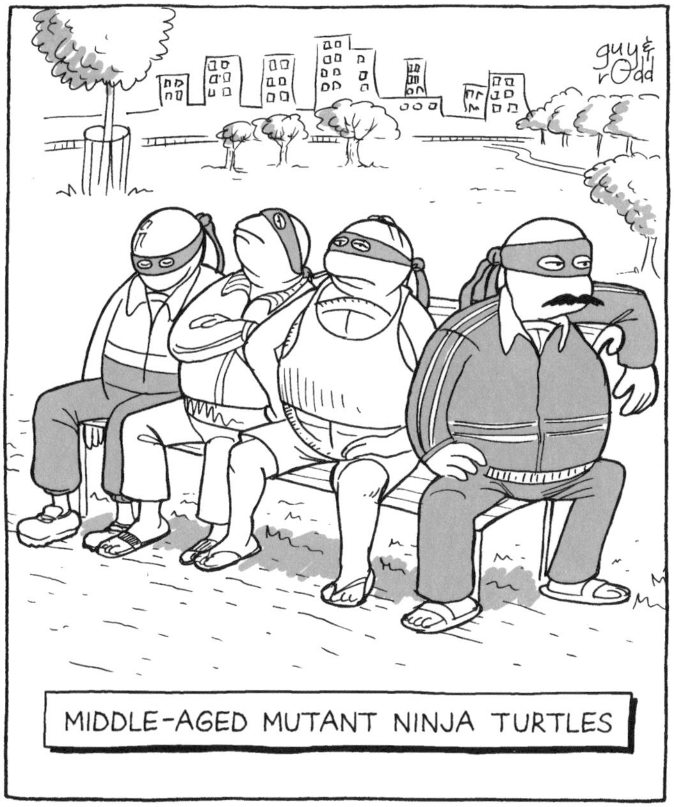
MIDDLE-AGED MUTANT NINJA TURTLES

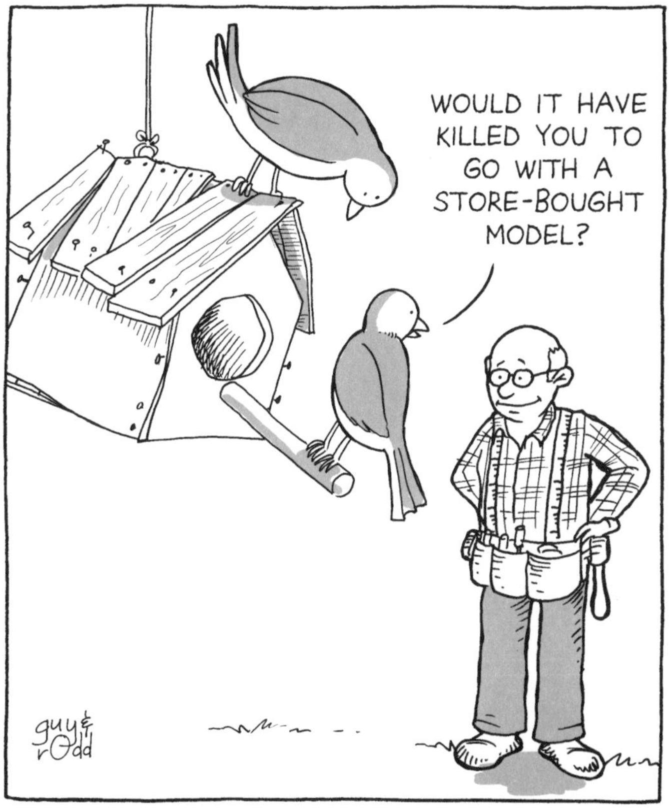
WOULD IT HAVE KILLED YOU TO GO WITH A STORE-BOUGHT MODEL?

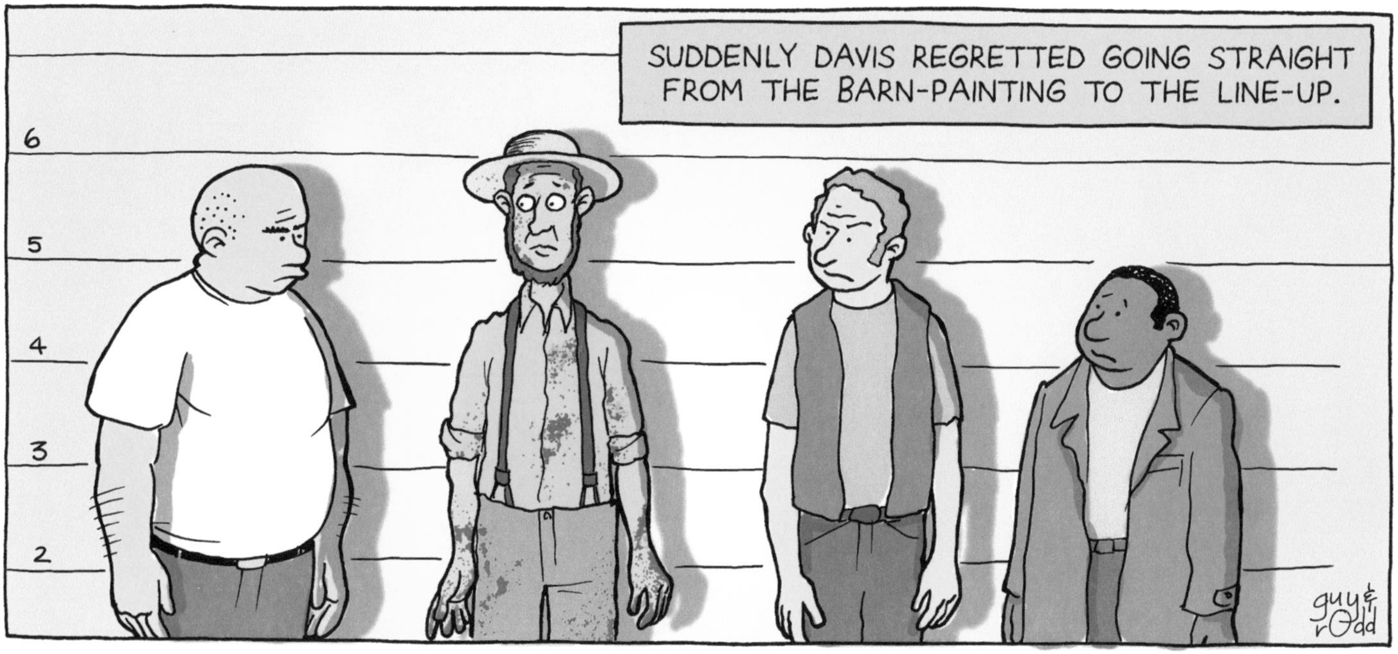
6
5
4
3
2
SUDDENLY DAVIS REGRETTED GOING STRAIGHT FROM THE BARN-PAINTING TO THE LINE-UP.

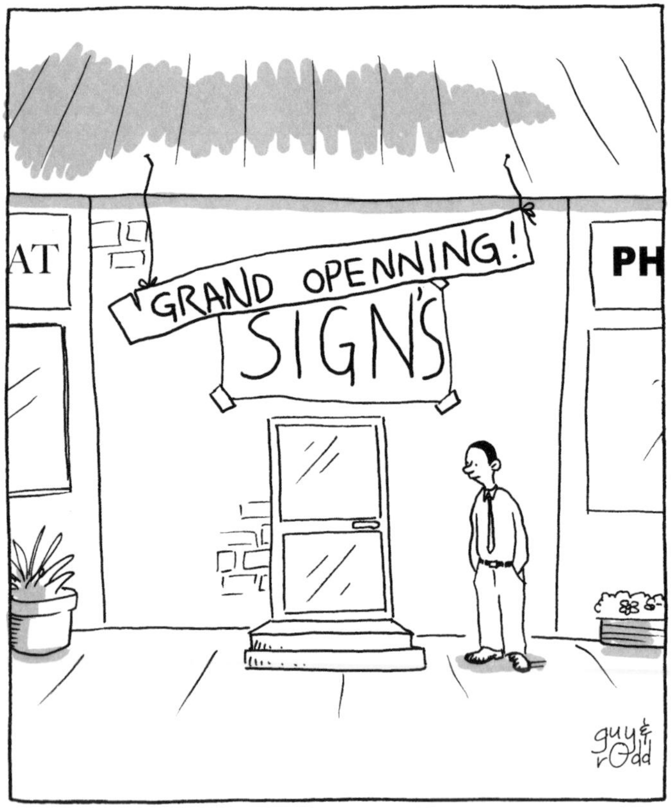
GRAND OPENNING!
SIGN'S
AT
PH
guy & rOdd

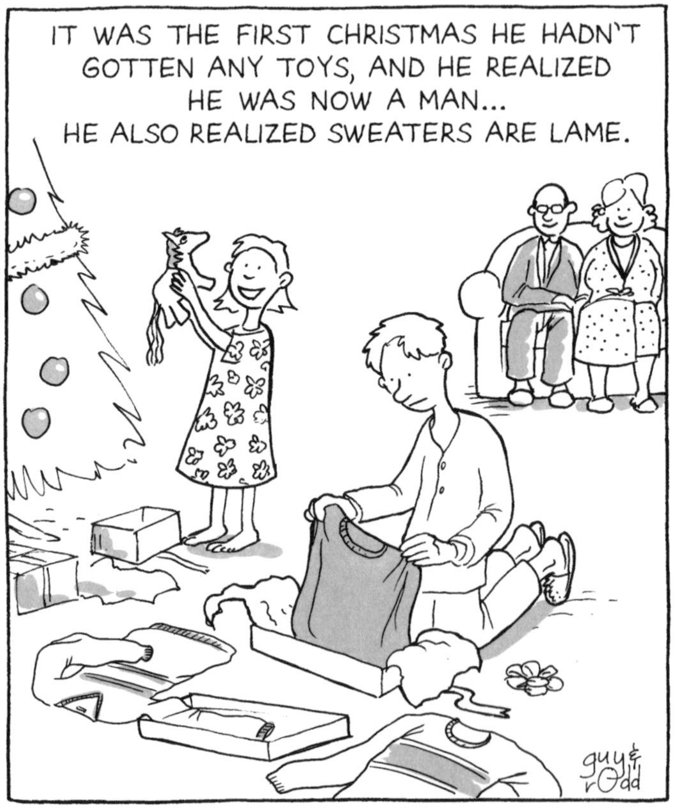
IT WAS THE FIRST CHRISTMAS HE HADN'T GOTTEN ANY TOYS, AND HE REALIZED HE WAS NOW A MAN...
HE ALSO REALIZED SWEATERS ARE LAME.
guy & rOdd

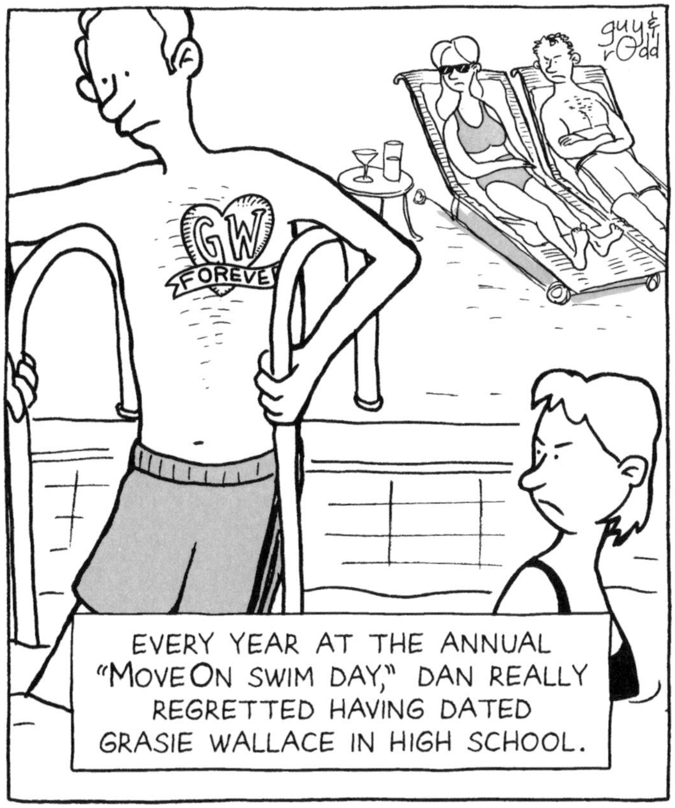
guy & rodd
GW
FOREVER
EVERY YEAR AT THE ANNUAL "MOVEON SWIM DAY," DAN REALLY REGRETTED HAVING DATED GRASIE WALLACE IN HIGH SCHOOL.

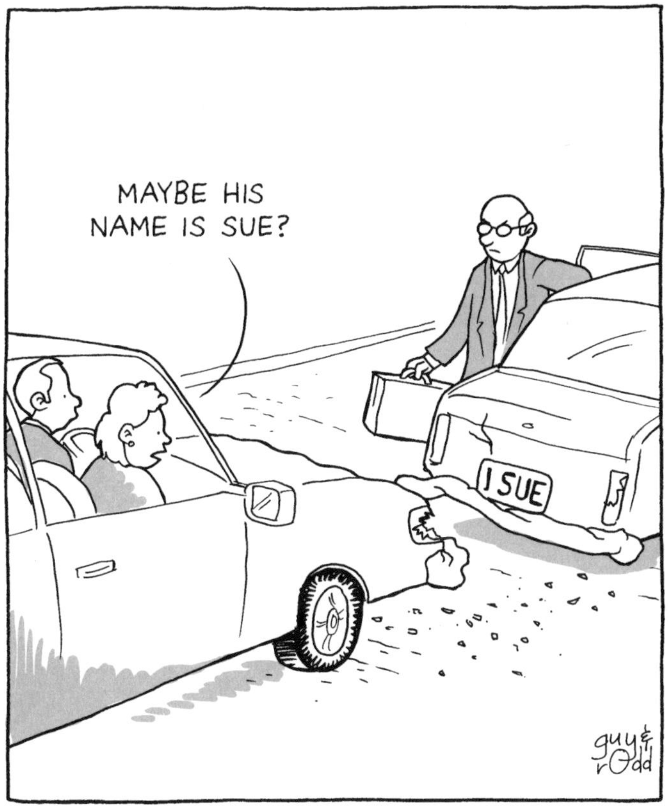
MAYBE HIS NAME IS SUE?
I SUE
guy & rodd

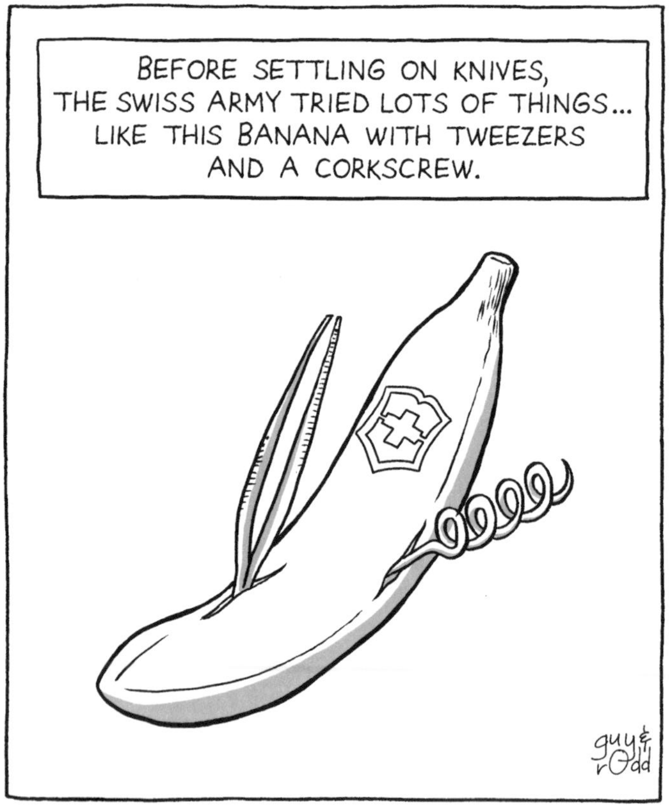
BEFORE SETTLING ON KNIVES, THE SWISS ARMY TRIED LOTS OF THINGS... LIKE THIS BANANA WITH TWEEZERS AND A CORKSCREW.
guy & rOdd

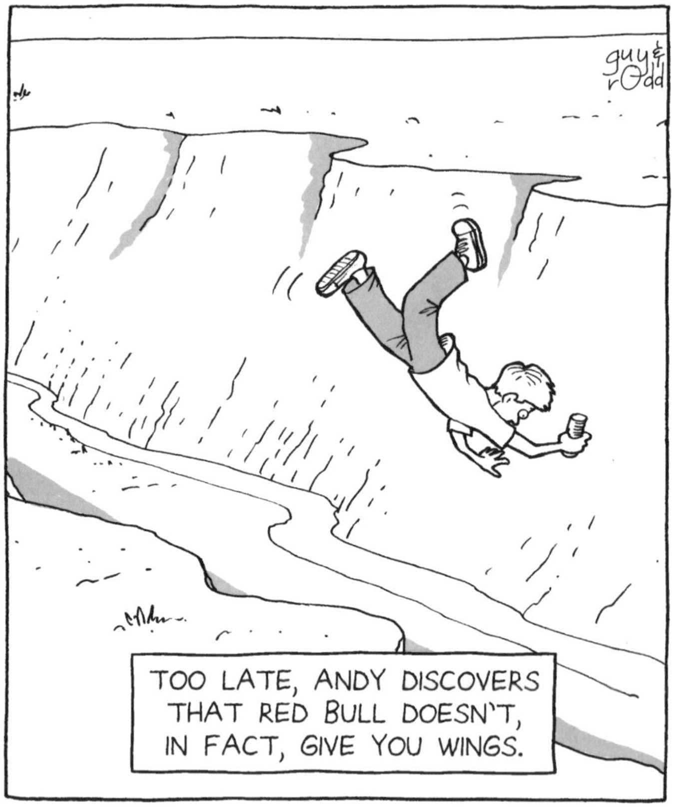
guy & rOdd
TOO LATE, ANDY DISCOVERS THAT RED BULL DOESN'T, IN FACT, GIVE YOU WINGS.

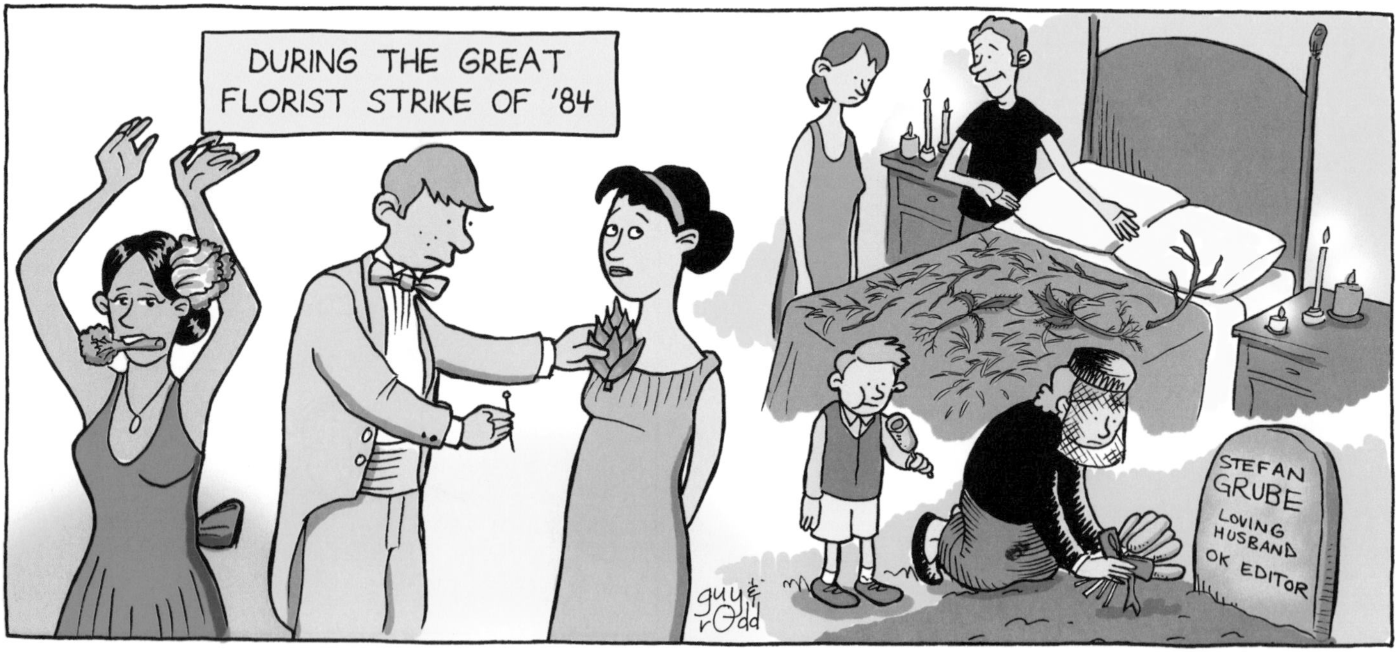
DURING THE GREAT FLORIST STRIKE OF '84
guy & rOdd
STEFAN GRUBE
LOVING HUSBAND
OK EDITOR

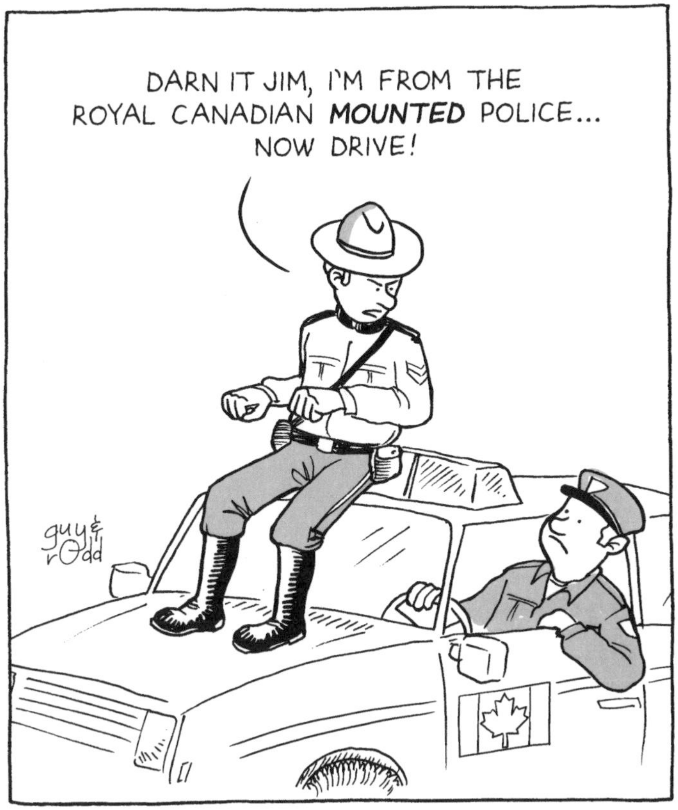
DARN IT JIM, I'M FROM THE ROYAL CANADIAN **MOUNTED** POLICE... NOW DRIVE!
guy & rodd

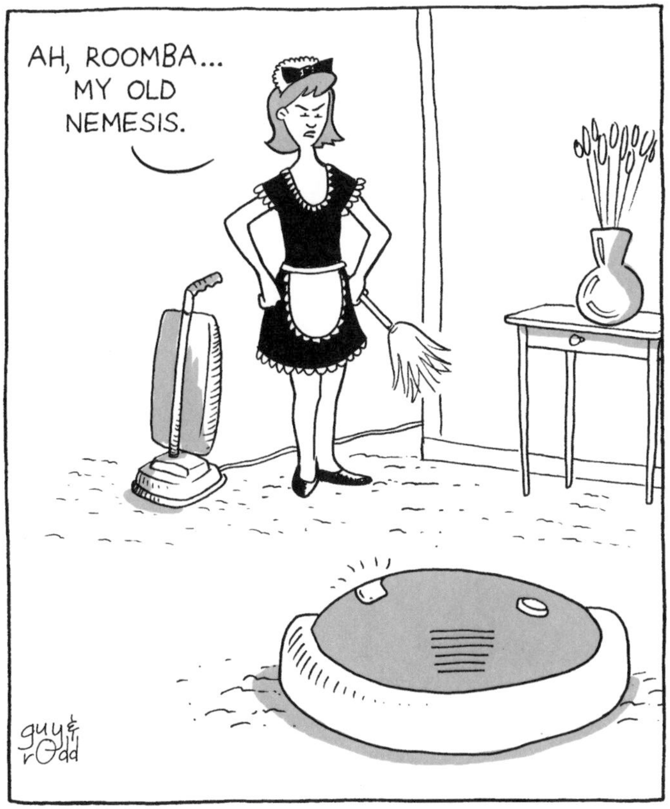
AH, ROOMBA... MY OLD NEMESIS.
guy & rodd

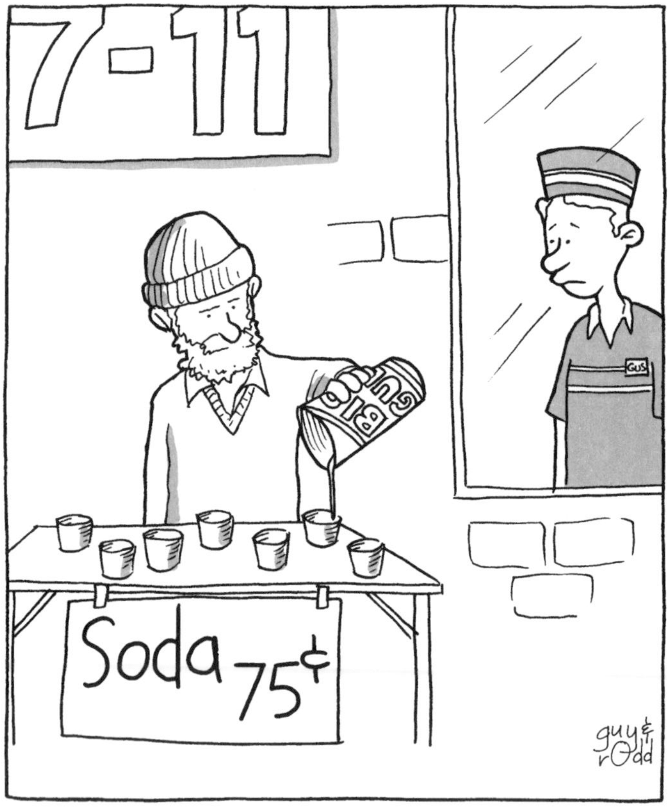
7-11
GUS
Soda 75¢
guy & rodd

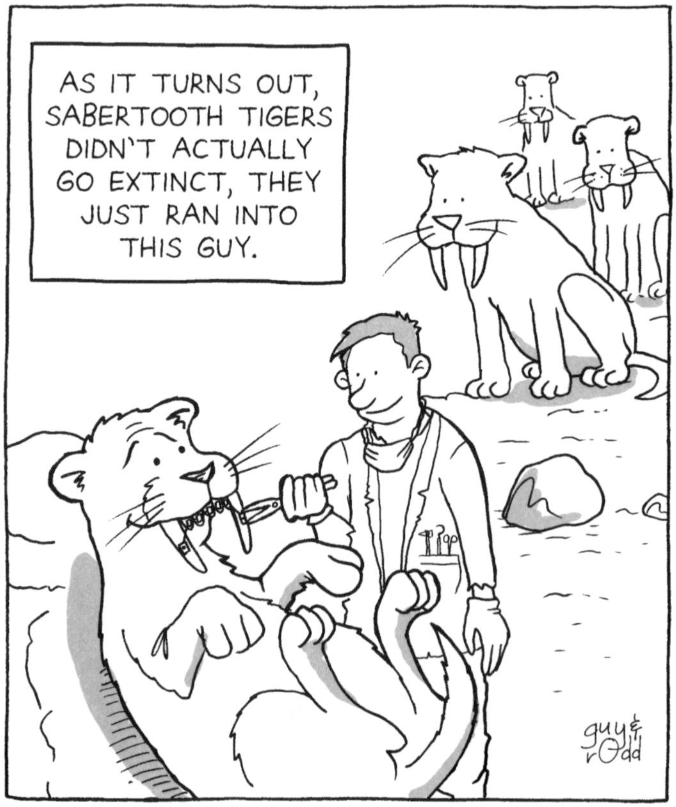
AS IT TURNS OUT, SABERTOOTH TIGERS DIDN'T ACTUALLY GO EXTINCT, THEY JUST RAN INTO THIS GUY.
guy & rodd

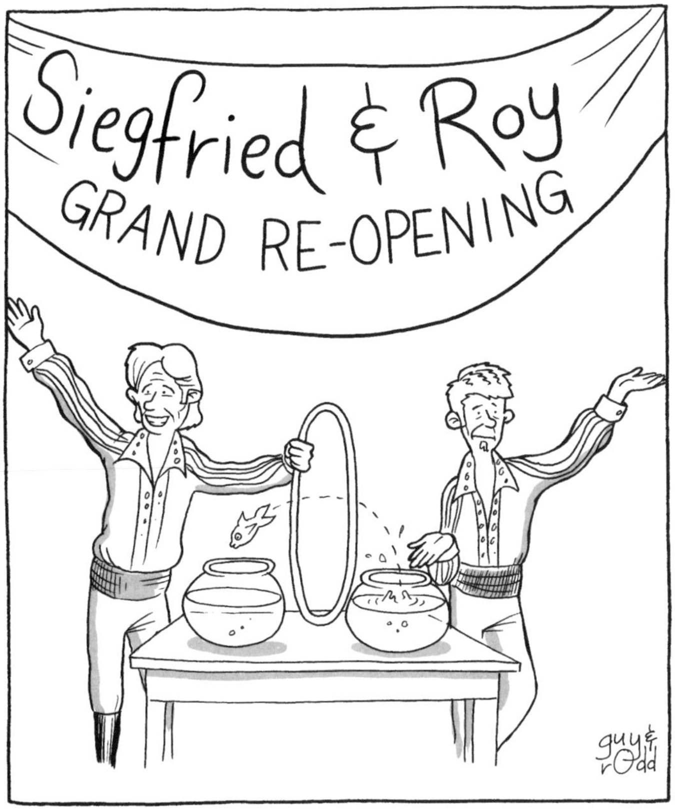
Siegfried & Roy
GRAND RE-OPENING
guy & rOdd

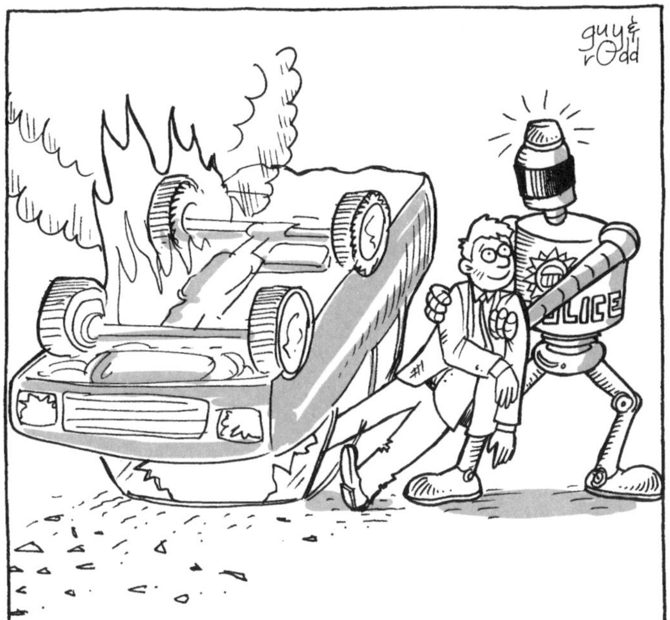
guy & rOdd

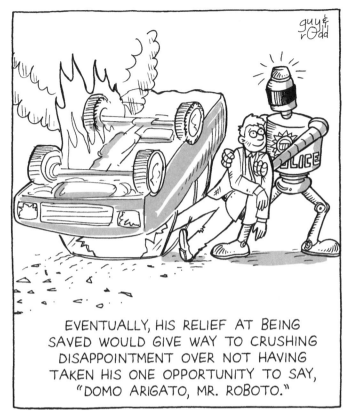

EVENTUALLY, HIS RELIEF AT BEING SAVED WOULD GIVE WAY TO CRUSHING DISAPPOINTMENT OVER NOT HAVING TAKEN HIS ONE OPPORTUNITY TO SAY, "DOMO ARIGATO, MR. ROBOTO."

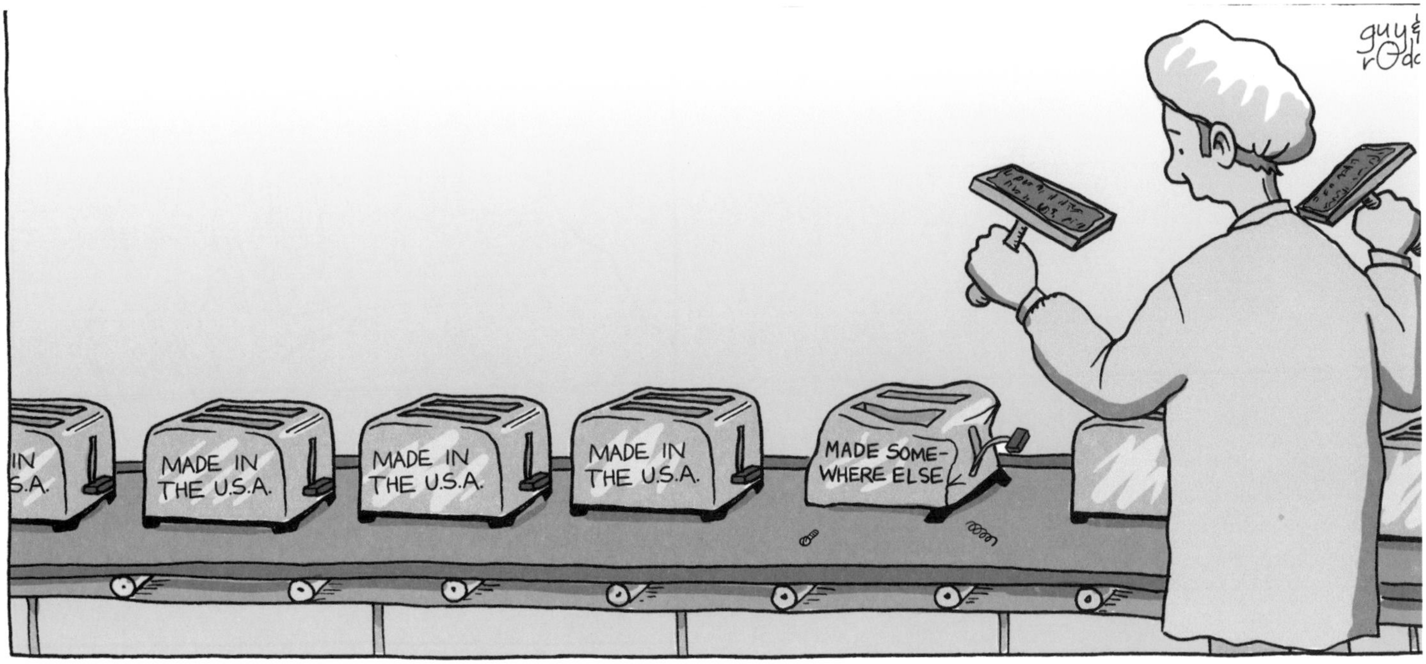
guy & rOdd
MADE IN THE U.S.A.
MADE IN THE U.S.A.
MADE IN THE U.S.A.
MADE SOME-WHERE ELSE

WHY ENTOMOLOGISTS HAVE, BY FAR, THE HIGHEST DIVORCE RATE OF ANY PROFESSION.
YOU KNOW, TERMITE QUEENS HAVE OVER 100 MILLION OFFSPRING. I MEAN, I'M JUST SAYING...
guy & rOdd

NO, YOU'RE LOOKING FOR THE HOTEL EVER-REST... BOY, YOU REALLY DID GET LOST.
guy & rOdd

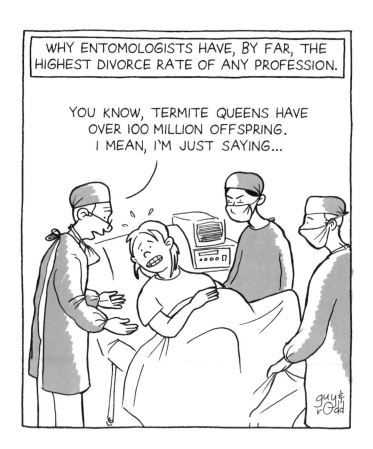

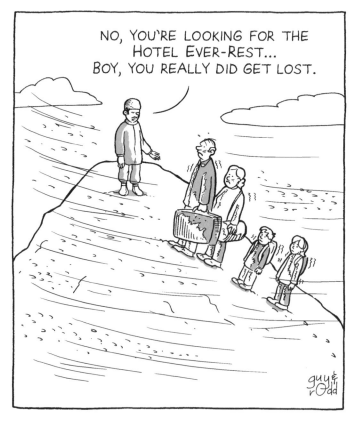

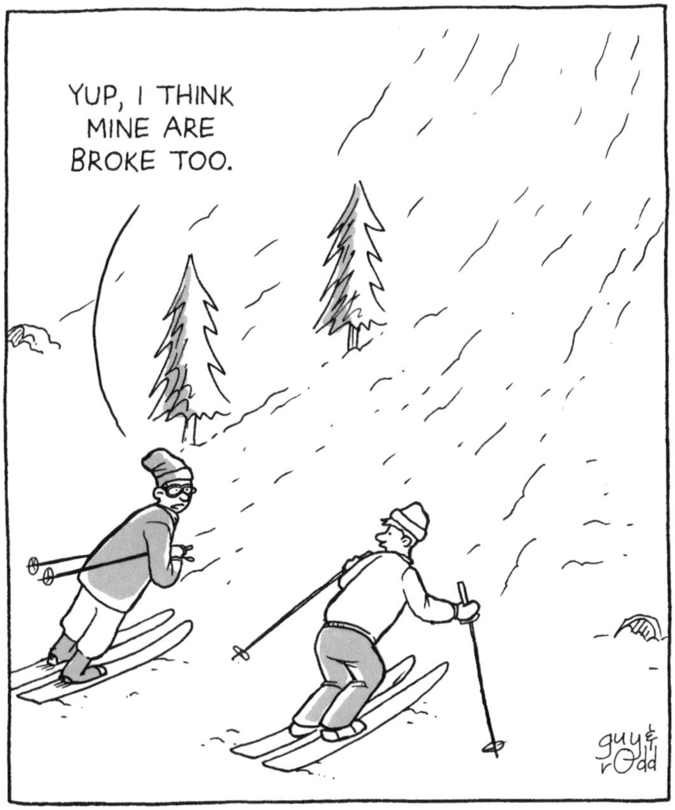
YUP, I THINK MINE ARE BROKE TOO.

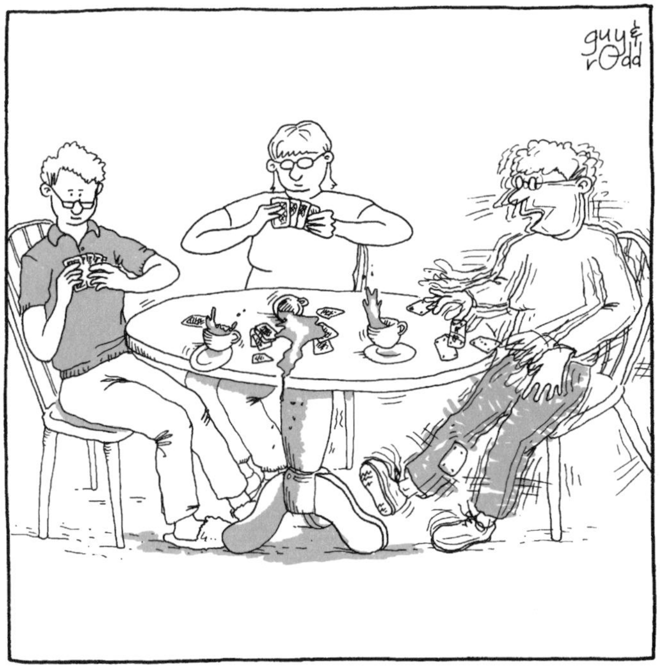

FOR SEVERAL MINUTES, NORMA'S BODY IS POSSESSED BY THE SPIRIT OF HER DEAD WASHING MACHINE.

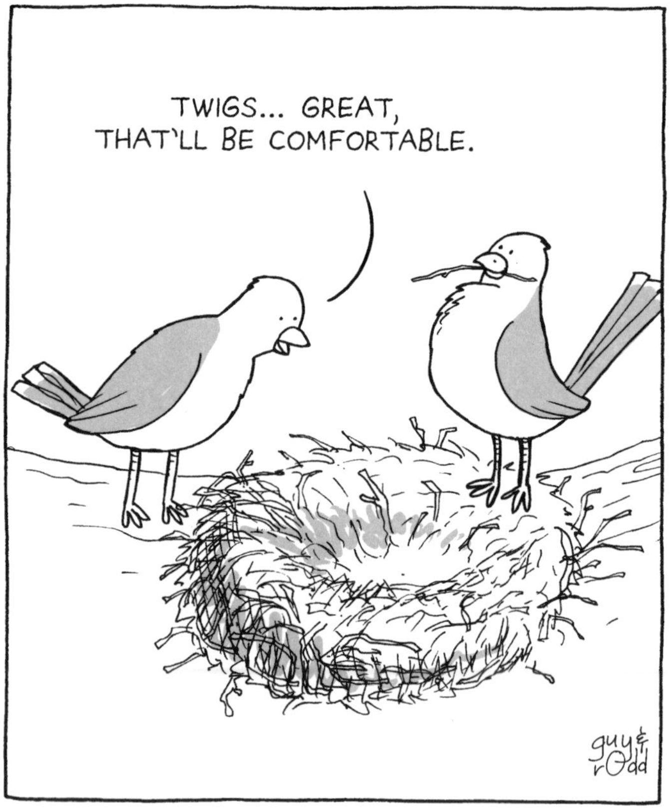
TWIGS... GREAT,
THAT'LL BE COMFORTABLE.

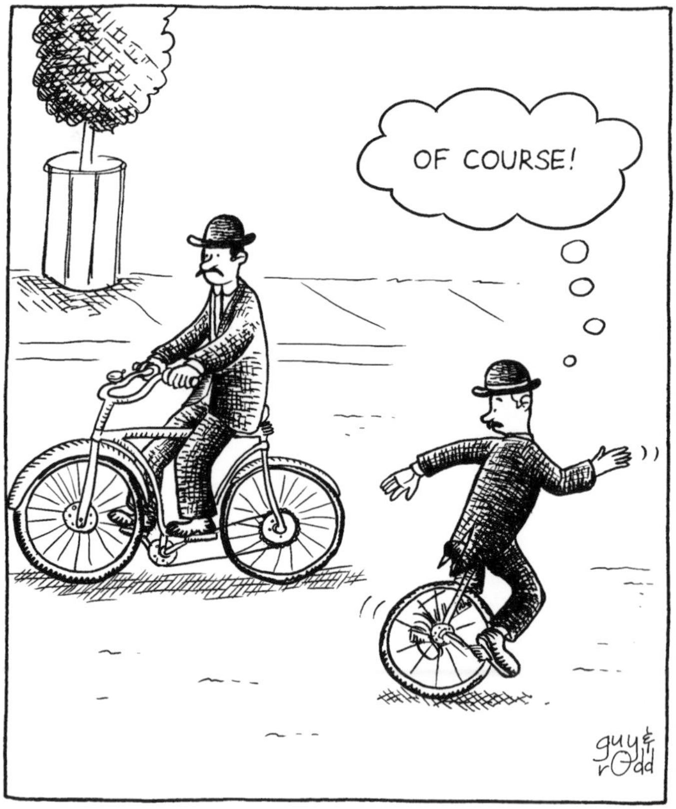
OF COURSE!

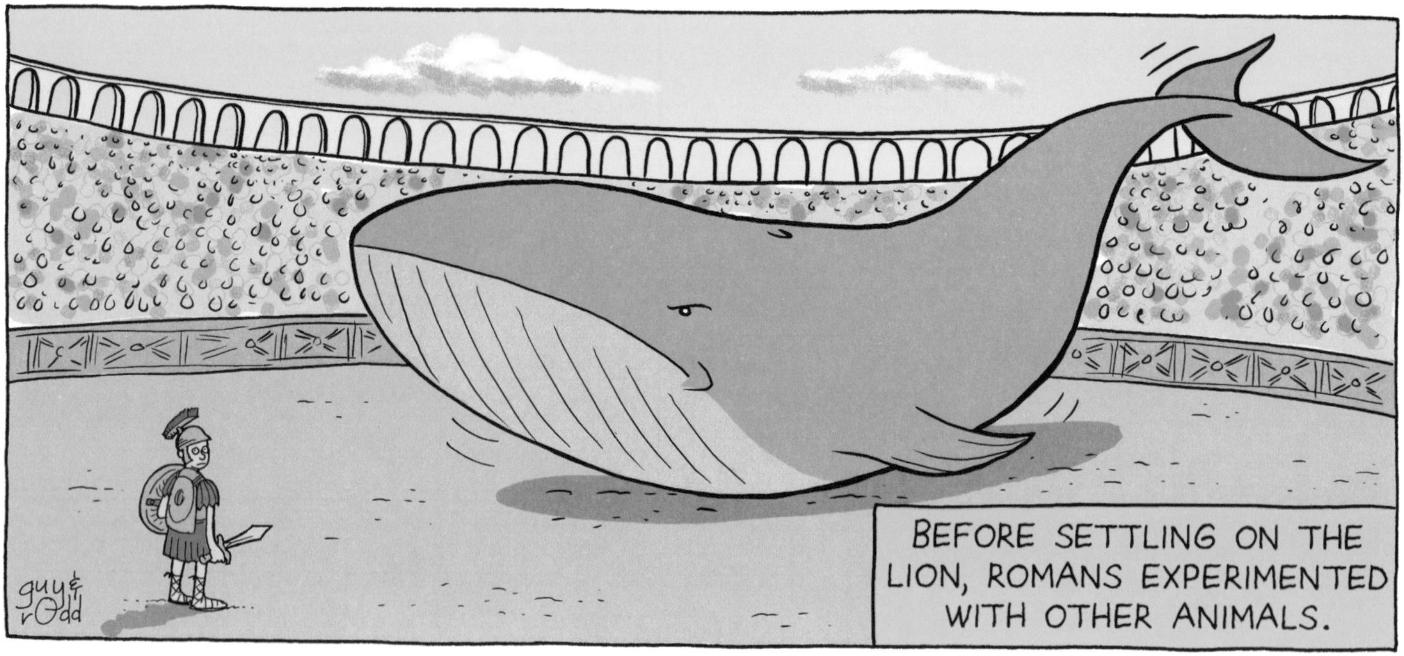
BEFORE SETTLING ON THE LION, ROMANS EXPERIMENTED WITH OTHER ANIMALS.

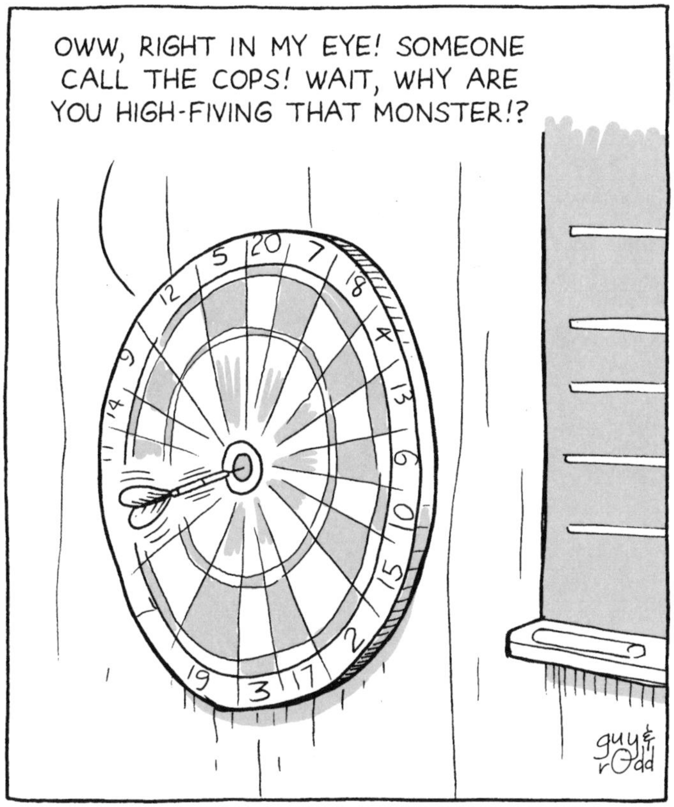
OWW, RIGHT IN MY EYE! SOMEONE CALL THE COPS! WAIT, WHY ARE YOU HIGH-FIVING THAT MONSTER!?

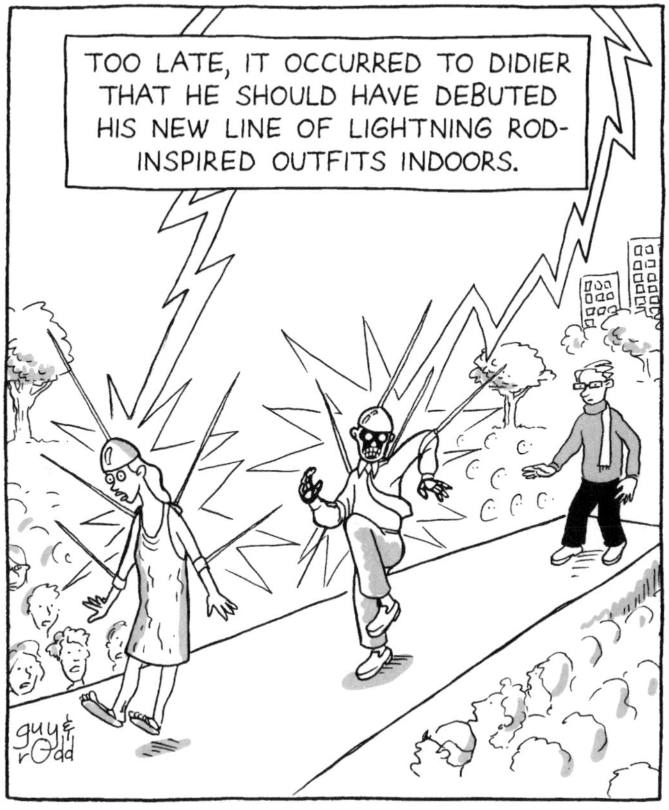
TOO LATE, IT OCCURRED TO DIDIER THAT HE SHOULD HAVE DEBUTED HIS NEW LINE OF LIGHTNING ROD-INSPIRED OUTFITS INDOORS.

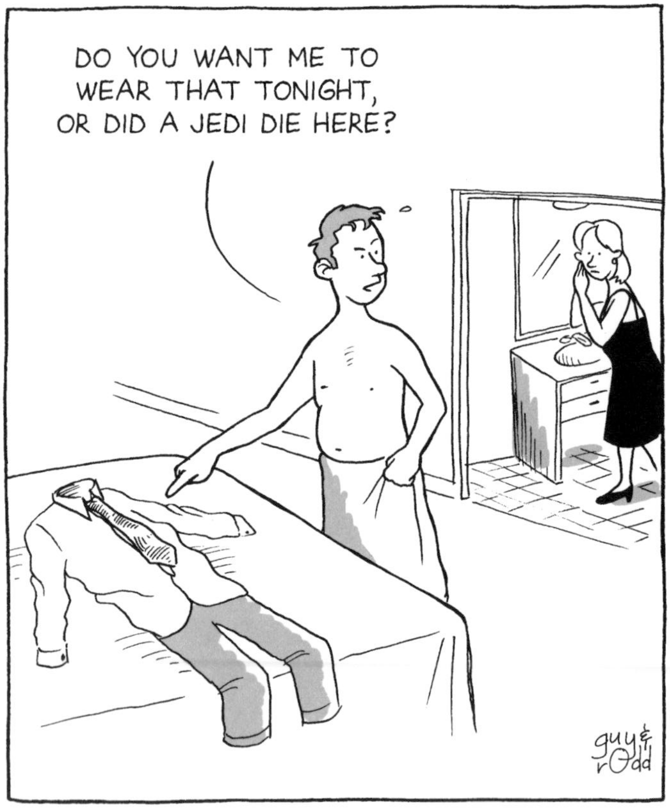
DO YOU WANT ME TO WEAR THAT TONIGHT, OR DID A JEDI DIE HERE?

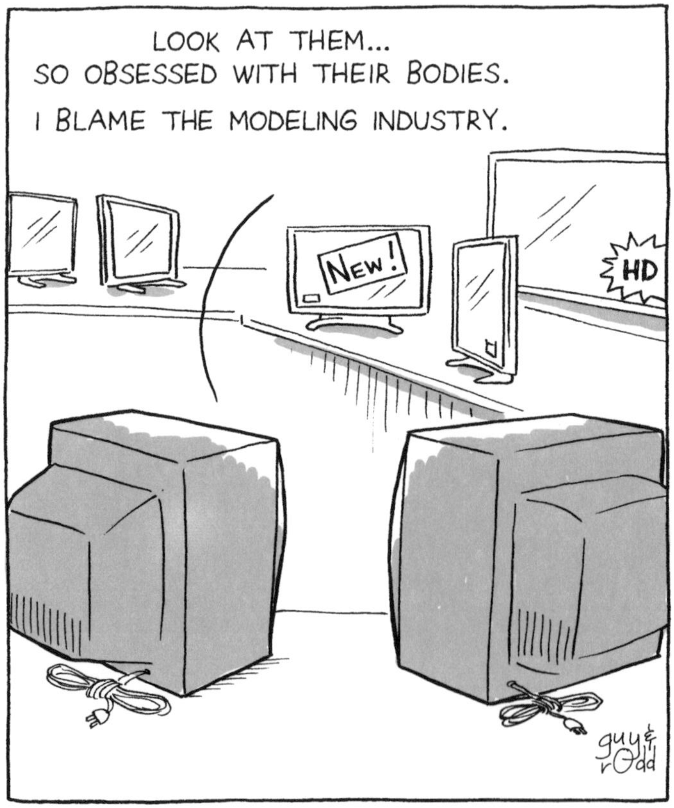
LOOK AT THEM... SO OBSESSED WITH THEIR BODIES. I BLAME THE MODELING INDUSTRY.
NEW!
HD

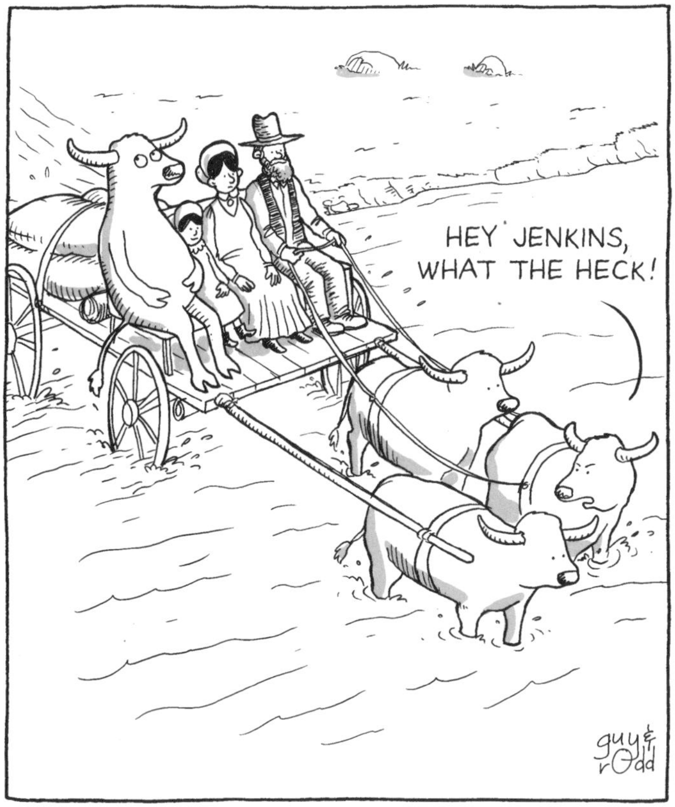
HEY JENKINS,
WHAT THE HECK!
guy & rOdd

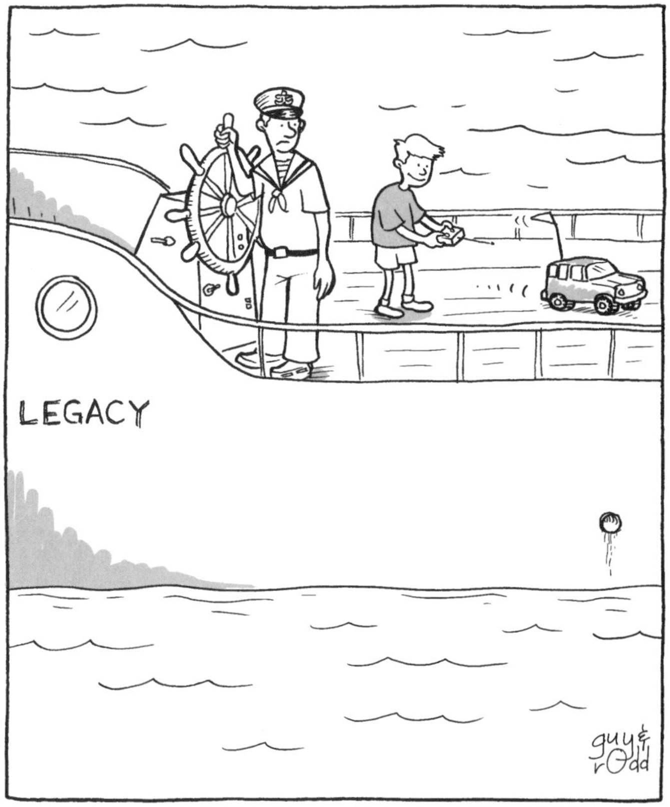
LEGACY
guy & rOdd

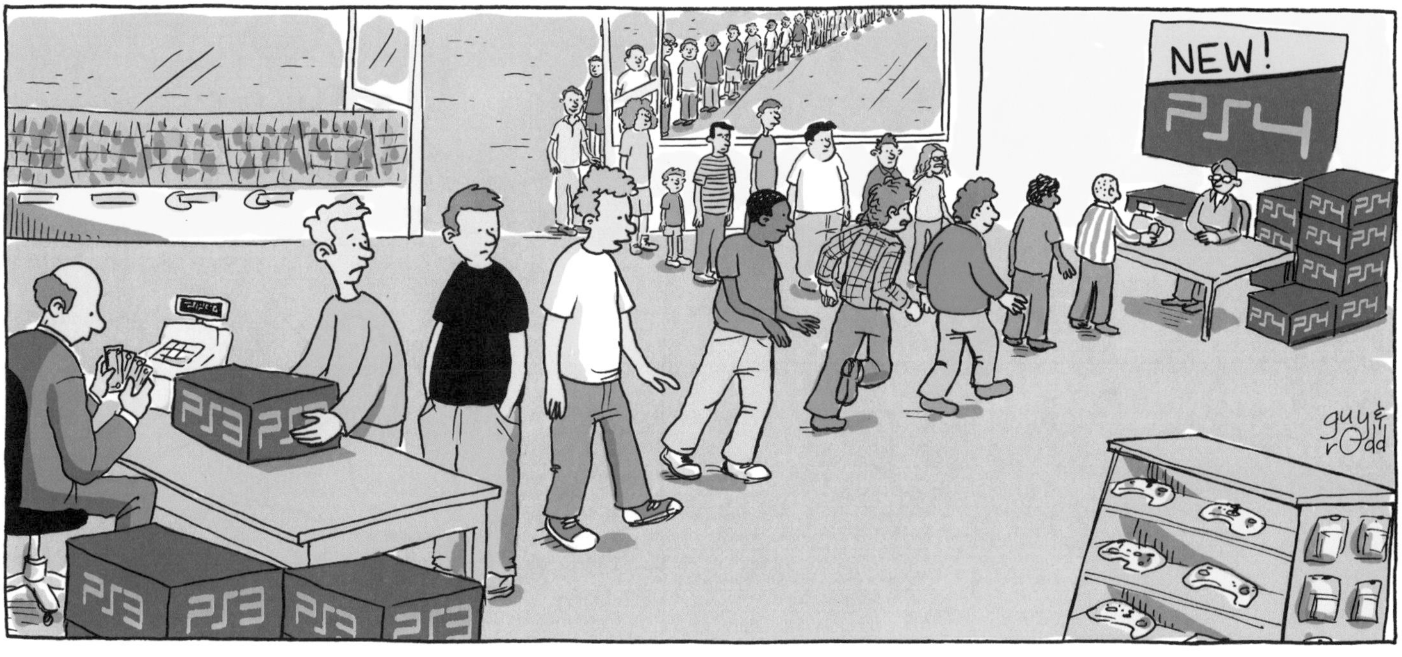
NEW!
PS4
PS3
guy & rOdd

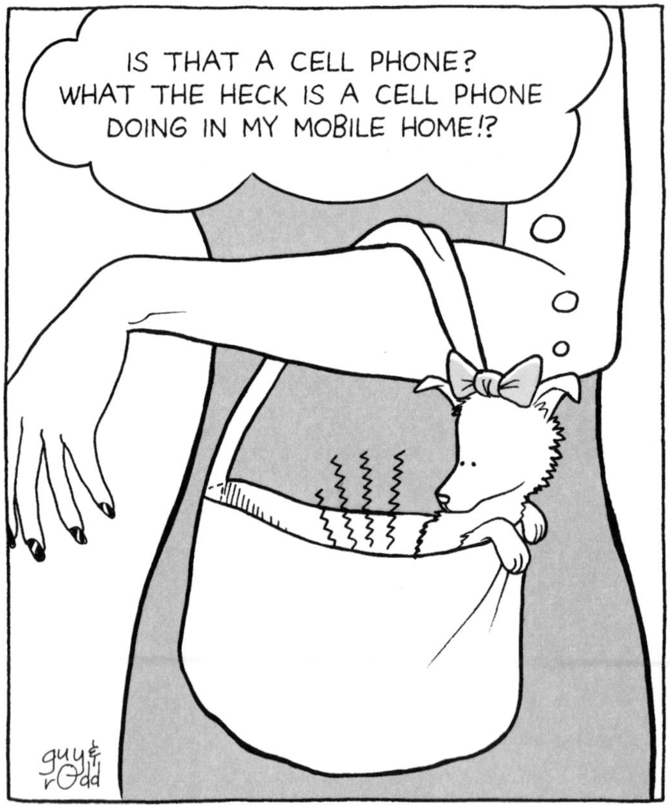
IS THAT A CELL PHONE?
WHAT THE HECK IS A CELL PHONE
DOING IN MY MOBILE HOME!?

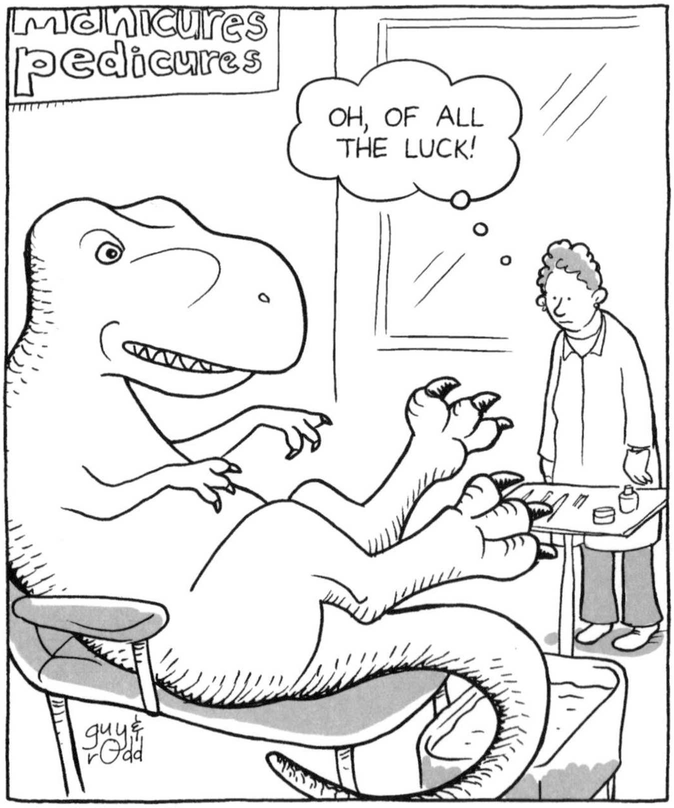
manicures
pedicures
OH, OF ALL
THE LUCK!

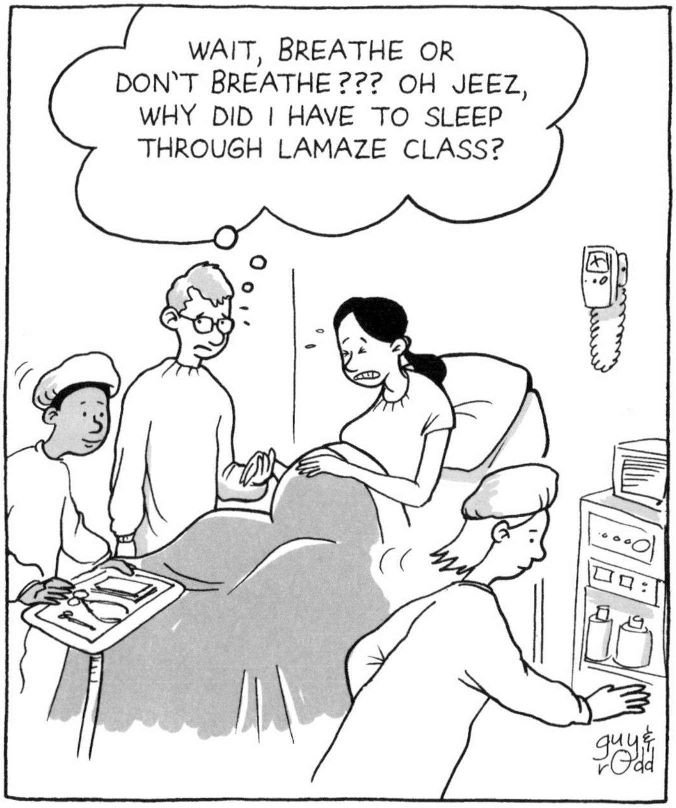
WAIT, BREATHE OR DON'T BREATHE??? OH JEEZ, WHY DID I HAVE TO SLEEP THROUGH LAMAZE CLASS?

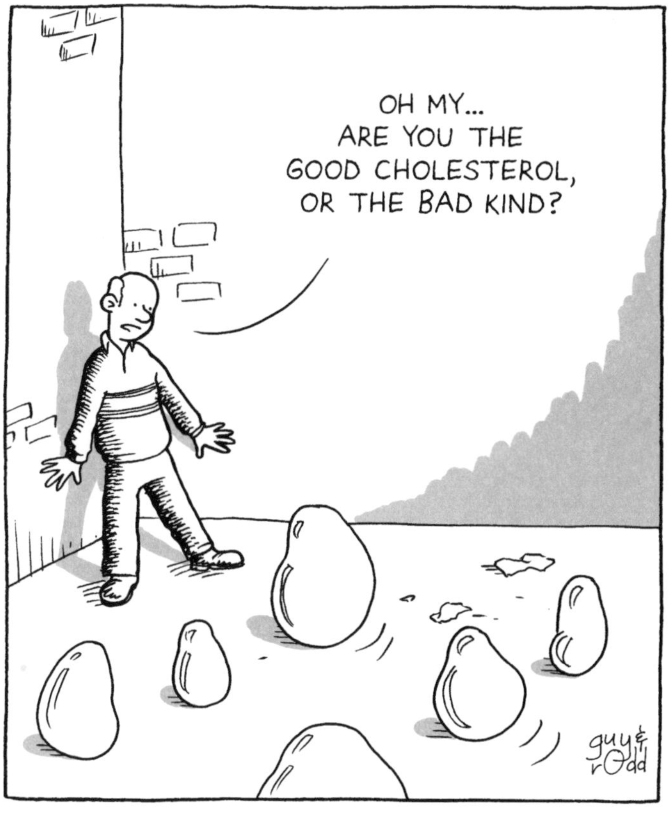
OH MY... ARE YOU THE GOOD CHOLESTEROL, OR THE BAD KIND?

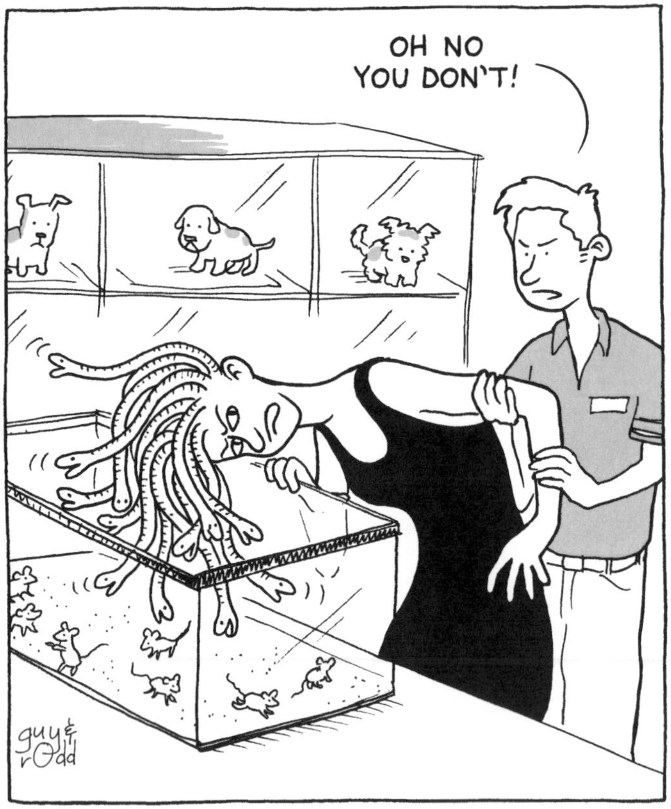
OH NO YOU DON'T!

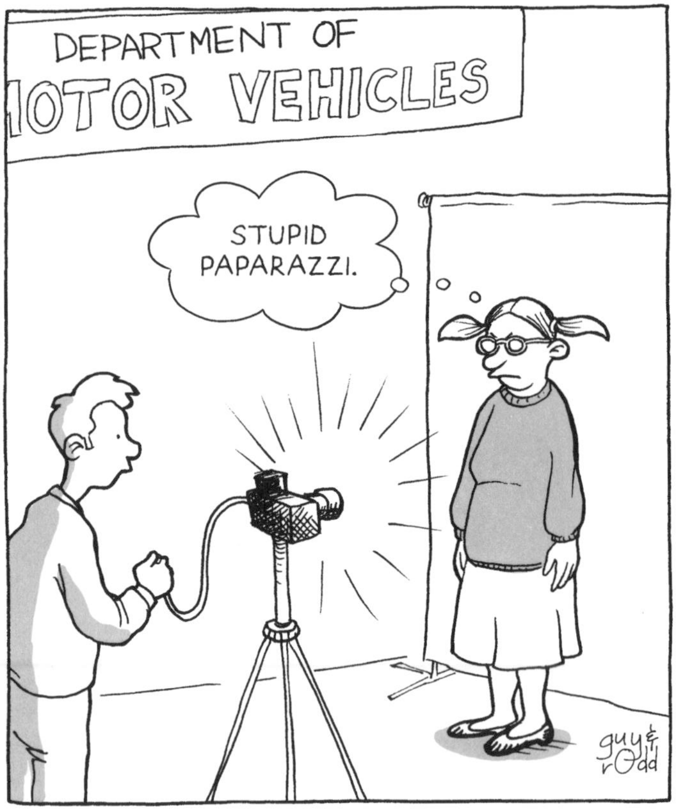
DEPARTMENT OF
MOTOR VEHICLES
STUPID PAPARAZZI.

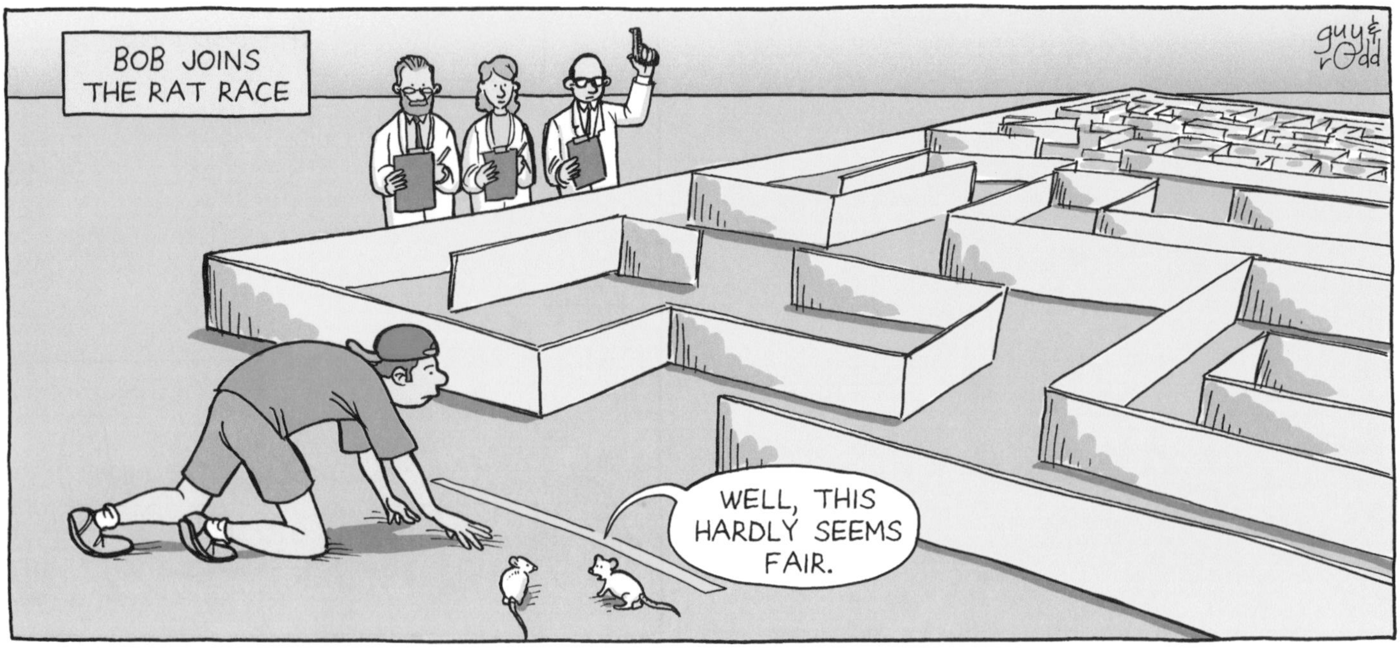
BOB JOINS THE RAT RACE
WELL, THIS HARDLY SEEMS FAIR.

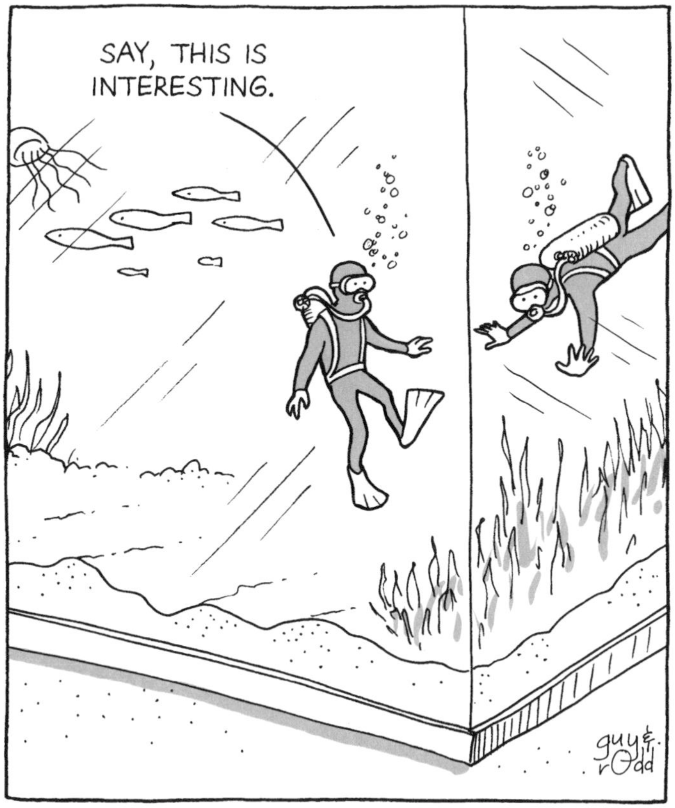
SAY, THIS IS
INTERESTING.

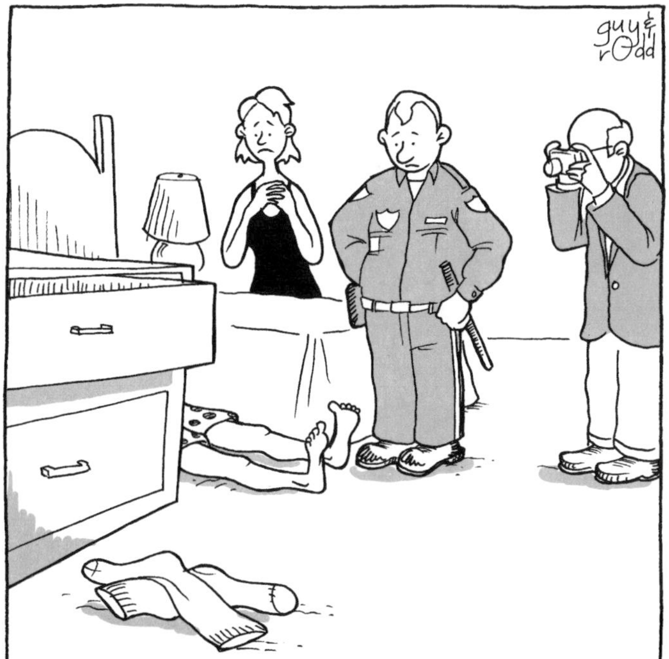

THE PAIR OF SOCKS WAITED CONFIDENTLY IN THE CORNER, SECURE IN THE KNOWLEDGE THAT NO MATTER WHAT HAPPENS, NO ONE EVER SUSPECTS THE SOCKS.

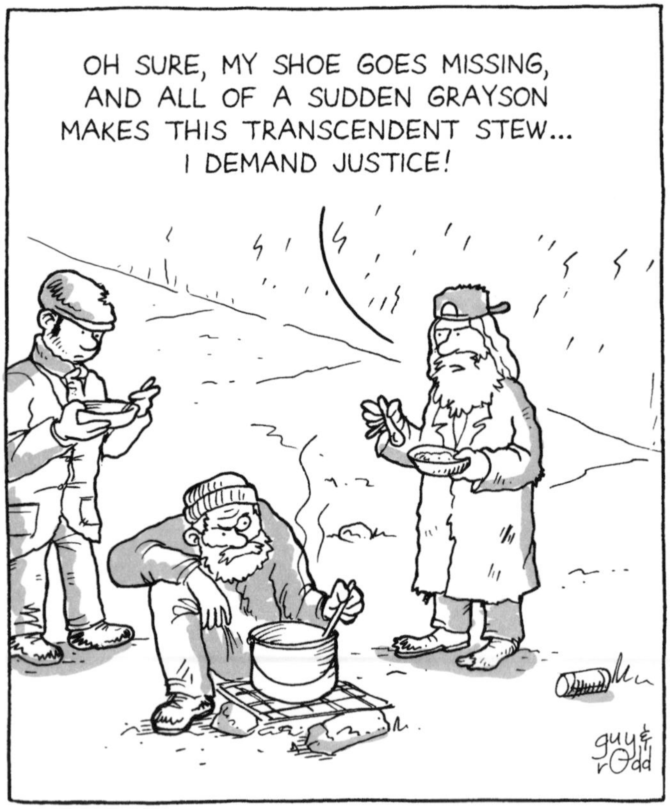
OH SURE, MY SHOE GOES MISSING, AND ALL OF A SUDDEN GRAYSON MAKES THIS TRANSCENDENT STEW... I DEMAND JUSTICE!

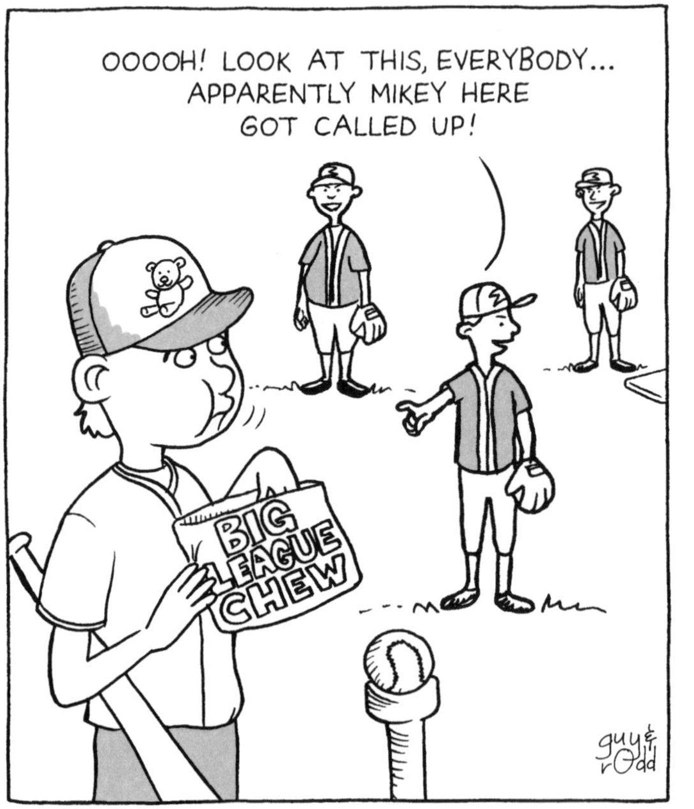
OOOOH! LOOK AT THIS, EVERYBODY... APPARENTLY MIKEY HERE GOT CALLED UP!
BIG LEAGUE CHEW

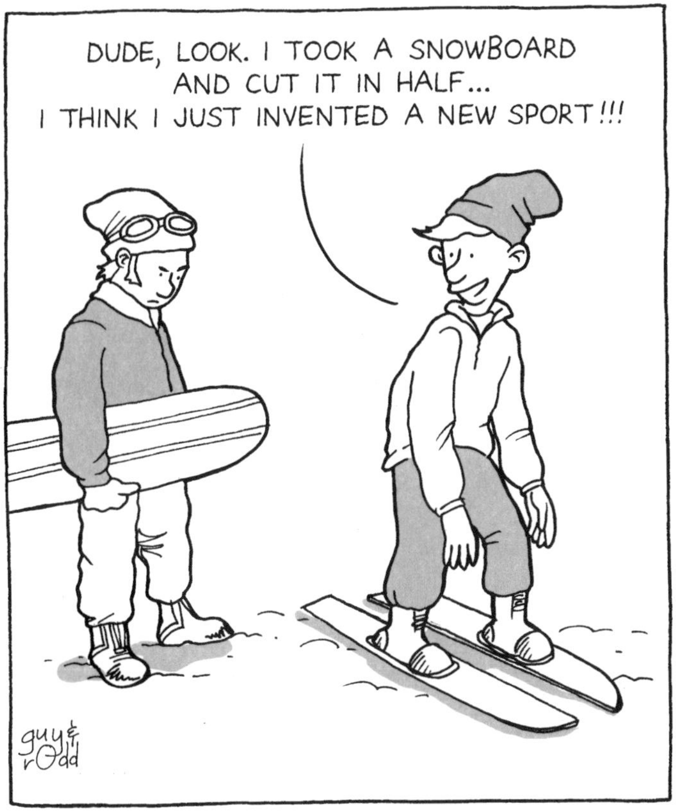
DUDE, LOOK. I TOOK A SNOWBOARD AND CUT IT IN HALF... I THINK I JUST INVENTED A NEW SPORT!!!
guy & rOdd

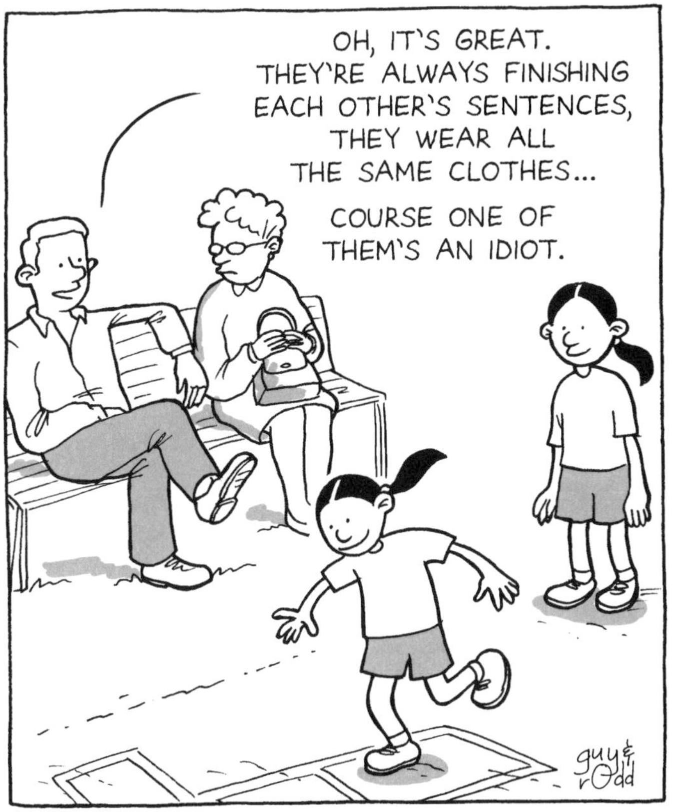
OH, IT'S GREAT. THEY'RE ALWAYS FINISHING EACH OTHER'S SENTENCES, THEY WEAR ALL THE SAME CLOTHES...
COURSE ONE OF THEM'S AN IDIOT.
guy & rOdd

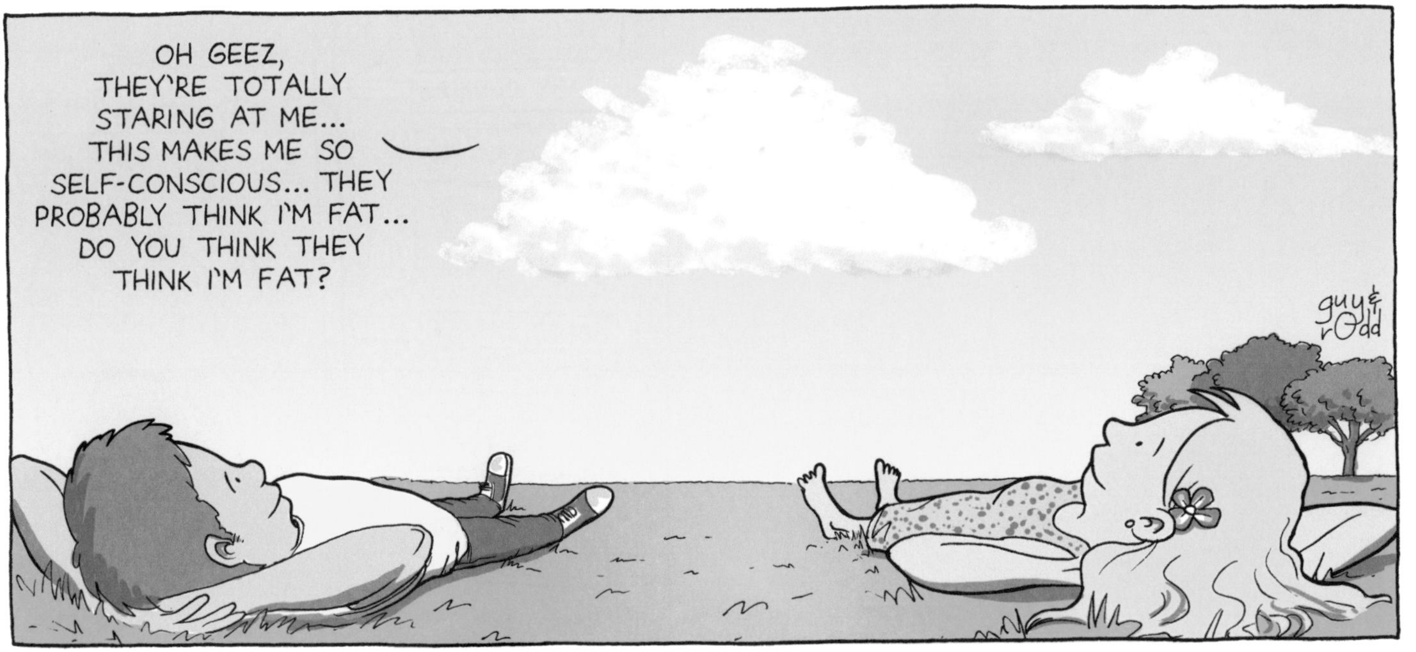
OH GEEZ, THEY'RE TOTALLY STARING AT ME... THIS MAKES ME SO SELF-CONSCIOUS... THEY PROBABLY THINK I'M FAT... DO YOU THINK THEY THINK I'M FAT?
guy & rOdd

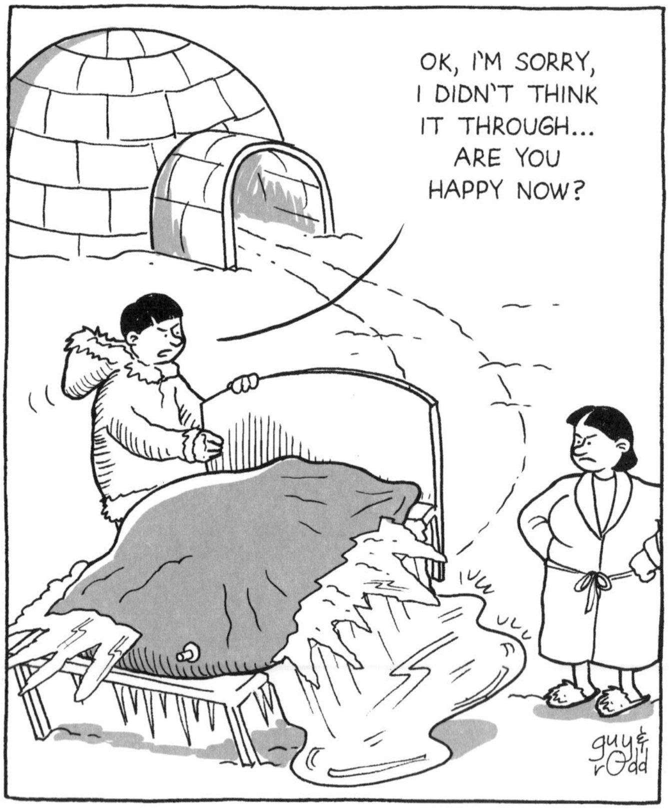
OK, I'M SORRY, I DIDN'T THINK IT THROUGH... ARE YOU HAPPY NOW?
guy & rOdd

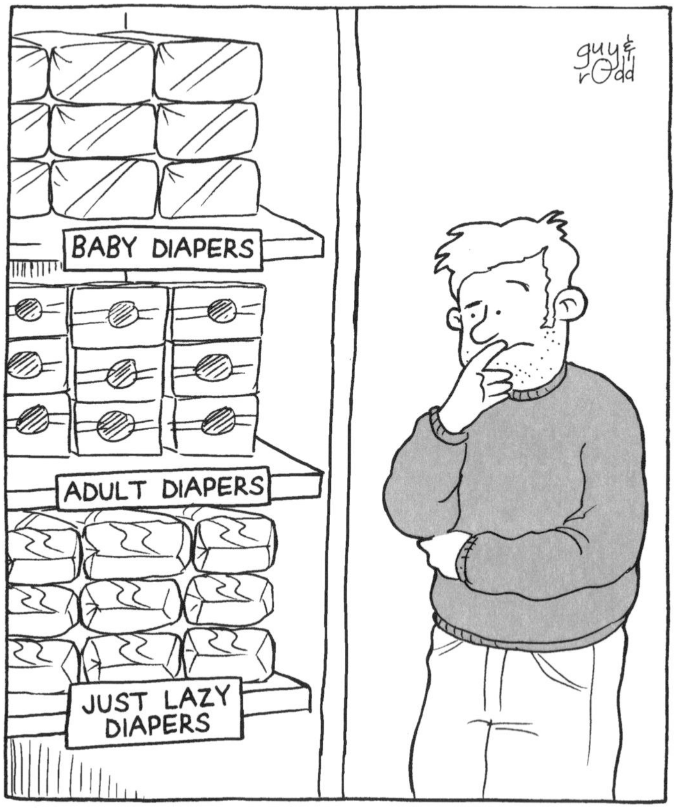
guy & rOdd
BABY DIAPERS
ADULT DIAPERS
JUST LAZY DIAPERS

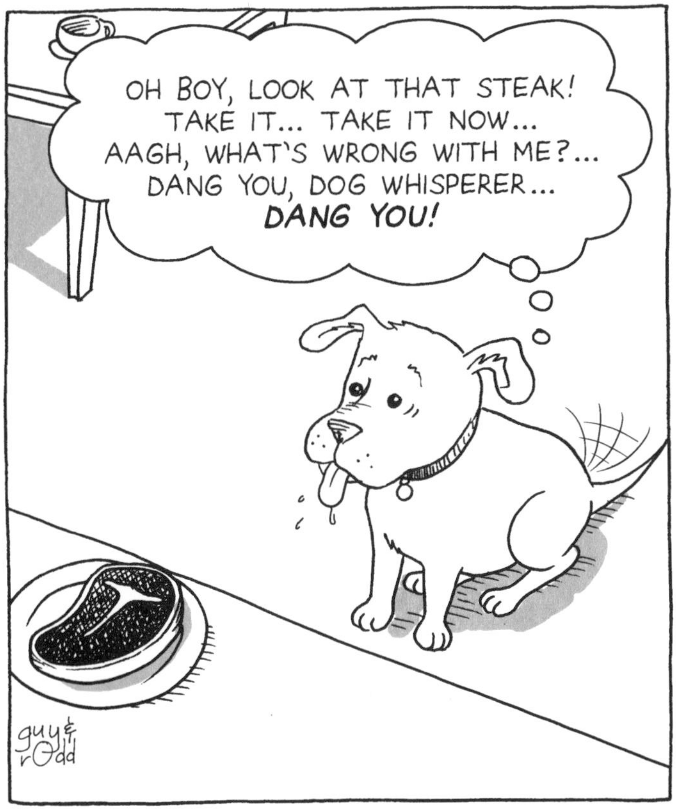
OH BOY, LOOK AT THAT STEAK! TAKE IT... TAKE IT NOW... AAGH, WHAT'S WRONG WITH ME?... DANG YOU, DOG WHISPERER... **DANG YOU!**
guy & rOdd

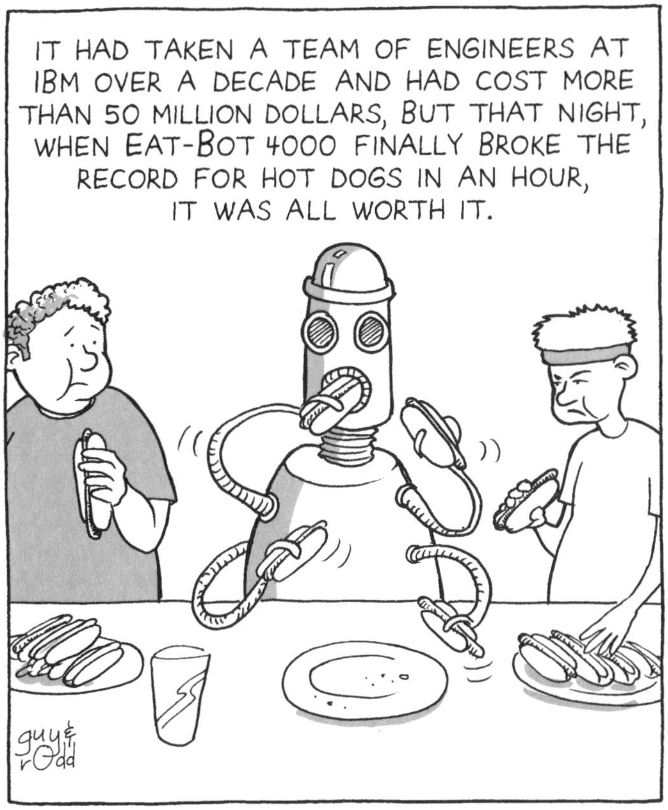
IT HAD TAKEN A TEAM OF ENGINEERS AT IBM OVER A DECADE AND HAD COST MORE THAN 50 MILLION DOLLARS, BUT THAT NIGHT, WHEN EAT-BOT 4000 FINALLY BROKE THE RECORD FOR HOT DOGS IN AN HOUR, IT WAS ALL WORTH IT.
guy & rOdd

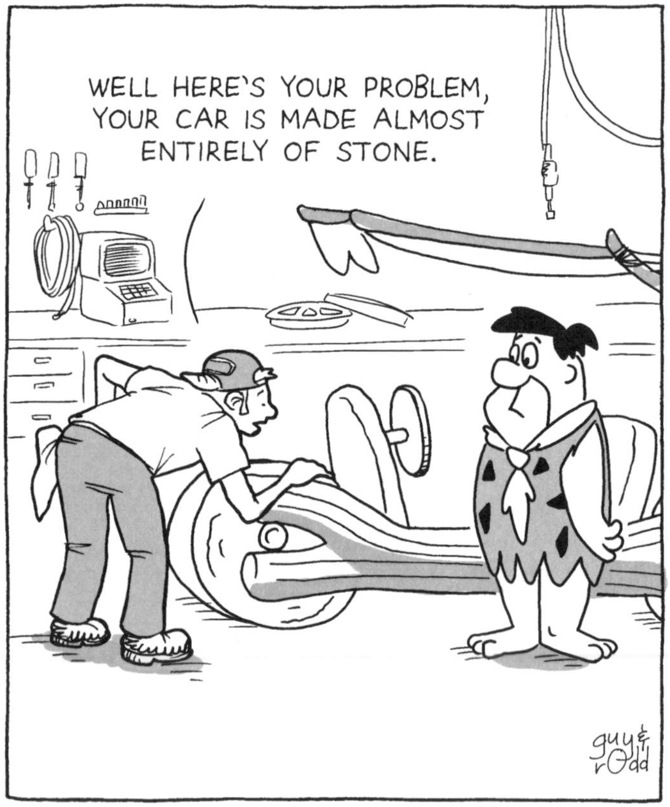
WELL HERE'S YOUR PROBLEM, YOUR CAR IS MADE ALMOST ENTIRELY OF STONE.
guy & rOdd

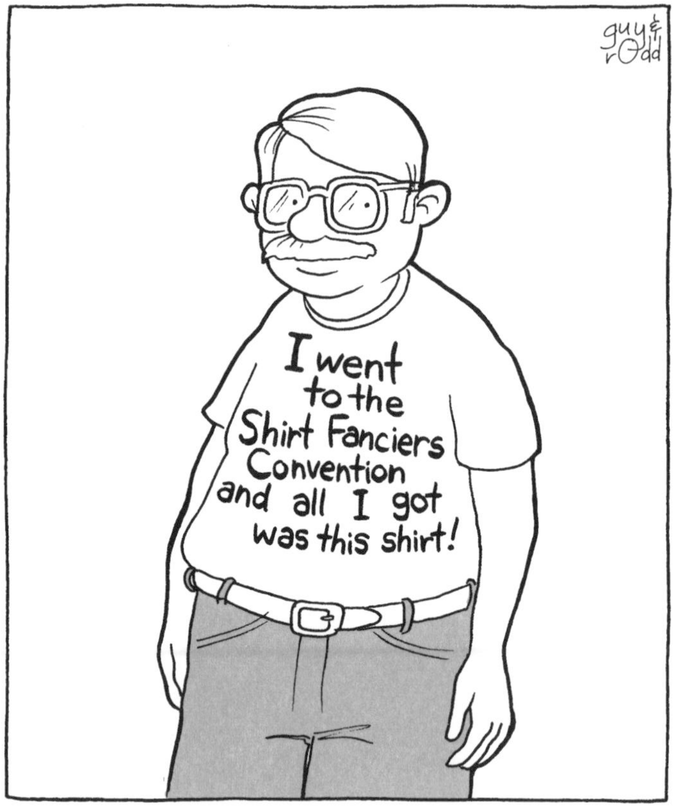
guy & rOdd
I went to the Shirt Fanciers Convention and all I got was this shirt!

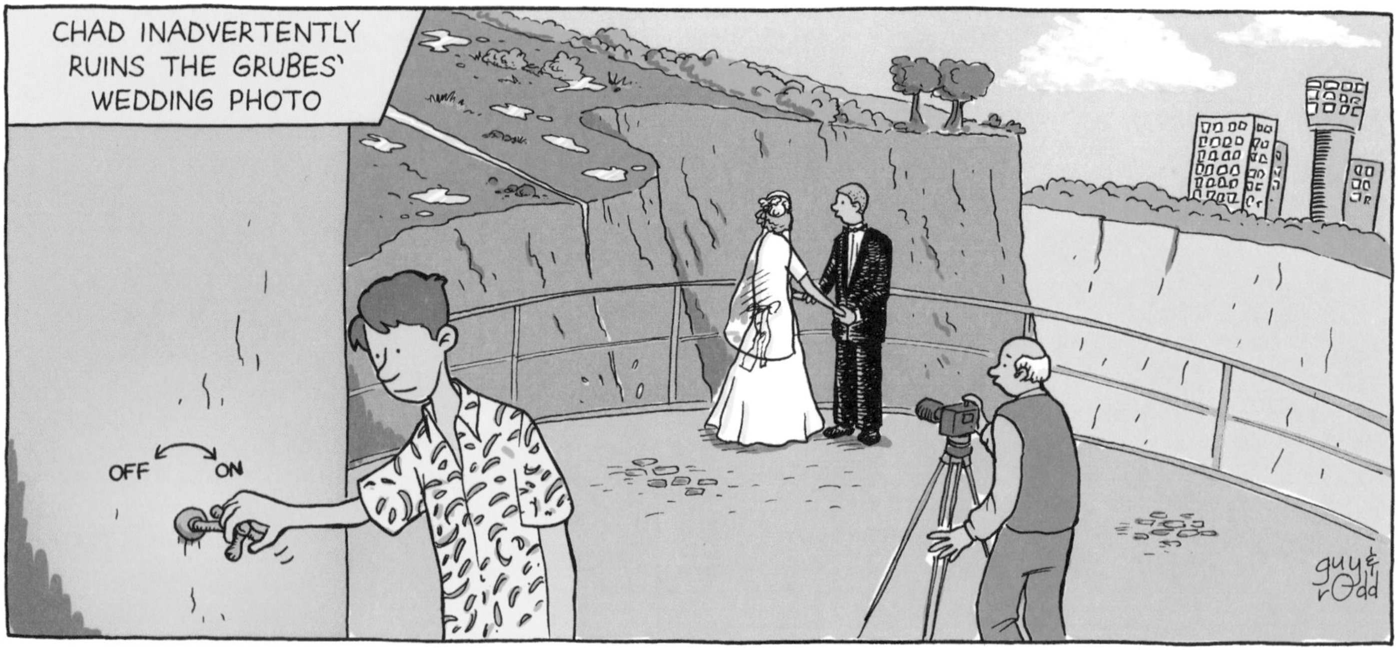
CHAD INADVERTENTLY RUINS THE GRUBES' WEDDING PHOTO
OFF
ON
guy & rOdd

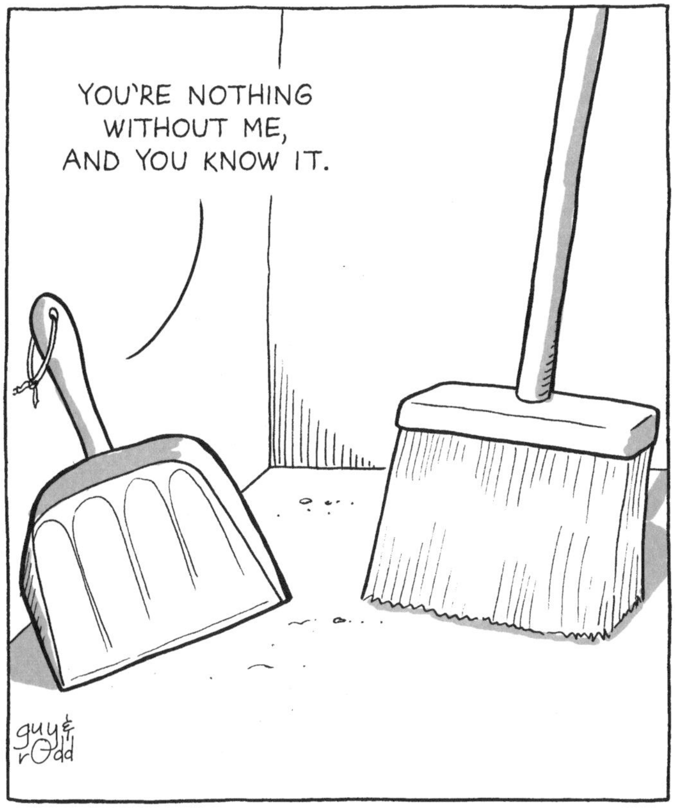
YOU'RE NOTHING WITHOUT ME, AND YOU KNOW IT.
guy & rodd

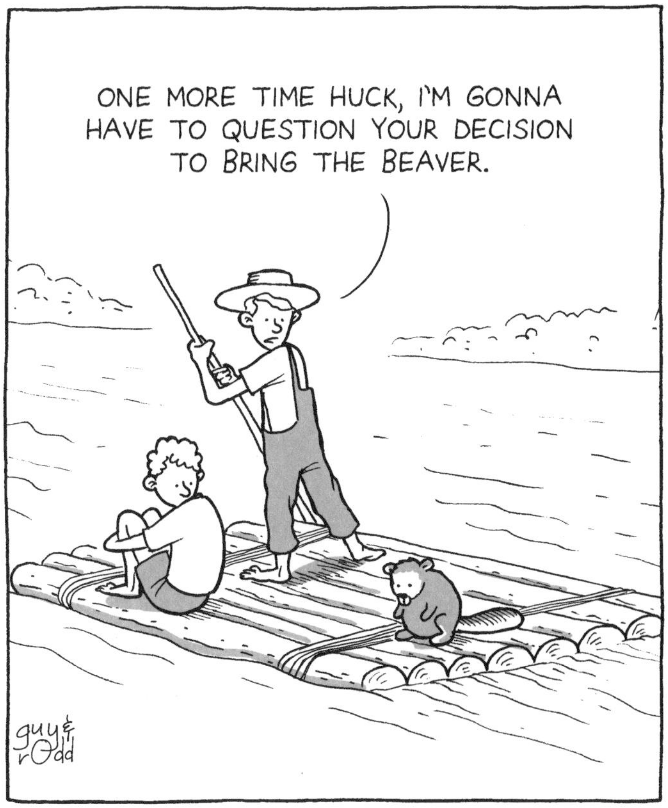
ONE MORE TIME HUCK, I'M GONNA HAVE TO QUESTION YOUR DECISION TO BRING THE BEAVER.
guy & rodd

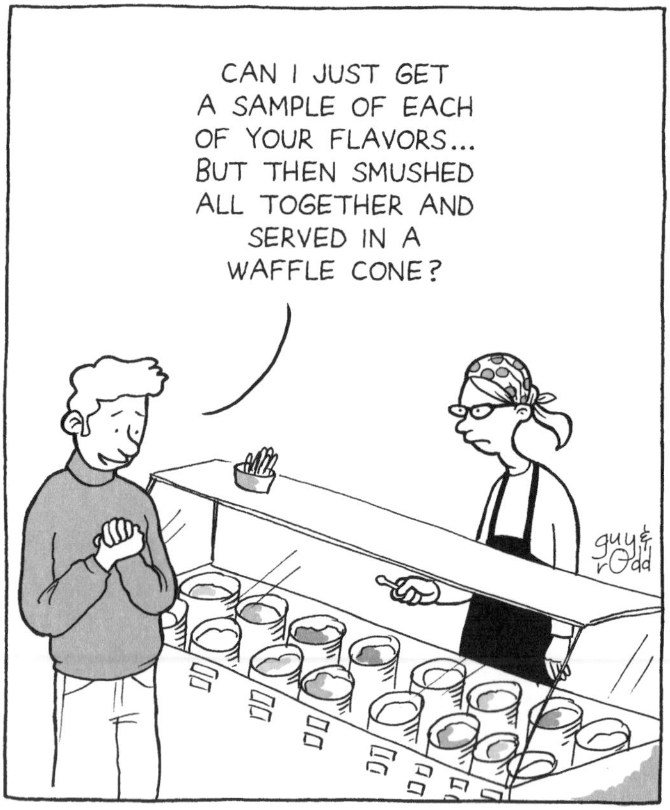
CAN I JUST GET A SAMPLE OF EACH OF YOUR FLAVORS... BUT THEN SMUSHED ALL TOGETHER AND SERVED IN A WAFFLE CONE?

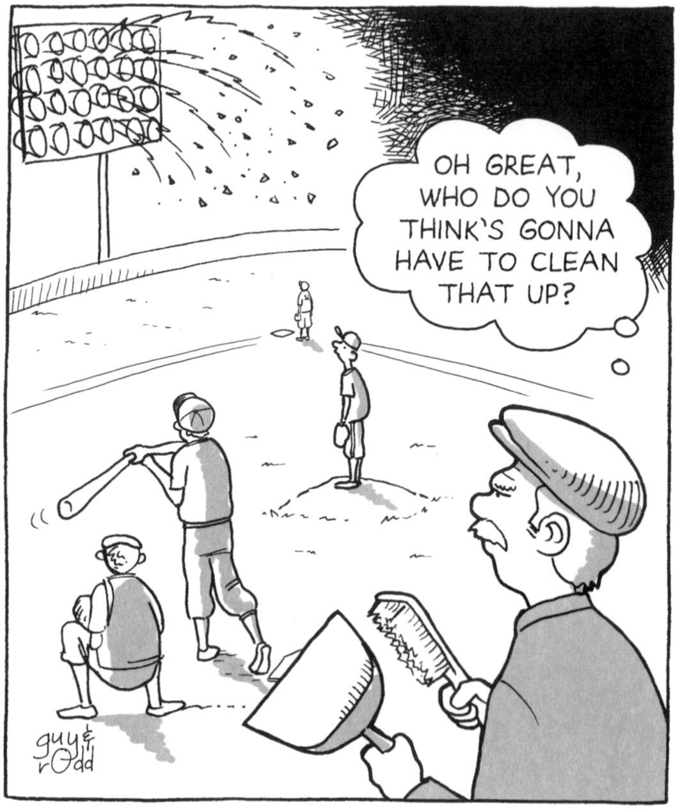
OH GREAT, WHO DO YOU THINK'S GONNA HAVE TO CLEAN THAT UP?

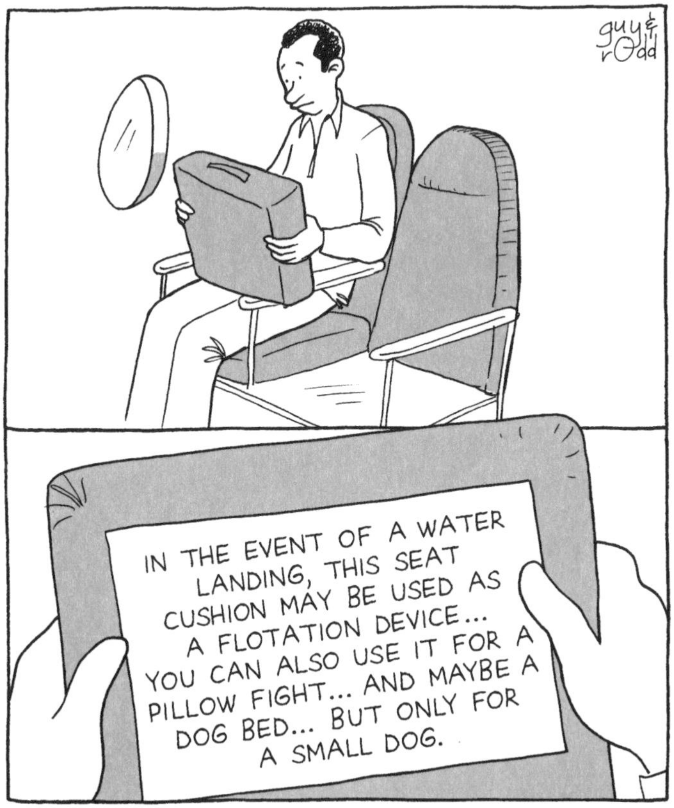
IN THE EVENT OF A WATER LANDING, THIS SEAT CUSHION MAY BE USED AS A FLOTATION DEVICE... YOU CAN ALSO USE IT FOR A PILLOW FIGHT... AND MAYBE A DOG BED... BUT ONLY FOR A SMALL DOG.

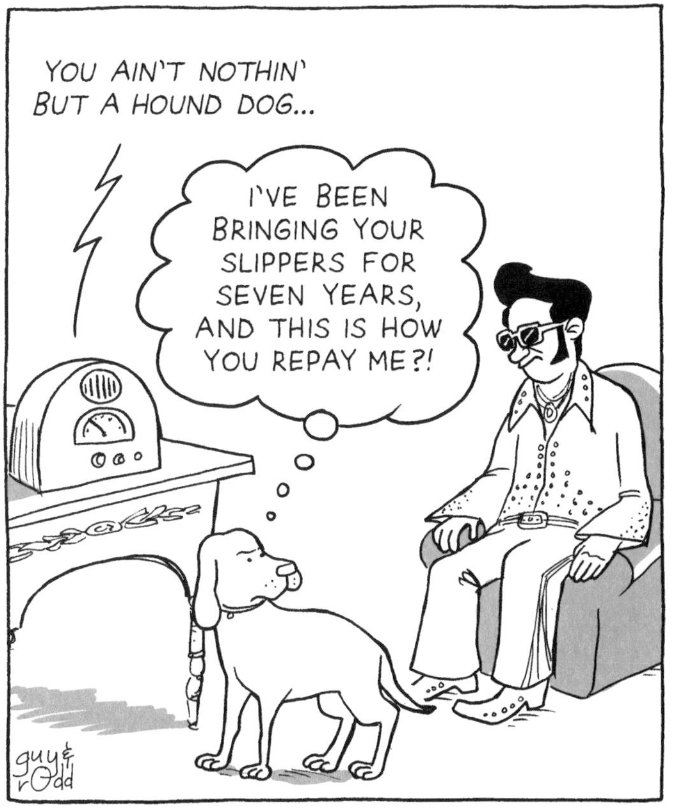
YOU AIN'T NOTHIN' BUT A HOUND DOG...
I'VE BEEN BRINGING YOUR SLIPPERS FOR SEVEN YEARS, AND THIS IS HOW YOU REPAY ME?!

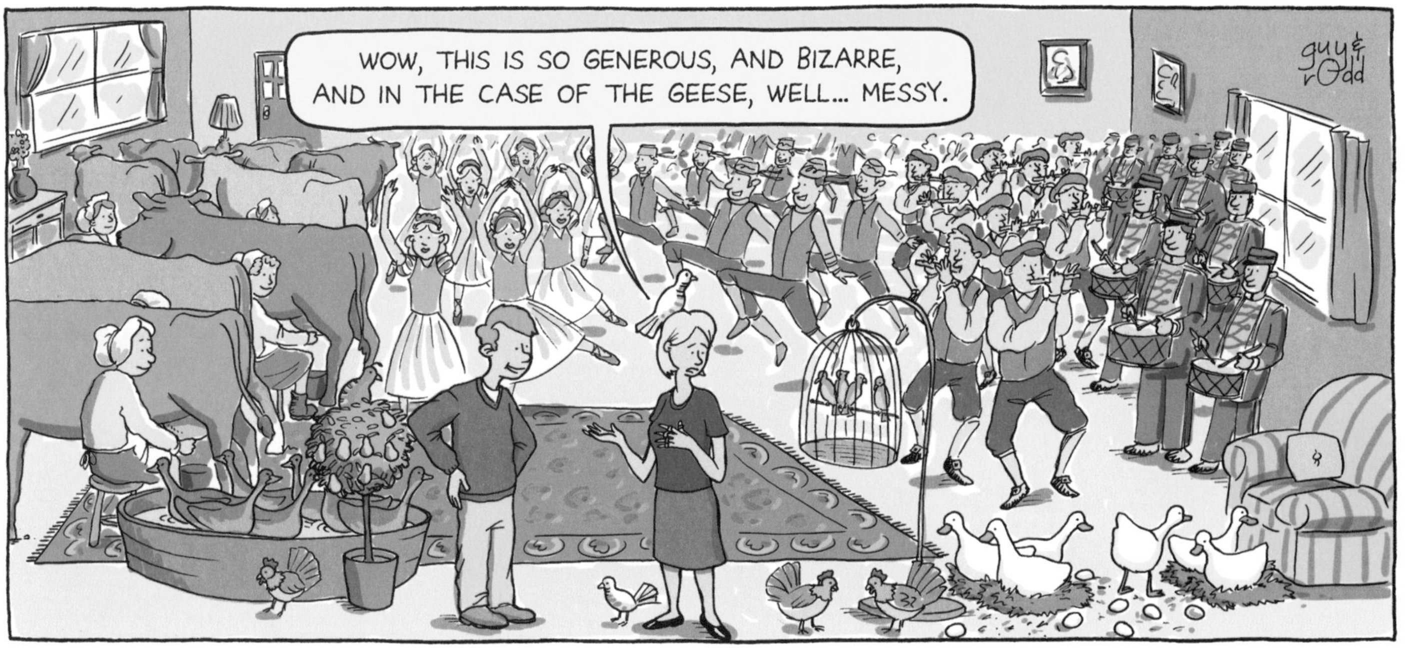
WOW, THIS IS SO GENEROUS, AND BIZARRE, AND IN THE CASE OF THE GEESE, WELL... MESSY.

BEDELIA WAS TORN. ON THE ONE HAND, SHE HAD NEVER MET A MAN SO GENEROUS...

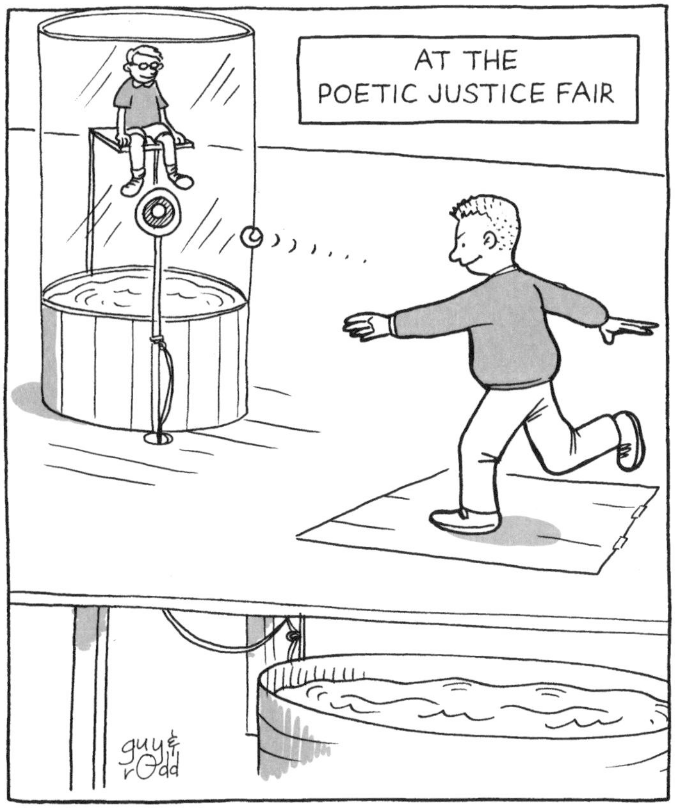
AT THE
POETIC JUSTICE FAIR
guy & rodd

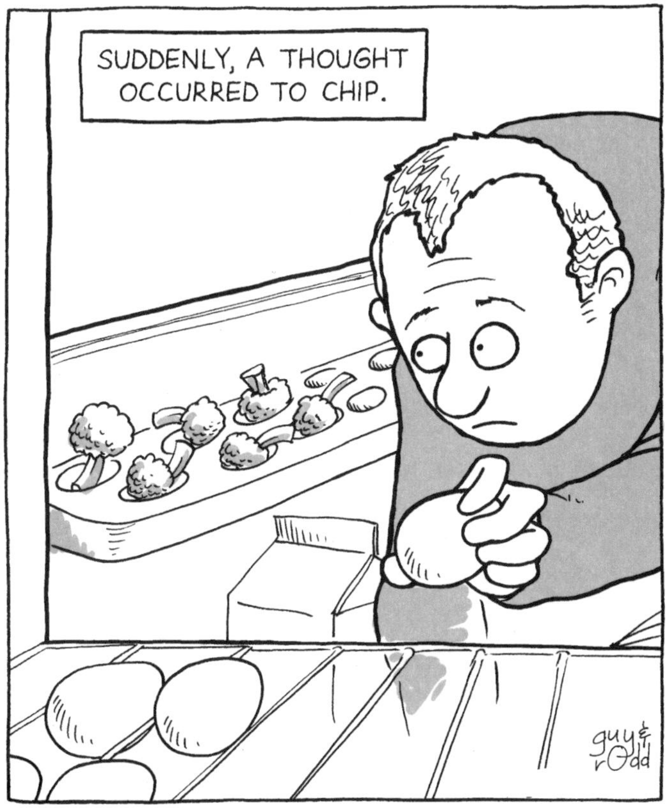
SUDDENLY, A THOUGHT
OCCURRED TO CHIP.
guy & rodd

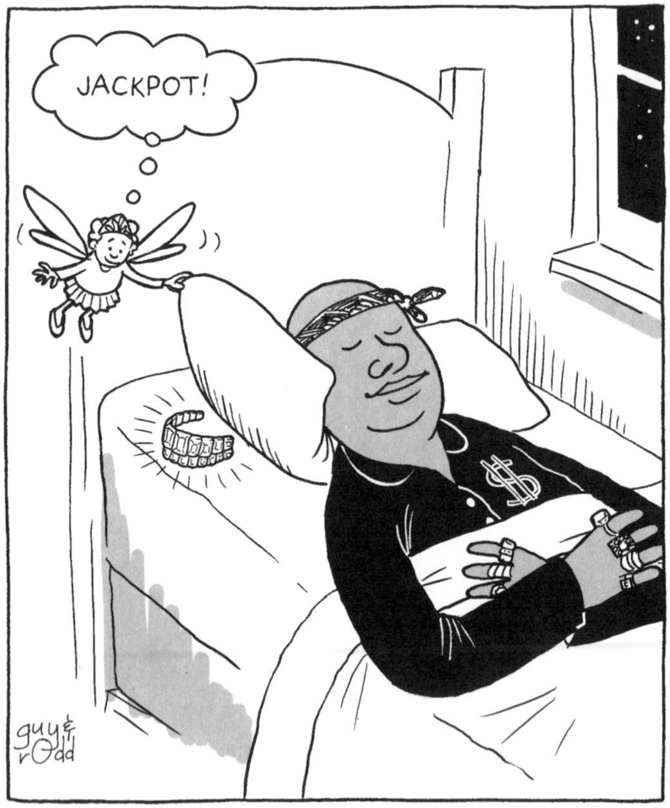
JACKPOT!

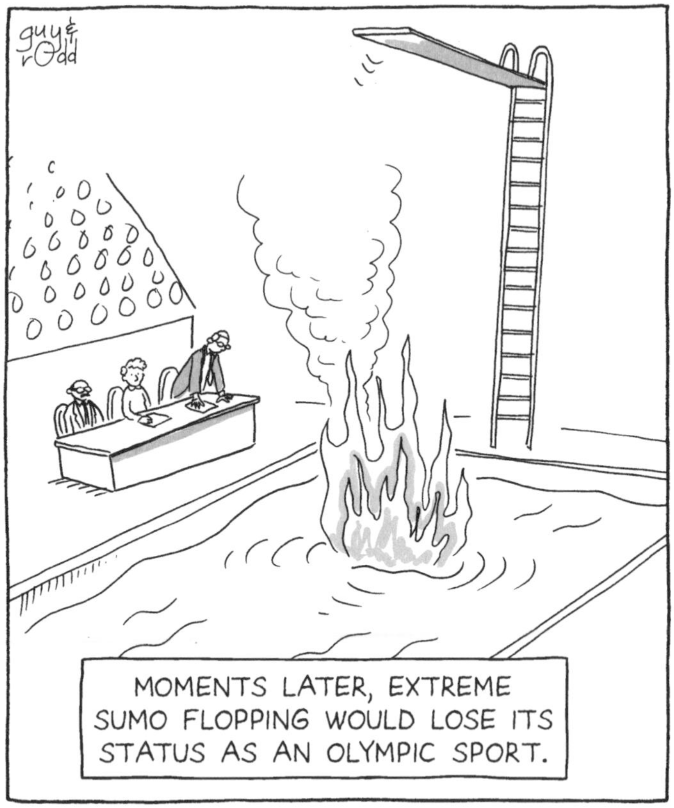
MOMENTS LATER, EXTREME SUMO FLOPPING WOULD LOSE ITS STATUS AS AN OLYMPIC SPORT.

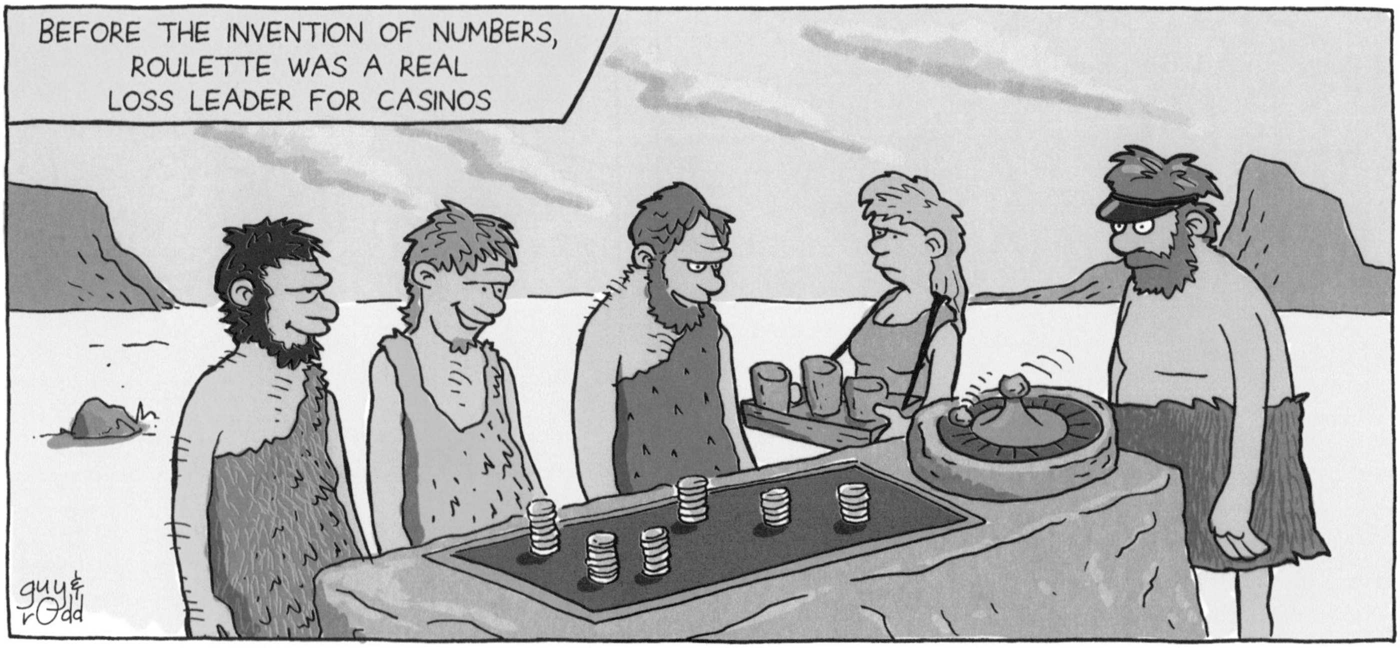
BEFORE THE INVENTION OF NUMBERS, ROULETTE WAS A REAL LOSS LEADER FOR CASINOS

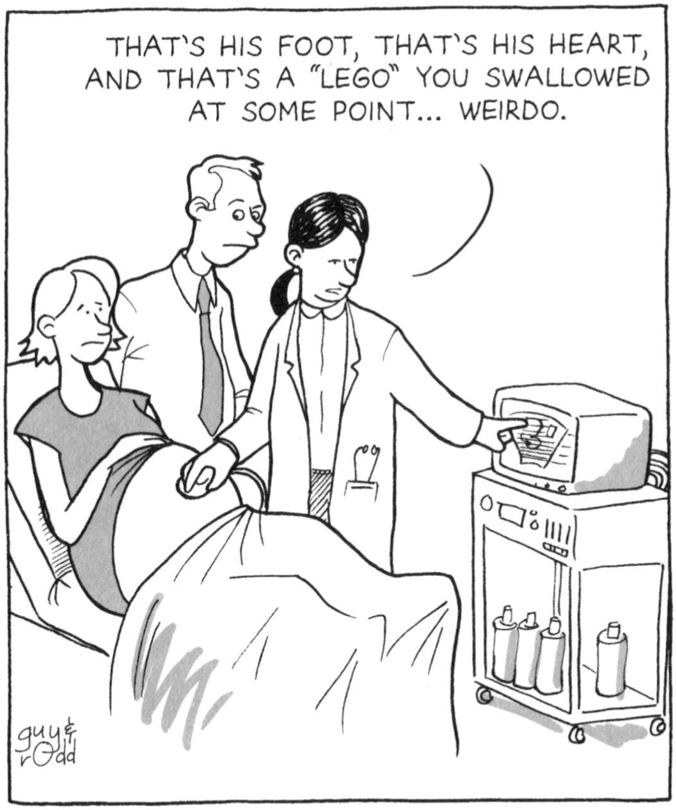
THAT'S HIS FOOT, THAT'S HIS HEART, AND THAT'S A "LEGO" YOU SWALLOWED AT SOME POINT... WEIRDO.

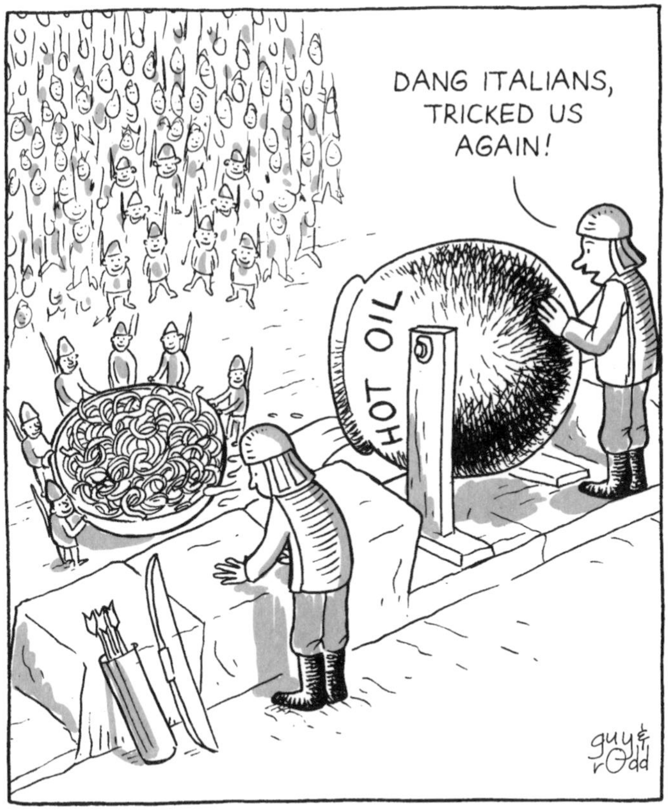
DANG ITALIANS, TRICKED US AGAIN!
HOT OIL

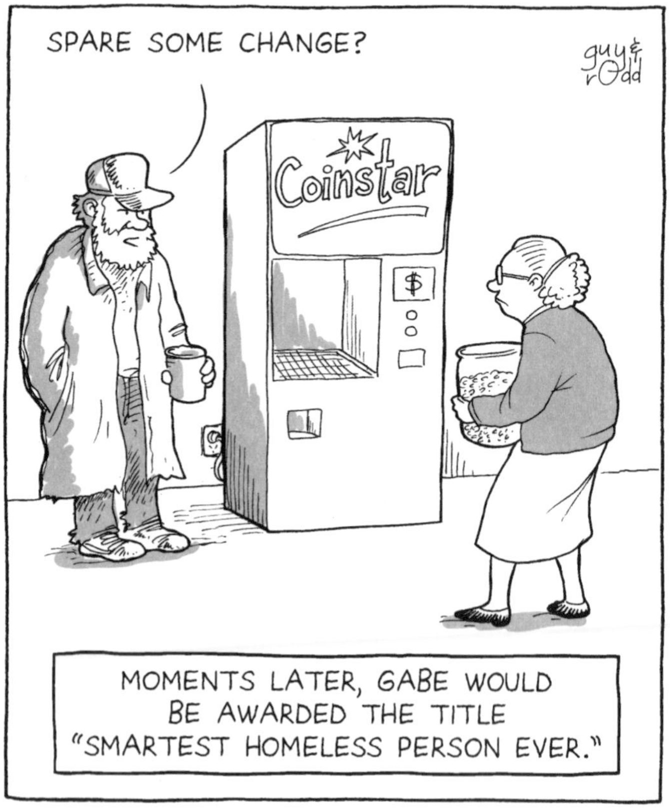
SPARE SOME CHANGE?
guy & rOdd
Coinstar
$
MOMENTS LATER, GABE WOULD BE AWARDED THE TITLE "SMARTEST HOMELESS PERSON EVER."

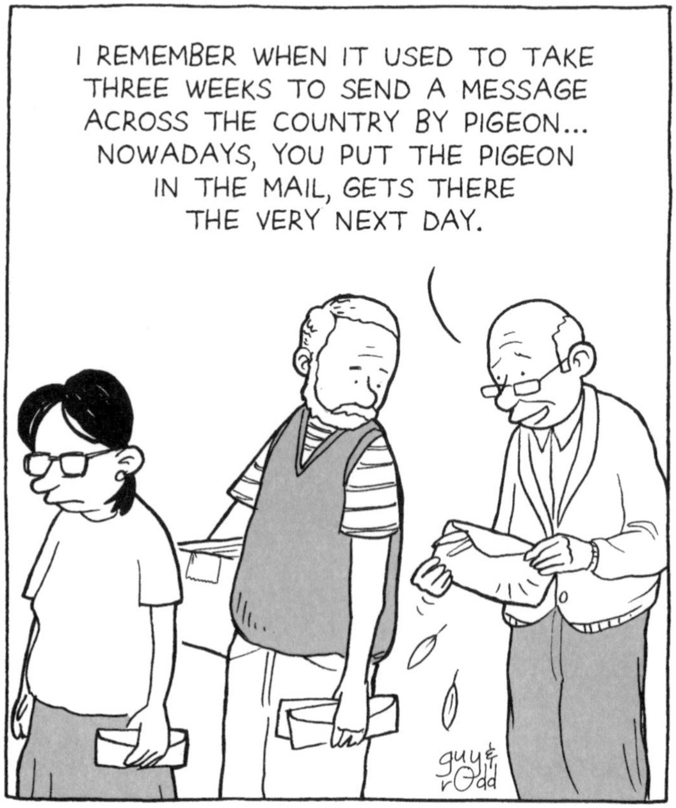
I REMEMBER WHEN IT USED TO TAKE THREE WEEKS TO SEND A MESSAGE ACROSS THE COUNTRY BY PIGEON... NOWADAYS, YOU PUT THE PIGEON IN THE MAIL, GETS THERE THE VERY NEXT DAY.
guy & rOdd

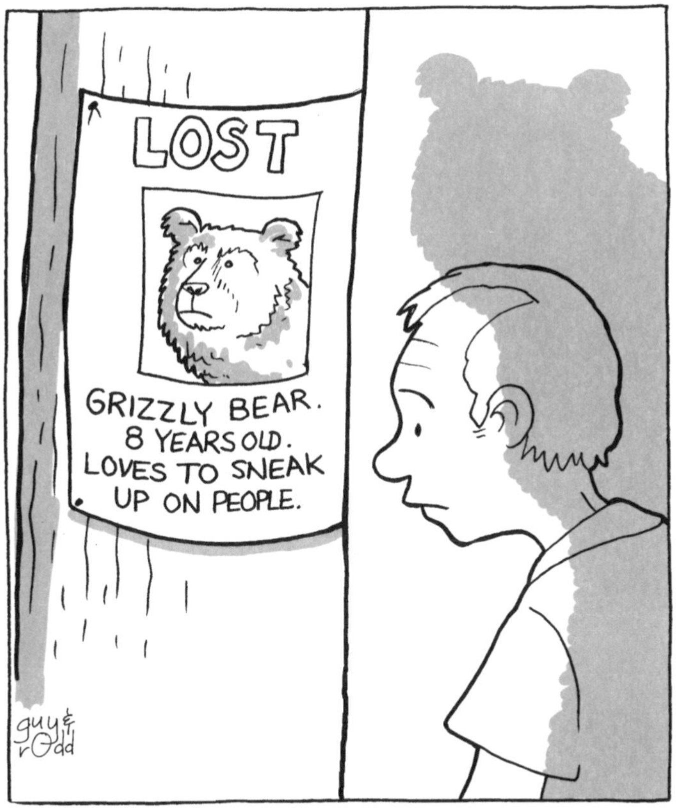
LOST
GRIZZLY BEAR. 8 YEARS OLD. LOVES TO SNEAK UP ON PEOPLE.

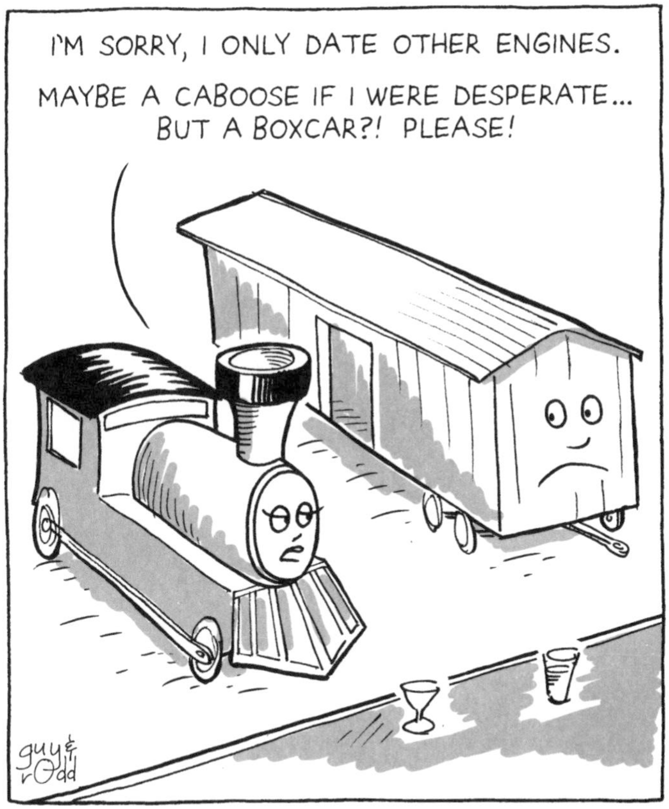
I'M SORRY, I ONLY DATE OTHER ENGINES.
MAYBE A CABOOSE IF I WERE DESPERATE... BUT A BOXCAR?! PLEASE!

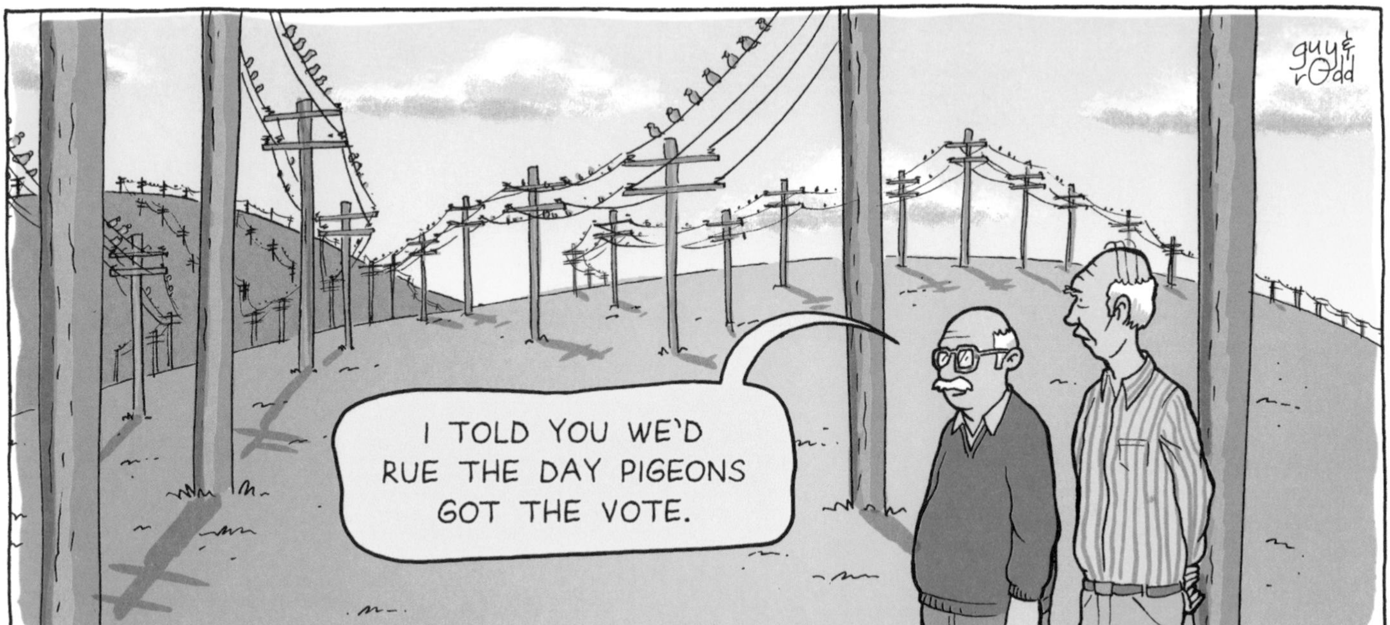
I TOLD YOU WE'D RUE THE DAY PIGEONS GOT THE VOTE.

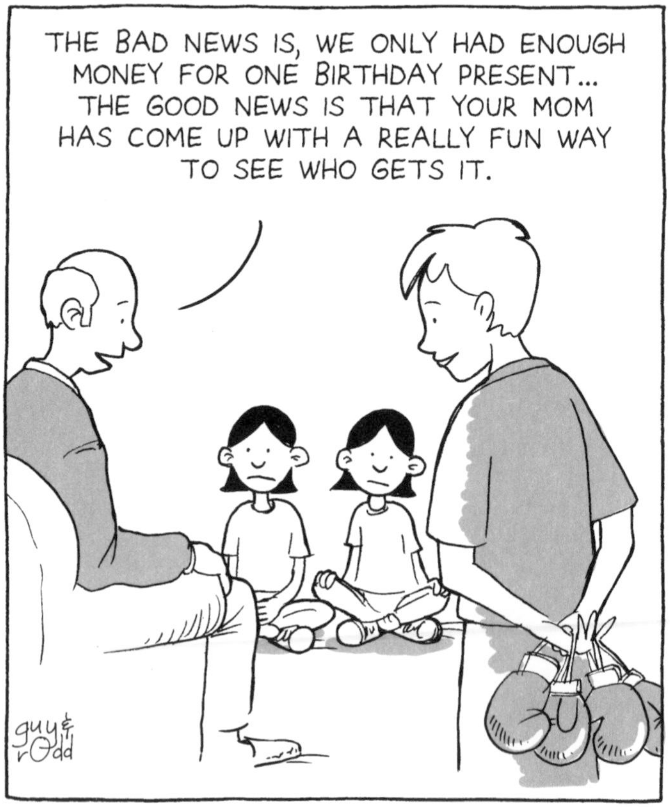
THE BAD NEWS IS, WE ONLY HAD ENOUGH MONEY FOR ONE BIRTHDAY PRESENT... THE GOOD NEWS IS THAT YOUR MOM HAS COME UP WITH A REALLY FUN WAY TO SEE WHO GETS IT.

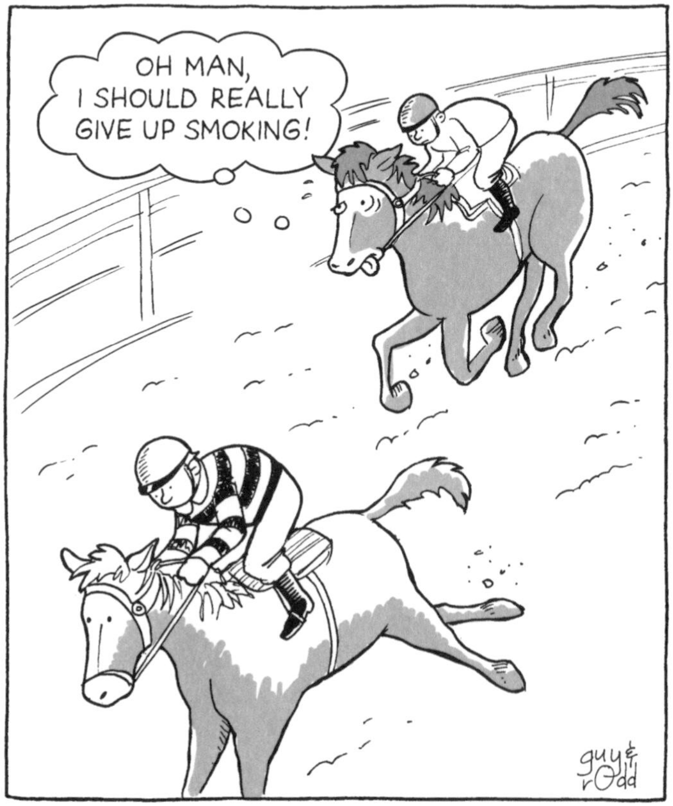
OH MAN, I SHOULD REALLY GIVE UP SMOKING!

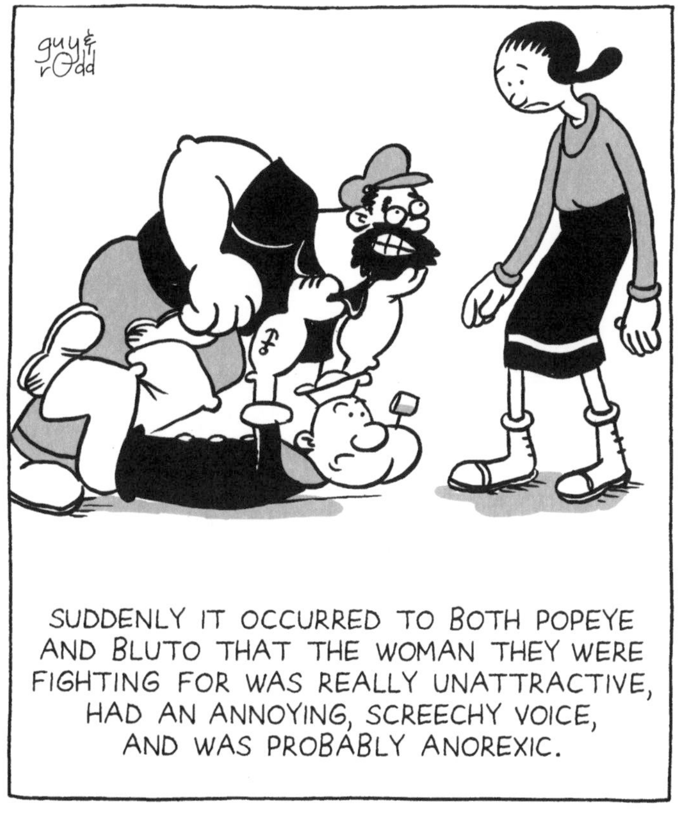
guy & rOdd

SUDDENLY IT OCCURRED TO BOTH POPEYE AND BLUTO THAT THE WOMAN THEY WERE FIGHTING FOR WAS REALLY UNATTRACTIVE, HAD AN ANNOYING, SCREECHY VOICE, AND WAS PROBABLY ANOREXIC.

"LARRY THIS" AND "LARRY THAT"... AND NO ONE HAS ANYTHING NICE TO SAY ABOUT THE HOLE.

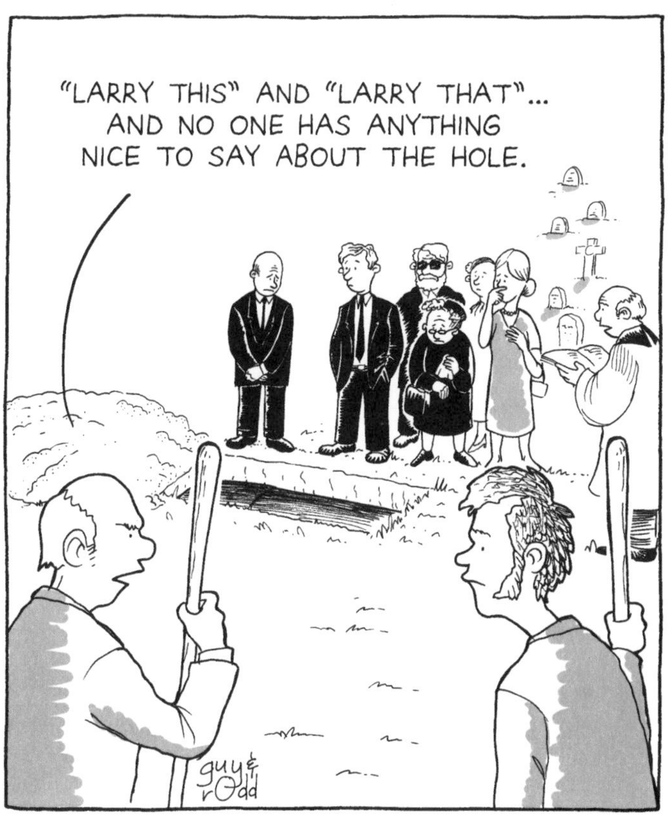
guy & rOdd

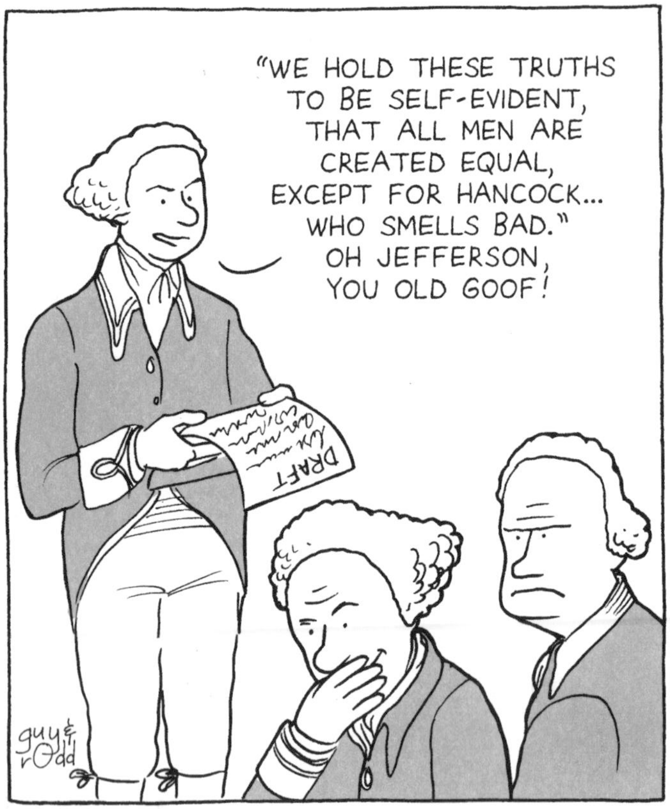
"WE HOLD THESE TRUTHS TO BE SELF-EVIDENT, THAT ALL MEN ARE CREATED EQUAL, EXCEPT FOR HANCOCK... WHO SMELLS BAD." OH JEFFERSON, YOU OLD GOOF!
DRAFT

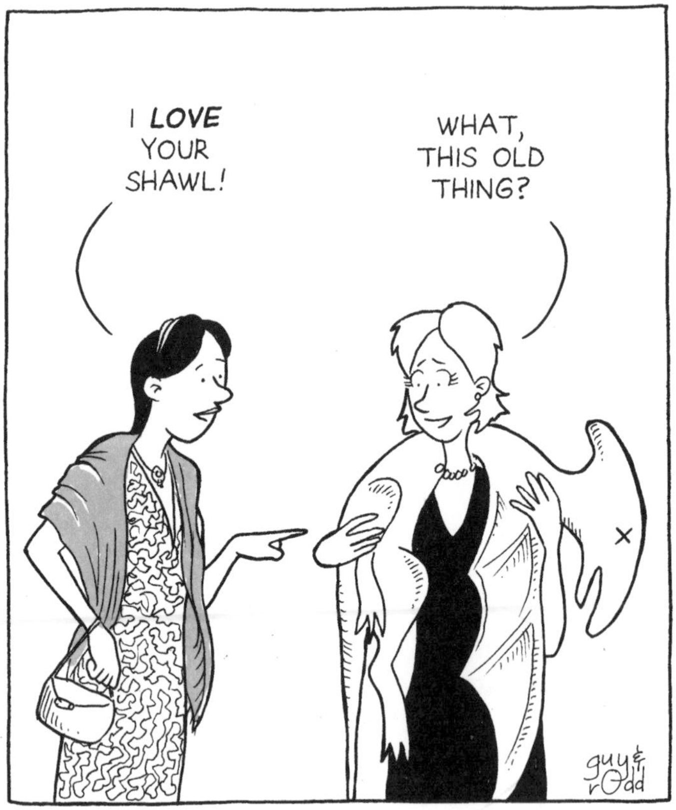
I **LOVE** YOUR SHAWL!
WHAT, THIS OLD THING?

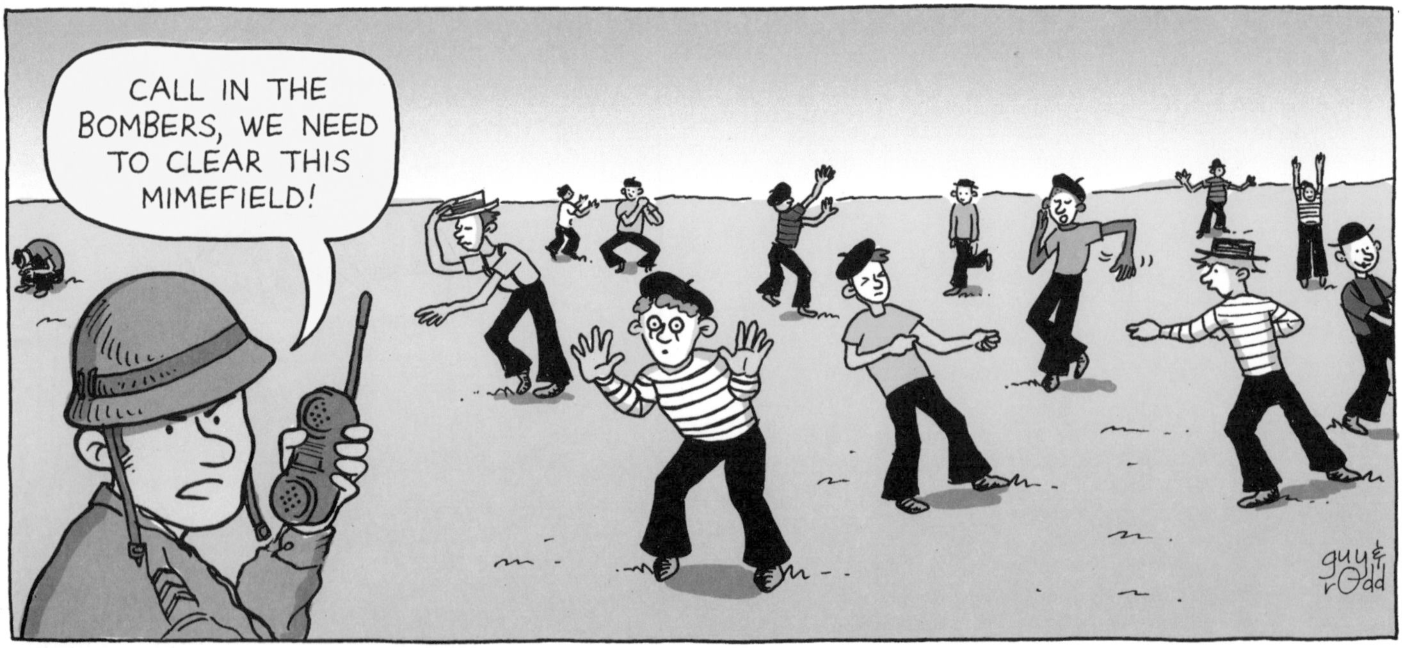
CALL IN THE BOMBERS, WE NEED TO CLEAR THIS MIMEFIELD!